P9-CEY-834

POLITICS

"More than any other people in the world, Americans identify with their own government. They see it as their own. They want to make it better. Participation is the fundamental strength of politics in America. There are those, and many times they are the best among us, who want to participate actively in the process of government. They want to give something *back* to America, so they make themselves available to the political process.

"Winning in politics and getting to the top of government is a special trip that few people take. I have been one of the lucky ones.

"This is how it happened..."
—Edward I. Koch

Please turn this page for the critics' response to Edward I. Koch's first bestseller, *Mayor*.

The Press Hails

"Outrageous...engrossing...not merely a chronicle of Koch's achievements. It is, more remarkably, an idiosyncratic collection of Koch's observations on just about everyone."   —*People*

"A portrait of a politician who loves his job...it's hard to name another memoir that seems so self-revealing."   —*Fortune*

"Not only revealing but also readable... with a candor that is refreshing for its audacity."
                    —**Russell Baker,** *New York Times*

"Koch proves he's an original...I love it— the whole frolic of Ed Koch and his mayoral memoirs. I relish the sheer enjoyment of his earthy judgment of foe and friend alike."
                    —**Max Lerner,** *New York Post*

"The book by the mayor of New York that has flabbergasted just about everybody in publishing...almost makes us believe the romance of La Guardia and the promise of Lindsay have returned at last. He is impish, funny, street smart...which is to say, he represents New York very well."
                    —*San Francisco Chronicle*

Edward I. Koch

ALSO BY EDWARD I. KOCH

<u>Mayor</u>

Published by
WARNER BOOKS

POLITICS

EDWARD I. KOCH

WITH
WILLIAM RAUCH

WARNER BOOKS

A Warner Communications Company

Warner Books, Inc.
666 Fifth Avenue
New York, N.Y. 10103

Ⓦ A Warner Communications Company

Printed in the United States of America

First Warner Books Printing: November, 1986

10 9 8 7 6 5 4 3 2 1

To David Garth
A media wizard without whom
I couldn't have been elected in 1977.
And, more important, my friend.

To Ron Dellums
A brilliant congressman and politician,
a credit to his constituency,
and a colleague in the Congress.

Contents

Introduction

IF YOU HAVE READ MY FIRST BOOK, *Mayor,* I hope you liked my candid writing style—for this book is no different. But this second book is not simply more of the same. It examines different issues and shows the way the art of politics is practiced. Most of all it probes further, at least from my point of view, into interesting and complex people who govern or seek to govern. Many are people you know. They are people who have affected all of our lives through their judgments.

What I've tried to do in these pages is to relate by example and anecdote my philosophy and approach to political·problems. *Politics* takes the form of a mélange of political and governmental experiences most of which occurred before I became mayor.

This is the most interesting of professions. Politics

can have intimate, seminal, exhilarating and depressing impacts upon both the politician and the constituent. Politics may be the only vehicle by which you can reach the heights or the depths, all in what seems to be a single moment, while the things that are accomplished, or left undone, last lifetimes.

I have tried in the course of my political career never to tack to the wind. That does not mean, however, that I have not compromised positions in order to achieve goals. Nor does it mean I haven't given up when I thought the fight was too great, or the energy required was too much to deliver at that moment.

I have found, and it is something we in politics have all heard about, that the enemies of yesterday can become the associates of today and the friends of tomorrow.

In truth many of the best people come into politics and government. Few but the best could withstand the scrutiny at the top. They do it because they know there is no other field of endeavor that can provide the same satisfaction—albeit not the same large sums of money that are to be made in the private sector. They come because it is exciting, challenging and fulfilling like no other job.

I hope that this book becomes a primer for those who might be considering an entrance into the fray by running for public office, and even a guide for those who wish to be less directly involved.

A political life requires courage. It requires an ability to roll with the punches. It rewards those who have learned to punch back. It takes a special commitment. Most people are satisfied to enjoy politics vicariously. Some just read about it. Some volunteer their time to work on campaigns. Others seek a more direct stake in the outcome by making large political contributions.

Political contributors are a lot like horse players. They try to predict the future and pick a winner. They are willing to take a chance and back up their beliefs with their money. As with the bettor who backs a winning horse, a financial contributor to a successful political campaign can also get an enormous sense of satisfaction. But that's where the analogy ends for me. If a campaign contributor is looking for a financial return on his/her money, if they think it will assist them in their business or professional dealings with me, they are making a big mistake. Those people obviously don't yet know me. In this area I have been accused of monumental ingratitude. I'm guilty. I try to judge every issue on the merits. There are no quid pro quos. The vast majority of public officials believe and act ₋ne same way. That doesn't mean there aren't substantial rewards for political contributors who back candidates they truly believe in. They may leave a positive mark on the generations to come. They may find that in that sense they get back much more than they give. They may be the one who got it started, made it happen.

I have said time and time again as a son of the City of New York, born in the Bronx, that I believe public service is the noblest of professions if done honestly and done well. I know I do it honestly. I believe that most people think I have done it well. This city and this country have given me so much. They opened their arms to my parents from Poland as immigrants in the early 1900s. They permitted me to rise to one of the highest positions in government in this country. I am motivated by the wish to give something back to this city and country, to the best of my ability, greater than that given to me. While I can never possibly repay this country for the opportunities I have received, I will continue to try.

I hope this book inspires others to enter politics and government. We all owe so much.

E.I.K.

1

"On the Merits"

Patronage is not illegal, and patronage does not necessarily corrupt. It is simply not the best way to run a government.

Patronage was best described by Meade Esposito when he retired as Brooklyn Democratic county chairman in 1984 and, waxing philosophical, decided to tell the reporters exactly how patronage had worked for him. He gave the following illustration: In 1973 he had supported Abraham Beame for mayor, and immediately after Abe Beame had won the primary Beame called him and said, "Meade, you have six commissionerships."* What that in fact means is one of

*See *The New York Times*, Jan. 27, 1984, p. B3.

two things. It could mean that whatever six people Meade Esposito might have sent to Beame for the six commissionerships that had been given to him, Beame would have appointed those six people without further inquiry. That is one form of patronage. Or, a better form from the point of view of the government, and probably what was intended, would be that these positions "belonged" to Meade Esposito and that they would not be filled until he, Meade Esposito, had sent someone who was qualified to hold the position, insofar as Abe Beame decided what "qualified" meant. It was by these rules that the game was played in the City of New York for many years.

I decided early on, and I have never deviated from this, that patronage was not going to be helpful to providing the best government for the City of New York at least in the difficult times in which I governed. And so I said to the Democratic county leaders at our first meeting at City Hall, "I want everybody to know, and I hope everybody understands it, that my government will not deal in patronage with respect to jobs in government. With respect to jobs in government, I'm happy to receive your recommendations, but I will make the determination as to who gets the positions, basically commissioner and deputy commissioner jobs, and will fill jobs on the basis of who's best irrespective of where they come from. I'm happy to have your resumés for the purposes of interviewing people, and I will interview them. But the ultimate selection will be on the basis of who's most qualified. With respect to judgeships I don't want your resumés, because judgeships will not be filled through any political procedure whatsoever. It will not be held against candidates if they happen to be involved politically. They have to go through the Mayor's Judiciary Committee, and if you want to recommend them to that committee feel free to do so. But you should know now that there will undoubtedly be mostly self-initiating applications there. Most applicants will be qualified lawyers who will just say that they want to be considered.''

There was a silent gasp in the room, because this surely was not what the county leaders expected. And then I said to them, ''In order to make up for what I've just said to you now, I also want you to know that I will be doing two things for you. I will support your candidates for public office unless I have reason to believe they're corrupt, but other than that I'm not going to go into the question as to whether or not they are equal to, better than or worse than their opponents. If they're yours, I'm for them. And, secondly, I will come to your fund-raisers, and if my name is helpful in raising money, fine.''

I have never deviated from either of these two positions. I also said to the commissioners at about the same time, ''You are given the authority by me to pick your subordinates. I want you to look at the whole field of prospective applicants. If I ever find out that you've discriminated based on race, religion, sex, sexual orientation, et cetera, I'll fire you. But if you don't discriminate on that basis and you take whoever you think is the best, I'm not going to clear those with you, they're yours. Don't call me when you hire and don't call me when you fire. The reason I'm doing this is I don't want you ever to be in the position that if I find fault with you you will say to me that I prevented you from doing your job because I sent you palookas whom you had to hire. If you have palookas on your staff, they're there because you put them on.

And I will tell you something else. I'm suggesting to you now that you look at all the people who work for you and those who are subject to being removed from the payroll because they are not civil service, or to being demoted because they are civil service but are working at higher levels than those at which they are protected by civil service—that you take the action to remove or demote now, in the first thirty days of your appointment, because after that you're going to come to love these people. You're going to get to know their wives and children and you're not going to fire them or demote them. That's the nature of the world.''

I know that every one of my commissioners, with maybe a few exceptions, makes deals with the county chairmen and the district leaders and the members of the City Council, not in any corrupt way but because they believe it is in their interest to maintain good relationships in getting legislation or budgets through or getting the assistance of district or county leaders. I'm not blind to that. Nevertheless, the practice is vastly reduced and I'm not part of it. And it's not as though I want to be like Caesar's wife. It's just that I believe that handling it this way reduces the incompetence and the corruption, notwithstanding the fact that both will be present in every administration.

Having established the rules, I then had to deal with the appeals for exceptions and so forth. That was inevitable, politicians being what they are, the ego, etc. And some of the appeals were memorable experiences. One I remember now clearly eight years later (there have been several refresher appeals on this one since then) is the case of Gurston Goldin, Jay Goldin's brother.

Jay Goldin had been elected comptroller, the second-highest job in the city government, in 1973. That was the year in which Beame was elected mayor. And sometime after that Abe Beame had appointed Gurston Goldin to the Board of Higher Education. Gurston Goldin is a psychiatrist. He is probably a very good psychiatrist.

Early on this became an issue, and Jay came in. He said to me, "I would like you, as a personal favor, to reappoint my brother to the Board of Higher Education."

I said, "Well, Jay, I'll think about it, but I can't make you a promise on that. I'll determine that after I inquire as to what's in the best interest of the composition of that board and the city."

He then said that to him this was "the most important matter of any matter" that we would ever discuss and that Abe Beame had obliged him in a similar conversation and that being on the Board of Higher Education was the most important agenda item for his brother Gurston.

I said, "Jay, I'll certainly give that consideration." I subsequently inquired about the board and, without in any way disparaging Gurston Goldin's abilities, I must say that others felt that I should make a new appointment. I called Jay and told him. He was beside himself with rage, repeating that this was the most important matter that he would ever ask me about; that if I did this for him he would never ask me for anything else; and, in effect, probably without using the words, that I would regret not obliging him.

I said, "Jay, I'm sorry about that, but I'm not reappointing your brother." There is no question in my mind that had I reappointed his brother and kept that appointment dangling, as a reminder of things past and of what I might do in the future, he might have been much more supportive than he subsequently was of me and my programs before the Board of Estimate.*

---

*The Board of Estimate is a hybrid political body that is unique to the City of New York. It is composed of three citywide officials—each with two votes on the board—Mayor, Comptroller and Council President; and of the five Borough Presidents—from the Bronx, Brooklyn, Manhattan, Staten Island and Queens—each with one vote on the board. The Borough Presidents have little direct authority in their own boroughs. The power of the Borough Presidents, and that of the citywide officials, exclusive of the Mayor, is (in addition to their voting on city contracts and land use matters) primarily premised on their having to vote on the city's expense and capital budgets. For the city budget to be adopted it must be concurred in by a majority (5 or more) vote on the Board of Estimate (the Mayor, in this single instance, has no vote), and a majority vote (18 or more) on the city's 35-member City Council. Then, of course, it must be signed into law by the Mayor.

I didn't think I should do it and I still don't regret not having done it. But I will tell you this: it made a difference.

The question will always be when someone does things that are unconventional and that occasion animus among others, Well, why? How did he get like that? So let me go into some of that, because I would be the first to say that the way I learned politics was unconventional and that what we were trying to do in the reform days of the 1950s and '60s was unconventional.

•   •   •

I got my start in politics when I became enthused about Adlai Stevenson and his speeches in 1952. I spoke for him in 1952 in the streets, as I did again in 1956. He was not, however, someone on whom I could model myself. He was very cool and patrician. But he was a magnificent writer and speaker, and his speeches were extraordinary in their clarity and depth.

Before I became enthusiastic about Adlai Stevenson, although my enthusiasm was not quite so dramatic, there was my admiration for Harry Truman. In retrospect there is no question but that Harry Truman is someone whom I still admire and have admired over the years more than Stevenson. That is because of Truman's ordinariness. He was a first-rate President who was ordinary. And when I say ordinary, I mean that he bled like everybody else; and got angry like everybody else; and responded in a commonsense way on most occasions. The most endearing story about Harry Truman is the one about his threatening to beat up the newspaper critic who panned his daughter's concert debut.

There was a third person who had an impact on my public life, simply because I am a New Yorker. That was Fiorello La Guardia. His career was quite similar to mine. He came into office in 1934 during the Great Depression. The city was at the edge of a fiscal abyss. He had enormous union problems. I came into office in 1978 when the city was at the edge of bankruptcy. And I had enormous union problems, although mine were with the public-sector unions. He had a lot of style. And today we look back and we like it, but at that time he was probably perceived as eccentric. He had a squeaky voice and people were passionately for him or against him. I think it is fair to say that my voice is too high and that few people are for long in doubt about me. They either like me or dislike me intensely. There was never any question about his fiscal and intellectual honesty, and I believe it is also fair to say that people do not question mine.

What is it that makes me tick in government? I perceive my career and opportunities in government as unique. I want to use them to exercise the maximum effort so as to leave this city better than it was before I became the Mayor. That means bettering the lives of the people who make up this town.

When I ran for the first time—in 1962 for nomination as Democratic candidate for state assemblyman—I ran with great trepidation and only because the political club of which I was a part could not find any other candidate to run in the primary. I was the lawyer who made sure that the required election petitions of the candidates we ran fulfilled the requirements of the law. Since there were no other candidates available, I decided that I would run. I lost that, my first, election. And I lost it because of what I believed to be the betrayal of several leading figures then active in public life here in the city, to wit, Mayor Robert F. Wagner and former Senator Herbert H. Lehman. They came out for my opponent, William F. Passannante, the incumbent Democratic Assemblyman. And it was devastating to me because I believed that I was the better of the two who were running and that I deserved their support. They, on the other hand, believed it was wrong to oppose an incumbent who was decent and hard-working. In retrospect, they were right and I was wrong. But at that time I felt so betrayed that on primary night when I lost I wept as I made my concession speech to the three hundred or so campaign workers in a crowded upstairs loft off Sheridan Square in Greenwich Village. And I said to them, "I will never run again. Politics is a dirty business."

I meant that at that time. Nevertheless, the next year I ran again. And this time I ran for Democratic district leader against Carmine De Sapio, who was seeking to come back, having been defeated two years earlier. The state of politics being what it was in 1963, most people thought I would not win. And, in fact, I won only by 41 votes out of the 9,000 that were cast. I defeated

Carmine De Sapio two more times—in a rerun election held in 1964, when I won by 164 votes, and then in a regular election in 1965, when I won by 518 votes out of the 11,000 votes cast.

In 1966 I ran for the City Council and took a seat that had been held by Republicans for thirty-eight years—and in an upset victory I won by 2,500 votes.

In 1968 I ran for Congress for the first time. And in another upset victory, in a Republican district on the Upper East Side of Manhattan known nationally as the Silk Stocking District, which had been held by the GOP for thirty-one years, I won with 51 percent of the vote. I served in the Congress for five terms, and in my fourth and fifth terms I received 75 percent of the vote.

In 1977 I ran for mayor. I was the sixth in the field of seven during much of the primary. I reached the runoff by winning in the primary election with 21 percent of the vote. In second place was Mario M. Cuomo, now Governor of the State of New York, who had 20 percent; and Abe Beame, who was running for reelection, received 19 percent. In the two-way primary runoff ten days later between Mario Cuomo and myself, I won with 60 percent of the vote. Then in the general election, with Cuomo running on the Liberal Party line and with me on the Democratic Party line, I won with 50 percent and Cuomo received 42 percent and the other two candidates split 8 percent between them.

In 1981 I ran for reelection. I received in two contested primaries the designation of both the Democratic Party and the Republican Party. In the general election I got 75 percent of the vote, the highest in the history of the City of New York. Four years later, in 1985, I broke that record again by getting 76 percent of the general election vote.

I believe that in every one of these elections what I had going for me was my personal integrity, both fiscally and intellectually. I had large numbers of supporters who believed in me and who knew that I would never succumb to any unreasonable pressures even if they were brought to bear in a good cause and never to pressures from causes that were not in the best interests of my constituents. And I never have. In every one of these elections, except for reelection as congressman and as mayor, I always had some personal anxiety about whether or not I would prevail. That's normal, particularly because I was relying primarily on volunteers, and not on the party organizations.

It was not until I was in the City Council that I was able to hire staff people. And I must say that one of the most important things I have ever done in my political life was to hire, in both political and governmental posts, overwhelmingly on the merits, and to fire solely on the merits. The latter is far more difficult than the former, but it is necessary to do. In the City Council I took $5,000 of the total allocation of my own salary and office expenses totaling $13,000 and advertised for ten consultants who would each receive an honorarium of $500 to help me, I hoped, to become the best member of the Council.

I remember interviewing someone who had applied

for one of these honorarium positions. His name was Phil Trimble. Phil was then a lawyer with a first-rate Wall Street firm. He said to me that he could "only give thirty-five hours a week to the position." You have to understand that this was in addition to his working for his firm. I hired him. Subsequently we became very good friends, and during my mayoralty he became my counsel and later he became a deputy mayor.

When I was in Congress, David W. Brown was my counsel and in effect ran my Washington office. I sent him to Washington to pick my staff when I was first elected to Congress. I was then going to hire the first five people of the eighteen authorized. He interviewed many people and provided me with ten applicants from whom I would make my selection. The first person I saw was Ronay Menschel. She later became a deputy mayor in my first mayoral administration. At that time she was between jobs, having worked for a Democratic Congressman from Connecticut, Representative Donald Irwin, who had been defeated in the year I was elected. She had run his Washington office. She was twenty-two years old. David Brown said, "She is very good, but she wants too much money. She wants fourteen thousand a year." David and I had agreed we would not pay anyone more than $10,000. So we told her that. She said, "I'll take it, but in six weeks you'll be paying me fourteen thousand." I think it took five weeks! She was and is superb and ultimately became the administrator and chief assistant in my Washington office when David

12

Brown moved back to New York to run the New York office.

I really didn't hire many people in Congress, because the staff allocation was for eighteen people and I hired only the best and they didn't leave to go elsewhere. It was generally perceived that my office in Washington was one of the most efficient and most competent. Everybody worked very hard because I worked very hard and they loved their work, as I did mine. From the very beginning I had the kind of relationship with my staff that was on a first-name basis whether you were an intern or the top administrator. And everybody had access to me and could walk into my office at any time. Picking eighteen people even with the changes that occurred over nine years is no big deal. But I learned some things about staffing early on, and I have carried them with me.

When I was first elected to Congress I owed that election to the votes cast on the Liberal Party line. As I said, I decided to hire the best people I could find for my congressional staff, without regard to their political affiliation. Of the eighteen employees that were to be hired, five were to serve in my district office in New York City. One day I received a call from Edward Morrison, who was then a vice-chairman of the Liberal Party. My recollection is that the conversation went something like this:

He said, "Ed, I know that you don't believe in patronage, and I certainly understand that. But how will it look if when you hire your staff there is no one there from the Liberal Party? And, of course, if you decided to hire such a person, I know you would only do it on the merits, so we would certainly send you a very good person.''

I thought to myself, That is not unfair. I do owe them a lot.

They sent me a very pleasant young woman. She was to act in the capacity, as all of the people in my office did, of both receptionist and caseworker. It was required that all the staff members type their own letters, because no one other than me had a secretary. Indeed, this young woman was to be my secretary in addition to her other duties. I quickly found that she did not type well and was not terribly energetic and that her cases fell behind. At the end of perhaps six months, I realized this could not go on unless I was willing to accept an office that would not be functioning at its optimum, with everyone sharing the responsibilities. So I called Ed Morrison.

I said, ''Ed, I have tried, but it cannot go on. She cannot do the job and I have to let her go. I am calling you to tell you of my decision.''

He said, ''How will it look for the Liberal Party and for you if the only person you get rid of is the person who came from the Liberal Party? That won't sit well with the members of the party.'' I wouldn't say there was a threatening note in his voice, but I will say it was clear to me that if I were to proceed that way it would be at my peril.

14

So I said, "Ed, I am telling you now that I will not tolerate incompetence, no matter what it costs me. We have to figure out a way for her to leave that is acceptable to you. But leave she must."

His response was, "There is a way."

I said, "How?"

He said, "You have to get her a better job."

I said, "I will do it."

I then spoke with Ronay Menschel. I said, "Ronay, I have to get rid of so-and-so and I have to find her a better job." And I explained the whole situation to her.

Ronay said, "Let me try."

A few days later she reported back to me and said, "It's done."

I said, "Tell me how you did it."

She said, "I called a friend of mine at HUD's regional office in New York and explained the situation to him." (The regional office of the U.S. Department of Housing and Urban Development was actually located in the same building as my congressional-district office—26 Federal Plaza.) "He said to me, 'I can help you. I'll take her.'"

Ronay added, "I had to be fair with him, so I told him that her office skills aren't very good—that she can hardly type, she can't take shorthand and she falls behind in her casework." The response of Ronay's friend was, "That's okay, we have a lot like that."

There are two occasions when one can engage in what used to be called the white lie. One is when you are getting rid of someone who is inadequate. I believe it is acceptable to tell them anything you want about how competent they are. And if you are asked to talk about that person publicly, I believe it is perfectly acceptable to make up laudatory statements and speak them straightfaced into the microphone. You are also allowed to say to the sick individual, "No, you don't have cancer."

This particular story of the secretary has a happy ending. Ronay and I managed to convince her that she was overqualified and that she should, in order to be challenged intellectually, take the new job at HUD. She said she wanted to think about it for a week, and in that intervening week she found an entirely different job at an even higher salary than she would have received at HUD. We parted friends.

As mayor I am in the position of appointing deputy mayors, commissioners and deputy commissioners. If I wanted to I could pick as many as three thousand people. In fact I appointed only about two hundred people, limiting myself in the beginning to deputy mayors, of which I had seven—in retrospect four too many—and commissioners and their deputies. Later I usually allowed the commissioners to pick their own deputies, and from the very beginning they picked everyone else in positions below deputy.

I am proud of the fact that my appointments overwhelmingly have been of people whom I never knew before they came through the process. I would estimate that 70 percent fell into that category and 30 percent were of people I knew before I became mayor.

Some of them were from my staff in Washington, and others were people I had met through the years. The appointments were made without regard to race, religion or sex. And, worse still from a political point of view, they were made without regard to the political consideration of the county leaders and other political people who had helped me and now wanted me to select their choices. In the past, to the victor had belonged the spoils, and I instead had spoiled the system from their point of view.

The most demanding in terms of my selections were black leaders who had supported me and who believed they should appoint the black members of my administration in high office. I would not permit that. I appointed the blacks who served, in the same way that I appointed the whites. I mention this because there are classically two things in politics that enhance your prospects for reelection, at least in the City of New York. They are the political appointments (outside of civil service) to high and middle levels of government and the appointments to the judiciary. Every staff appointment that is made through the regular political system means an energetic volunteer and to a certain extent a contented county leader when you run for reelection. I once attended a dinner for the Borough President of the Bronx, Stanley Simon, and there were one thousand people at that dinner. I said to Stanley Friedman, the county leader who had arranged the dinner, "I don't know how you did it. I couldn't get a thousand people to attend one of my fund-raising dinners." He said, "If you give me a thousand jobs, I'll get them there for you.'' While that was an overstatement, he in fact could point out how each of those who attended, whether they were working in government or were in the private sector, owed something to him or to Stanley Simon— not in a corrupt way, but just in terms of the regular glue of politics.

The same thing is true in the selection of judges. The Mayor of the City of New York selects the Criminal Court and Family Court judges. A total of 149 judges are selected, to serve for a ten-year period. The normal procedure is that a committee does the examining. Prior mayors had such committees as well, but I handled it in a different way. The county leaders expected that their judicial designees, if they were honest and relatively competent, would be selected by the Mayor. But since I have been the Mayor I have refused to allow them to have any political involvement in the process. I have never sent a person to the committee, known as the Mayor's Committee on the Judiciary, for its approval. Instead, I have asked the committee to send me three qualified candidates for each open position. Those candidates are self-initiated. They simply ask to be interviewed. As a result of that, I have been commended for my appointments. And the best commendation was provided by the Judiciary Committee of the City Bar Association, which in its 1983 report said:

> The Mayor has exhibited great concerns for the quality of the Judiciary. The Committee keeps

no statistics as to race or sex. Yet it is our impression that the number of candidates of high quality who are female, black or Hispanic has been at an all-time high. If every American government official with the power to make judicial appointments adhered to the standards that Mayor Koch has followed, the quality of the bench in this country would be a matter of national pride.

This kind of government can be politically costly. It means that I cannot, with the expectation that they owe me, go to the county leaders and to the district leaders and be certain of their support. And yet I have been successful, to a far greater degree than anyone would have expected, without the glue of politics—to wit, patronage jobs and patronage judges. I have done it because it was finally accepted by the county leaders that I could not be intimidated or threatened with loss of political support, and that worked basically because I was popular in the City of New York. Even more overriding was an acceptance by the political leaders that what I was doing was in the best interest of the city even if it was not in the politicians' best interest. What they would seek to do was to wear me down a little so that I would bend on occasion and take their appointments. I assume that on occasion I did, but I cannot recall one such occasion. I also once said to Meade Esposito—who was the county leader of Brooklyn for six years during my administration and for many years

19

before that—when he was complaining to me, "Meade, I know that you're embarrassed when I announce judicial appointments and you have never heard of the people and had no involvement in their selection. But why don't you, when the announcement is màde, immediately say that you are the one who gave me the name and claim that the judge is yours? It's okay with me and I will never say no." He didn't laugh and I think he occasionally, out of pure vanity, did what I had suggested.

One of the negative effects of what I have done was demonstrated in the 1982 gubernatorial election, which I lost. There were few volunteers, and the best people who had been appointed by me in government didn't come out in large numbers to help. Commissioners did not feel obliged to work in my campaign, and I would not ask them to do so. That is unique. Moreover, they did not feel obliged to urge others who worked for them to work in my campaign. Again, that is unique. It is certainly not the reason I lost, but it is an interesting effect of good government.

Finally, I am sure I have made my decisions in an apolitical way in part because I am religious to the extent that I believe in God and the hereafter. I don't know what God looks like or the form of heaven or hell, but I know heaven is better than hell. I believe we will each be weighed on the scales and receive an appropriate second opportunity in the more important second chapter to come. Therefore, I want to do whatever it is that I can do to leave a major positive mark. I want my administration as Mayor to surpass that of La Guardia, simply because I am competitive and I believe I can do it. I want history to look at what I have done with an approving judgment.

Improving the quality of the lives of people will make it easier for me when I am weighed on those scales.

2

Reform Politics

IN 1952 THE STEVENSON FORCES, such as they were, had a street-speaking campaign operation, giving each volunteer speaker a flag and a real soapbox or its equivalent. I didn't do anything more than that.

In 1956 I moved from Brooklyn to the Village. I looked for the group that was supporting Stevenson, and I became their major street speaker. That group was called Citizens for Stevenson, I believe. It had been organized because Carmine De Sapio, the leader of the Democrats in Greenwich Village, would not support Stevenson. The pro-Stevenson group ultimately became the Village Independent Democrats.

I began in politics with this Stevenson group but I left them, because I didn't think they were a particularly good group. Theirs was a very fractious operation headed by one of the group's founders, Dick Kuh—an assistant district attorney at the time, in Manhattan DA Frank Hogan's office—as president.

So I left what was to become the VID and for a year or so I didn't do anything politically. Carmine meanwhile had issued sort of a statement to the effect that he really wanted to change his political operation and he was looking for young people. I was approached by two guys, George Delaney and Ed Hale, who were both young and already with Carmine at the Tamawa Club, and I agreed to give De Sapio's operation a try. Both of them ultimately joined me in going back to the VID, but at the time in question they asked me if I wouldn't go up to the Tamawa Club, where they were election-district captains and where they said new people were wanted.

So I went up sometime in 1957 or 1958, and George Tombini, who was Carmine's uncle and who ran that club—well, he and all the others just recognized me, that's all. I mean they were friendly in the sense that they were courteous, but they didn't let me do anything. I just stood by standing out like a sore thumb. I stayed for about six months and then I said, "The hell with it," and I dropped out. They missed the boat, because if they had let me participate, who knows what might have happened? And I think it's fair to say I probably wouldn't have become mayor—I didn't have enough seniority with them.

In any event, I dropped out of politics after that for

maybe six months or a year, and then in 1959 I decided I'd go to a public meeting of the VID, and I'm sitting in the audience and some people come over—I think actually it was Gwen Worth, who was then one of the leading personalities in the club. She said, "Why don't you help us?"

I said, "I'd love to. I was just hoping someone would ask me. I thought that maybe because I had broken away from the club I would not be welcome here."

She said, "Oh no."

So I joined the club again and I became a pretty good political organizer. In 1960 I became the law chairman. I had been chairman of the speaking committee in 1959. We had had district-leadership races in 1957 and 1959. Herman Greitzer had been the VID candidate in 1957, and Charlie McGuinness in 1959. Both had lost their races, and in 1960 we ran a race for state committee, with Jim Lanigan and Sarah Schoenkopf. We won that. That was the first fight we won against De Sapio. It was a rather strange fight, because it was one reform force against another. Eleanor Clark French was a candidate selected by Carmine to defeat us, and we beat her and Charlie Kinsolving, who were both reformers. Carmine had used them, and they had permitted themselves to be used to beat us, but we crushed them. That was the first victory for the Village reformers.

Then Jim Lanigan ran in 1961 for district leader and he won in a race that I think could only be described as a victory for Mayor Wagner. Wagner ran for reelection that same year against the bosses and pulled in most of the reform forces in Manhattan. In fact, the only club that didn't win its race was the New Chelsea Club, which had refused to support Wagner. Bob Clampitt was the head of that. I don't know what he's doing now, but at the time he used very bad judgment.

That was 1961. As I said, Jim Lanigan was the first person to beat Carmine De Sapio, but nobody remembers him now. He's sort of like a nonperson. Personally I thought he was weak in character. I've seen him on two or three occasions since that time, and he looks so woebegone that I no longer dislike him as much as I did then.

The next year, 1962, I ran for the Assembly nomination, and in that primary race we were faced by the following situation: the Village Independent Democrats at the time were probably the strongest of the reform clubs, and we thought we would like to run somebody against Assemblyman William Passannante, whose base was De Sapio's stronghold in the South Village. Nobody seemed to want to run against Passannante, but I, because I wanted ultimately to be in public office and believed the club should have a candidate, said, "I'll run."

However, I could not get universal support in the district. The VID, of course, supported me, as did the Murray Hill Club. But it was a very divided operation. Passannante was well liked by people. He had a reasonably good record, and a reasonably liberal record for one who came out of the South Village and whose constituency in great part was conservative. In any event, I lost, and I lost as a result of the intervention of Senator Lehman and Mayor Wagner.

Let me see how I can put it: I was the reform candidate; Lanigan was the district leader and very supportive of me—he owed me a lot for my having helped him in his race for district leader. There was a Democratic state convention that year to select candidates for statewide office (that was before the days of statewide primaries). We elected delegates to the state convention in 1962. James A. Farley, a former U.S. Postmaster General and statewide leader, former national chairman of the Democratic Party, wanted to go to the convention, but he had not run to be a delegate, he wanted simply to be put up on a slate that had to be agreed upon among the political leadership in that assembly district, all of whom happened to be at that time reformers. Edward Costikyan, Manhattan county chairman, and Wagner and Lehman, none of whom was from the First A.D., all wanted him appointed. But the Village Independent Democrats, who had to approve the designation, said, "No, we will not appoint him as one of the delegates. He doesn't stand for our philosophy, and we won't do it." The other two clubs in the area, the Tilden and Murray Hill clubs, both were willing to designate Farley, but they were locked in with us. The delegates came out of one package, and it required our consent if Farley was to be seated in place of someone who had won, and we said, "No."

So then Lehman and Wagner began to work on Jim

Lanigan, because they had decided that the Village Independent Democrats ought to fold up their tent and leave. Indeed, from their point of view, what we were doing was simply running against every officeholder in the borough of Manhattan, good or bad, and many of them were Italian; and of the candidates that we were running, most were Jewish—so it looked like a Jewish–Italian vendetta. It wasn't intended that way. It is a fact, though, that most of the reform candidates were Jewish.

Lehman and Wagner wanted to reduce our impact if not eliminate us. What they did was this: Lehman sent a letter opposing me to every Democratic voter in the district, and Wagner came out against me and got Lanigan to attack the club. What happened with Lanigan was this: after Lehman and Wagner had called repeatedly and tried to get Farley on the slate and we had refused, they just assumed, after all, inasmuch as Lanigan is the leader, how come he can't accomplish this? And, of course, that's not the way the VID worked at that time or indeed probably works today. So Lanigan sort of removed himself from the club and didn't participate with us. Then, when Lehman came out against me, he tried to get Lanigan to line up support against me. The club reformers were still for me for the Assembly nomination notwithstanding Senator Lehman's attack, but we couldn't get hold of Lanigan. I think it was August by then. I remember it was near Labor Day weekend. And we decided what we would do (because we had heard rumors, too, that Lanigan was going to resign from the club, and obviously that would be very destructive for us in that election; God knows how you'd explain the resignation of a district leader): Sarah Schoenkopf went to his house—he lived on West Fourth Street—and knocked on his door. Nobody was there or else nobody would answer the door, wouldn't answer the telephone, and it was Sarah Schoenkopf's idea (she's now Sarah Kovner, Mrs. Victor Kovner) that we send him a telegram. The telegram read something like this: "Jim, unless you call the club within the next hour, we are issuing a telegram denouncing Senator Lehman and signing your name to it."

Well, he called the club in ten minutes. I got on and said, "Look, Jim, can we get together? I just want to talk to you." At first he didn't want to, but I persisted. Finally he said, "All right, but I just want to meet you. I don't want to meet anybody else, and we can do that at midnight and we'll meet in Jack Delaney's"—a well-known former Village restaurant that was located at Sheridan Square across the avenue from the VID headquarters. It's now maybe seven or eight o'clock in the evening when I have this conversation.

So I said, "Fine." Then what we plotted at the club was: I would go over to Jack Delaney's. We knew where Lanigan lived and how he would get there, and the others (Carol Greitzer, and I think Ed Gold was there, too—Sarah Schoenkopf certainly was) would be on the lookout, and when they saw him enter Delaney's they would come in, too. That was the plot.

So I went over to Delaney's at about midnight and sat down at a table, and just on time Lanigan walks in with his wife, Mary. I was their friend; they were my friends; I'd been to their house; I'd helped them. I really had what I considered to be a good relationship with them. In any event, he sits down and immediately in walk Carol Greitzer and Sarah Schoenkopf. They sit down on the same banquette, and he can't get out. And he is shocked, but he doesn't say much.

I say, "Look, Jim, we need your help."

He says, "Well Ed, I'm of a different breed." I'm paraphrasing what he said. "I'm of a different breed, and these are the people I relate to, Lehman and Wagner, and I just can't do anything that would be against them."

I say, "I understand that, Jim, and we don't want you to do anything against them. All we want you to do is not to do anything against me. Just don't do anything. Why don't you just get out of town for the weekend? Just don't do anything that would hurt me." This is on the eve of the primary election—maybe four or five days before. The primary that year was very close to Labor Day. This was probably Thursday, and maybe the next Tuesday would be the primary election.

He says, "You know, I'll resign from the club. I'll withdraw. In fact, I have a little note here, and I'll just withdraw and that will be the end of it."

I say, "No, no, no, that's not helpful to us. We don't want you to withdraw. We just want you to not attack us."

So he says, "Okay, Ed, I'll never attack you." And that's the way the meeting ended. This might be a conversation that took place on a Wednesday or Thursday night before that weekend, the Labor Day weekend.

So I think, Well, okay, it's tough, but we could still maybe win. Then a day or two later we get a call from Eddie Katcher of the New York *Post*. This is probably Saturday—I can't remember the date. Katcher, who was supportive of De Sapio in his columns, an old-line reporter, calls and he says, "We have a letter here from Lanigan in which he is resigning from the club, and he calls the club dialectically involved." The thrust of Lanigan's comments, as reported to us by Katcher, are that the club is a Commie club—you know, engaged in dialectics and that sort of thing, whatever that meant.

We just didn't know what to do. We said, "We don't believe it. We just don't believe it."

Katcher said, "Well, the letter also indicates that a copy has been sent to Stanley Geller," who was then the president of the club. So we waited. You see, it was Labor Day weekend: no mail. I think one of our people was a copyboy or something at the *Post*, and we sent him up there to see if he couldn't get hold of the letter in some covert way so that we could find out whether we should have a press conference to respond to it, because we didn't want to respond to something that maybe had never taken place, and we just didn't want to believe Ed Katcher.

We didn't get the letter until Tuesday morning, so what we did was: prior to that, we called a press conference. We didn't tell people who were being notified of the press conference what it was about, only that there was a press conference scheduled for Tuesday morning. In the event that we got the letter on Tuesday morning, we would be able to respond to it. And, sure enough, the letter came Tuesday morning to Stanley Geller's house, a copy of the letter of resignation that had been sent to the *Post*. It appeared in the *Post,* and we had our press conference. But it didn't save me.

I lost. And I lost in a way that was devastating. I think I got 32 percent of the vote, which is an all-time low in the Village. Even Herman Greitzer, in the first district-leader race against De Sapio, had gotten about 37 percent. I think I got 40 percent overall in the assembly district, which is also a devastating loss, because a 5 percent differential is generally considered a huge victory—and here Passannante wins by 20 percent. It was devastating.

I remember the night of the primary: I was broken-hearted. I was finished with politics. I made a farewell speech that would rival Richard Nixon's. I said, "Politics is a dirty business and I'll never run again and I'm through with the whole thing." I had tears in my eyes, no question about it, and everybody was very tearful in the room. It was just overwhelming.

The truth is it was the best thing that ever happened to me. Passannante is still in the Assembly twenty-three years later, and I went on to the Congress. Passannante was the only guy who could claim that he had beaten me until twenty years later when I was beaten for governor. If I had won in 1962, I might still be in the Assembly. That's really the heart of it. It was the best thing that ever happened to me.

•   •   •

Following that loss I picked myself up and ran for district leader. De Sapio's post. In 1963 I went up to see Steve Smith, President Kennedy's brother-in-law, who was running the Kennedy organization in New York. I remember it very well. It was at the Pan Am Building. I told him that we at the VID were going to beat Carmine—we didn't have a candidate yet, but we would—and urged him not to let the Kennedy people get involved against us on the grounds that the regular club was the De Sapio club at that time. Actually, that was not absolutely true. The official club was not the De Sapio club, it was the VID, because Lanigan had won the male district leadership and Carol Greitzer the female district leadership. But it was expected the De Sapio club would win simply because Lanigan wasn't running again, and Carmine was, and the VID had suffered this enormous defeat in the Assembly race. It was not only a defeat for me; it was a defeat for the VID. So there was great fear on our part that Steve Smith would in some way or other get involved against us and oppose us with the Kennedy machine. I said to him, "We will find somebody and we will beat De Sapio, and I just want you to be aware of that so you won't do something because you didn't have all the facts, that you will later find regrettable." I wanted to make it clear I wasn't threatening him; I was just trying to cajole him, to make him think about it rather than just jump in without having all the facts.

So then we started looking for candidates. You couldn't get anybody to run for district leader. And of course our club was so crazy—they came up with exotic ideas like getting James Baldwin, the writer, to run. If he had said yes, they probably would have taken him. And then they went to Theodore Bikel, the singer and actor, and they wanted to get him to run, and they went to every exotic personality that they could find. I'm not using "exotic" as a pejorative; I'm just referring to big-time names from their point of view—celebrity types. And they wouldn't run.

Finally I said, "I'm the president of this club. We're going to have a candidate. I don't want to run, but I will." I didn't want to run for district leader. Who wants to run against Carmine De Sapio? You literally worry about getting killed; you do. I really didn't want to run.

I lived then in the West Village, at 72 Barrow Street. I lived in the same building and even on the same floor as friends and relatives of Carmine De Sapio. There was always the fear that De Sapio would engage in illegality: tamper with the voting machines, kill people. But there was no violence when I ran against him in 1963. Well, maybe there was one time . . . It was about two o'clock in the morning and I was coming home from some political event prior to the election.

At 72 Barrow Street in the West Village, it's very

dark there. And this night I happened to meet a neighbor right in front of my building. We talked and I had just stepped away from the building when a flowerpot fell, and had it hit me on the head—and it would have had I not stepped away—I'd be dead.

I looked up: nobody's face. It could have been an accident. Who knows? But when you are running against a Carmine De Sapio you always remember you are running against someone who is capable of generating illegal activity.

The best illustration of Carmine De Sapio vis-à-vis corruption was the cash-in-the-cab incident. That was the time, in July 1957, when he left $11,000 in the back seat of a taxicab. That may have been the beginning of his downfall.

The story, as I recall it, is that he's the last passenger in a cab before the cab driver sweeps out the back. When the driver sweeps out the back he finds $11,000 in one-dollar bills, which is rather unusual. So this is an honest cab driver and he takes it to the police station. The law in the City of New York is if you find anything of value—my recollection is if it was over ten dollars at that time—you were legally required to turn it over to the cops, and then after a reasonable period of time, if it is not claimed, then it's your property.

Well, the cops inquired who was in the cab, and the driver said, "The last guy in the cab was Carmine De Sapio."

So they went to Carmine and he said, "Oh, that's not my money—definitely not, I never saw that money."

So the money went unclaimed and the driver ultimately got it. But everybody believed—I'm sure still believes that this was a wad that he was carrying around for God knows what purpose. And the smartest thing on his part would have been to say yes and give some explanation as to why it's in one-dollar bills. It isn't such a terrible thing for a guy like Carmine De Sapio to have $11,000. It's unusual, but it isn't impossible to have an honest explanation for it.

People never got over that little story.

And, of course, he went to jail, not for that, but for conspiring to commit bribery and to extort contracts. That was the end of his public life. The guy actually went to jail.

I remember being called the day he was sentenced, and being asked to go down to Sheridan Square and sit on a park bench nearby with a reporter. And I remember watching it later on TV.

The reporter said to me, "What do you think of De Sapio?"

"Oh," I said, "he is a crook. But I like him. And I'm really sorry that it's happened. But at this point I would have hoped there would be a suspended sentence." That was really the way I felt.

Then the reporter said, "What would you say if De Sapio walked across this street and walked up to you right now?"

I said, "I would say, 'Carmine, I'm sorry.'"

Well, they played that part of the tape in juxtaposition to the Italian barber who had the barbershop right underneath the Tamawa Club. That was the barbershop where De Sapio always got his haircuts. And the reporter is in the barber's chair, all lathered up, and going through the same kind of routine, and he closes by saying, "What would you do if Carmine De Sapio walked in that door?"

Well, the barber has been waxing eloquent about Carmine and is almost in tears about what has happened, and this barber says, "I woulda kissa him!"

It was sweet and . . . charming.

One of my joys in that district-leadership race was winning my own home election district. It was such a joy for me because it had been overwhelmingly for Carmine, but many of them voted for me because I was their neighbor.

Anyway, so I said <u>to</u> the club, "You can't get anybody else. So I will be the candidate." I remember one of the officers being very upset by this. He said, "Just by your saying that, you're keeping other people out."

I said, "So what? You run. Then I won't be the candidate." I was already getting tired of this operation, with all the internecine warfare that was taking place in the VID at that time. It was very troublesome and very enervating to have to fight your friends in addition to your enemies. It was a very difficult problem.

Anyway, they couldn't get anybody, so Carol Greitzer and I ran, and, as I've said, we won—by a margin of forty-one votes, which recalls another story.

Ed Costikyan was by then county chairman and very distressed by the thought that the De Sapio people and

De Sapio would make a comeback. He called me up to come up and see him. As I've indicated, he was not beloved by the reformers. He had been elected as county chairman by what they would consider to be a sort of third force. He was the candidate of Wagner and Lehman and not of the major forces in Manhattan as they saw themselves. In any case, he told me that he had taken a poll. The poll showed that I was going to lose by 1,500 votes if I ran, as I was then running, as a reformer against an old-liner; and that the only way there was a chance of my winning was if I ran on my record of community service. I had done a lot in the Village as a lawyer providing pro-bono service and was involved in many community matters. Costikyan recounts this story in his book *Behind Closed Doors,* which is his personal history of politics in the city. It happens to be a favorable report of the incident, and it amazed me that it was, since he was very angry with me at the time because I had come out for John Lindsay for mayor and Costikyan was campaign manager for Lindsay's opponent Abe Beame. He wrote: "Needless to say I acquired great respect for his [Koch's] intelligence and his courage. He was smart enough to turn his strategy inside out halfway through the campaign, strong enough to turn a losing campaign into one that could be won."* That was his story. He really didn't have much to do with changing what we were doing other than pointing out what he thought we should change in terms

Behind Closed Doors, by Edward N. Costikyan (New York: Harcourt, Brace, 1966), p. 218.

of strategy and plotting and so forth. But most of the work was done at the VID. And when we won, as we ultimately did, it was because of the hard work of the club, and the hard work of myself. I remember going down to the Italian South Village and getting eggs thrown at me. I'm glad it was only eggs. I worked very hard.

The night of the election at the VID was probably the most exciting night of my life. We thought that I had lost, because it was a dead heat and all of the election precincts had reported with the exception of Stewart House, a high-rise apartment building on East Tenth Street, which was so big it was an election district all by itself. It had not yet come in, but it was certain to go for Carmine because Diana Halle, his running mate for district leader (female), lived in that building and normally you expect that a building will support the candidate if that candidate lives there.

So we were sure it was over, and everybody was downcast. Then there was a telephone call from Costikyan and he says to me, "Don't concede. You've won."

I said, "Eddie, please don't tell me I've won. I'm looking at the board here and we have the results. I'm telling you—I lost."

He says, "We have the police results and you have won. Don't concede."

This was after the polls had closed. It was not as if he'd fixed the election. The police do get the results immediately. The returns are phoned right in from the precinct by the cop who's in charge of the poll, and

Costikyan had gotten them. He had Stewart House, which we didn't have. And a few minutes later in comes our captain from Stewart House: "We won! We won!" It was very exciting. We won the election by forty-one votes.

There was a lot of television there. You have to understand this is a big night. It's also raining outside. I remember that now. So the question then came: "Forty-one votes?..." Costikyan said, "Impound the election machines." So I get on the platform and I say, "We've won by forty-one votes. The De Sapio people are going to try to change the election. Go back to your posts and guard the machines and don't let them in." We meant every word of it. In retrospect it's really very funny. People streamed out of the VID—it's like midnight now—like they were going to the Battle of the Marne and defend Paris. They were going to guard those machines until those machines were taken away by the Board of Elections the next day. They stayed through the night, standing in front of the buildings to be sure that nobody went in to change votes. It was wonderful. It was the most exciting time.

3

Constituent Politics

I DON'T FIT ANY SPECIAL MOLD among those who seek high office. If anything I am more the anti-hero. Normally, in high political office, you want someone who is very cultured and sophisticated. Someone who comes from a well-placed family. Someone who has attended the right schools, gotten high marks, practiced in one of the best Wall Street law firms. All of those things I am not. Besides not being all that, I am not particularly good-looking, just ordinary. And all those things are what people have always said.

I find it bizarre when people say now that I am things that I am not. People occasionally say how well I dress. But I am wearing the same clothes I always did. I never throw away a suit. I am wearing the same Brooks

Brothers suits I've worn for years. Yes, I have some new ones. So, clearly, it is in the eye of the beholder.

The things I say now I said before. You don't get wittier as you get older. You either are or you aren't. My wit is sharp. It was before. But suddenly it's like, Gee, when did you develop it?

Now, there is one special element here. I am comfortable in front of a television camera. Why? Because I perceive it to be a very honest medium. It projects you the way you are. A lot of people are more comfortable watching things on a television set than they are watching them in person. They tend to elevate the people they see on television. I think that explains why people like my suits better than they used to.

Now for the pedigree reasons that I have mentioned. I was never popular with the radicals, the chi-chis or the goo-goos. And what that means is that in my early career I was the underdog every time I ran for a new office. I always ran with the humility of an adopted child.

●   ●   ●

The Manhattan skyline of 1960 told a lot about the city. Downtown and Midtown already had their towering skyscrapers. Between those mountains existed a saddle: Chelsea, Greenwich Village and the Lower East Side. These were the low-lying residential neighborhoods: predominantly mom-and-pop stores on the ground floor and five stories of tenement apartments above.

The pace of life was slower here than in Midtown or

up in the neighborhoods off Central Park. There was an Old World ambiance, and the architecture reflected it.

When I moved to Greenwich Village in 1956 it was still politically a district of three neighborhoods: the West Village, Lower Fifth Avenue and the South Village. The West Village was home to artists, anarchists and late sleepers from all over the world. The South Village—that area south of Washington Square Park—remained a densely populated mom-and-pop, thoroughly Italian neighborhood. And Lower Fifth Avenue was home to the richies and the upper middle class. Any Village district leader would have to find a bridge between these three neighborhoods or face becoming irrelevant.

As a Jewish lawyer born in the Bronx and now from Brooklyn, a VID reformer, I faced from the outset the problem of acceptance in the South Village. But the Italians are very tolerant and community-minded people. As a result, I became finally accepted by working harder on community issues than any Tammany district leader ever had worked.

I remember being on a platform at Sheridan Square in 1963 and saying, "You know it's true, Carmine was born here. And it is true that I moved here. I came in 1956."

And the hecklers would scream, "Go home! Go back where you came from. Go back to Brooklyn!"

I would then say, "But I'm like an adopted child. I love you more because you took me in."

What were the issues that I got involved in as district leader?

Carol and I got involved in everything—I'm talking about on the local level. That would mean being involved in preserving Washington Square Park, in getting the buses out of Washington Square Park. The park was the hub—everything revolved around Washington Square. Another issue was cleaning up Sixth Avenue. When I say "cleaning up" I mean the people who were bizarre or panhandlers—without violating anybody's civil rights; you always have to be conscious of that. We were also involved in getting better conditions at the Women's House of Detention, which was then located at Tenth Street and Greenwich Avenue. These were the local issues.

When we first started in '63, national issues did not predominate as such except for the atomic bomb and the hydrogen bomb. There we supported Adlai Stevenson's efforts to get nuclear testing stopped.

Prison reform—we got into prison reform. And we became famous in a very limited way. You have to understand there were eighty district leaders in Manhattan when we were first elected—forty men and forty women. But you rarely heard of the other district leaders. You often heard of Carol and me. Now, that wasn't because we were especially good, although I think we were. It was because we were from the Village.

The New York Times loved to do a story on Greenwich

43

Village. I guess the *Times* thought, Who cares about the Upper West Side? I'm talking about the uptown district leaders. You rarely saw their names in the *Times*.

In fact our name recognition made problems for Carol and me. The other leaders resented it bitterly. Here we were getting all this attention from the press and they're getting nothing.

If I had wanted to be sophisticated, I'd have said, "Oh, yes, the papers should have covered all of us equally." But bullshit! I loved it and so did Carol. And we appreciate the fact that ultimately we were each able to go on to other public offices as a result of the attention given us there by the media.

•   •   •

The Village had some kind of magnetic power for the whole city and still has it. New Yorkers love what happens down there. In 1963 they not only read about the Village; they also came downtown to see for themselves; to go to the coffeehouses or the jazz joints or just to hang out, and that made for problems.

One night we clocked ten thousand people in front of Harry Rissetto's liquor store, in the space of maybe an hour, walking back and forth on MacDougal Street. It may have been the same two hundred, but I'm telling you, ten thousand people were clocked passing his liquor store. You could hardly walk on MacDougal Street. It was an incredible scene there.

As the mess got worse Carmine made it the issue in

1963. This was the height of the coffeehouse operation and the guitar playing.

After the election I formed the MacDougal Area Neighborhood Association. I recognized that this was a legitimate issue. The problem was that this was a residential neighborhood. Fifteen hundred people lived in that three-block area, mostly Italian. And here people were coming in from all over the city and they had no regard for the neighborhood and they would piss in the doorways. The people who lived there were just incensed. They couldn't send their young kids out on the street. This was a residential neighborhood—this was not Times Square.

First I called up the pastor of the church on Carmine Street, Our Lady of Pompeii, and I said, "Father, I want to do something about MacDougal Street. I want to have a community meeting. Can I use the church's community room?"

He said, "Of course." So a couple of days later I get a call from the chairman of the trustees, who says, "You can't have the community room. We don't want to get involved in politics."

I say, "This isn't politics; it's civic. I'm the district leader and I want to have a community meeting."

"Sorry, you can't have it here," he says, and it's obvious that Carmine had opposed it and decided to stop it if he could. I had sent Carmine a letter, by the way. It said, "Dear Mr. De Sapio, I am holding a meeting of the community to discuss the problems of

MacDougal Street. The meeting will be held at Our Lady of Pompeii, which is located at..." It was hilarious—that's his church. It was really funny and I enjoyed it.

After that letter I got this cancellation. So I called up New York University and I asked if I could have one of their auditoriums, and they said yes. Then I announced that owing to the enormous response to the meeting, there would not be enough seats in Our Lady of Pompeii and that the place had been changed to the NYU Education Building.

Well, people were very worried at the VID. I remember one woman saying to me, "Don't go there; I hear that they may even kill you, they're so angry with you."

I said, "Oh, come on; don't worry about it. What can they do? I don't believe it."

So I go down there. It was a hot August night. And out in front on West Fourth Street, right in front of the Education Building, there are three blacks carrying picket signs. The signs read: "Koch must go." The Italians had hired them to picket me.

Well, the auditorium fills up. I had invited to this meeting every official who had any kind of jurisdiction. The city wanted to be helpful to me. Wagner was still the Mayor. We had maybe six commissioners, on the stage to answer questions, and I'm chairing the meeting. And one guy gets up who is not Italian—he's obviously sort of a hippie type. And he says in a very aggressive way, "I want to ask Bill Passannante why he has been so miserable on . . ."—six different issues that have nothing to do with MacDougal Street. And Bill and I were not friends.

But I said to the guy, "That question is out of order. That will not be asked. This is not a meeting where we're going to engage in personalities and political attacks."

He continues.

I say, "Sit down."

He says, "Who are you to tell me to sit down?"

I say, "I'm the chairman and I'm running this meeting. You will sit down." Then I say to this audience of 250 Italians, "Do I have your confidence?"

You have to understand they hated this hippie guy; they viewed him as the guy who was pissing in their doorways, and they began to roar and applaud me and yell, "Sit down! Sit down! He's the chairman."

It was wonderful.

There were some VID people there who were scared to death when I did that. I mean supposing they had yelled back, "No!"

Okay. So out of that meeting I formed the MacDougal Area Neighborhood Association, called MANA, and we met for a year. First we met over at the Village Gate. And on the committee I tried to put various interests that would be involved. I had a coffeehouse owner on, but he was no good—he didn't really care about the community, he only cared about his business. I asked Wally Popolizio to be the chairman and Harry Rissetto to be a member, because he was sort of like everybody's uncle in the area, and they brought in a lot of people. I think they brought in twenty or twenty-one people. And there were De Sapio people among them. There was one VID person as well, a woman who lived on MacDougal Street, Barbara Northrup.

Anyway, during the course of the meetings in 1965 an incident occurred that was just awful. The Democratic county organization redistricted for the district-leadership races, and they cut the Village in two. I went up to county headquarters—J. Raymond Jones was then the county chairman—and I looked at the lines, and I said, "These are bad lines" (the lines had been drawn by the county leader). I said, "I don't want the Village divided." What they had done was they had drawn two districts: everything west of Sixth Avenue and everything east of Sixth Avenue, give or take a few blocks here and there. And I didn't want to lose the West Village. I wanted it all to be one Village. They had also added 2,500 Italians by moving the southern boundary down to Spring Street as opposed to leaving it at Houston.

Actually, it was MacDougal Street that was involved, that had been taken out of my district. I said, "I want it back." MacDougal Street, regardless of its infamous reputation at the time, was an authentic part of the Village scene. The residents were Italian, but there were lots of weekend tourists who were the precursors of the yuppies—college students out for a good time, thinking they were going to meet Allen Ginsberg, the poet, in every coffeeshop, and occasionally they did.

J. Raymond Jones said, "You'll just be adding Italians to your district. What do you need it for?"

I said, "I don't care. I want the district kept as one district." And that was the way it was left.

But only temporarily. Jones was not interested in me or in keeping the Village together. What did that have to do with politics? And the other thing was, he wanted to help De Sapio, and dropping the lines down to Spring Street helped Carmine.

So when they held public hearings on the lines up in Albany I went up there to testify against the lines and said that they'd been drawn in the county headquarters—I said that I had gone there to see them—and that these were not lines that were drawn on the basis of anything other than political considerations.

That night I picked up the papers, early editions of *The New York Times* and the *News,* and on page one of the *Times* is J. Raymond Jones denouncing me as having asked him to cut the Italians out of my district, and conveying that I had made anti-Italian remarks to him. You can't imagine how devastating that was. I hadn't done it, just the contrary. J. Raymond Jones had made the story up. But how do you catch up with a headline on the front page of *The New York Times?*

Well, I thought, that's the end of my political career. So I consulted with my closest advisers—Micki Wolter, a young woman who is now director of *The City Record,* very bright, a good friend. She said, "Well, what you have to do: you've got to go down to the South Village every night and just show the flag, show them you're not afraid of them, talk to them, try to convince them."

So I went down to MacDougal Street every night, and the first night I went down she went with me. And I don't know whether it was in my mind or not, but everybody seemed to stop to stare—like all the windows went up on Thompson and MacDougal and Sullivan Streets. A woman came over and said, "Why do you hate Italians? Why do you want to put us in boxcars and ship us to concentration camps?" I mean it was insane what they were saying. This same woman talks to me in front of a pizzeria on MacDougal Street and begins to berate me and then she says as she looks into the store and sees a black guy with a white woman, obviously a couple, she says, "Just a minute," and she runs into the store and she yells at the woman, "Nigger lover! Nigger lover!" And then she comes back out and she says to me, so help me, "You are nothing but a bigot!" It's an unbelievable story, but it happens to be true.

Now, I won anyway—this would have been my reelection as district leader in 1965—and the people on this committee were very helpful to me. But I'm walking along the street a couple of days after the election and I meet Pete Canevari, a local guy, who was to have been Carmine's successor. He had been groomed personally by Carmine. He's not the smartest guy in the world, but he's all right. Of course he hated me, because, after all, I had taken away his prospective job and future. He stops me on the street and he says, "Ed,

I think you should resign from MANA. You can't help it anymore after what you've done. You really ought to resign.''

That bothered me. So I go to the next meeting. I can't even remember at whose house it is; I think it may have been at Barbara Northrup's house. There are maybe fifteen or so people—Wally Popolizio and Harry Rissetto and Dina Nolan and Nick Marucci, Marie del Gordio, a whole host of people. A lot of those people had come out of Carmine's club, too, but we now had been working together for close to a year. And I said to them as we're having Saturday breakfast, ''I think I must resign. I've had this conversation with Pete Canevari, and he thinks it's harmful to the committee for me to be on it. The committee is more important than my being on it. I'm not the chairman, in any event; Wally is. And I think I'll resign. I don't want to hurt what's taking place.'' I really felt quite distressed by what Canevari had said.

So Wally said, ''Just a minute. Let's figure out what everybody else wants to do.'' So he goes around the room. He says, ''What do you think?'' And everybody, *everybody,* the most pro–De Sapio people there, said, ''Certainly not. You're a member of this committee. You are not going to resign.'' And we get to Marie del Gordio, and she said, ''You were elected for two years and you are not resigning.''

It was really very sweet. So I stayed on.

•   •   •

But now to go back a little in time, eight months after I was elected district leader in 1963 the court set aside the election and there was a second election on the grounds that some of those forty-one votes didn't fulfill all of the requirements of law. It was outrageous. It was a political decision by the courts. The court found that some of the people who voted hadn't signed the book. Signing the book has nothing to do with it. Yes, there is a technical requirement to sign the book, but election after election some people don't sign the registration book, and it's not fraud but incompetence on the part of the election inspectors that is to blame. It wasn't a question that anybody who had voted was not a qualified voter. These people were legal voters who had not been asked to sign the book.

So the day the court's decision comes out there is an article in *The Villager*, which was supporting Carmine De Sapio. De Sapio was quoted as saying, "My opponent opened up the graves." The implication was that I had voted people who were not entitled to vote. It was an outrage. I mean here is a guy who ultimately served time, and I am an honest guy. His people were the people who were running the Board of Elections. We didn't appoint the clerks. We had, perhaps foolishly, kept on at the Board of Elections the inspectors who had been appointed originally by Carmine De Sapio.

So, I was going to be on a television program the following day with Carmine. It was a taping for Sunday. When I walk into the studio Carmine sees me and says, "Hello, Ed," and then holds out his hand. I refused to shake his hand.

I say, "Look, Carmine, you can't call me a crook on Thursday and shake my hand on Friday. This is not a football game."

The TV program was split fifteen minutes for each of us. Gabe Pressman was the moderator. Carmine went on first. The first thing he said was, "Mr. Pressman, I am really shocked. This is the first time in all of my days in politics that I have seen something happen that's just un-American: Mr. Koch refused to shake hands with me! How un-American can you get?"

Well, I get on and I say, "This is not a football game." Most people thought it was childish; some people didn't care; my ardent supporters thought it was wonderful. On reflection if I had to do it over I would probably shake his hand and say something along the lines of "Carmine, we are shaking hands, but this is such hypocrisy. How could you do what you did yesterday and want to shake hands? I don't really want to shake hands. We are doing it because it is considered gentlemanly, but I want you to know how I feel." That is what I would do twenty-one years later. But I am not ashamed of what I did. I thought it was right to do.

●   ●   ●

Notwithstanding the many problems as Village district leader, I succeeded in distinguishing myself as someone effective at getting things done in the community. It was a reputation that followed me to the City Council, to which I was elected in 1966. Once there, I did not change; and my role as mediator between the late sleepers of the West Village and the early risers of the South Village increased.

Possibly because my district covered Greenwich Village, with its mixture of old Italian families, hippies and assorted individualists, I got an unusually large number of calls for help. Some were sublime, like "Mr. Koch, could you please get the Pan Am helicopter pilots to stop hovering over my roof when I'm sunbathing?" Some were unbelievable, like "Would you get my son home from Vietnam for Mother's Day?"

One evening I picked up my telephone to hear a constituent complain, "There are beatniks living above me. Please get rid of them."

"No," I said. "You may not like people with long hair, but that's no reason for throwing them out on the street."

"It's not the long hair."

"Just because people may be dirty—"

"It's not the dirt."

"Well, what is it, then?"

"They ride motorcycles."

"You can't do anything to people because they ride motorcycles."

"In their apartment?"

"Now you're talking. Give me your name, address and apartment number."

After hanging up, I called the Fire Department to report a fire hazard: the presence in a residential building of a gasoline engine that was neither properly secured nor insulated.

* * *

One of the main constituent problems, as I've said, was Washington Square Park. We had problems in the park over the years when I was district leader and later when I was in Congress. For example, I will tell you one of the problems I had. In May 1972, about six o'clock on a Thursday evening, I was going through the park to go over to Sixth Avenue and take a subway up to an American Jewish Committee dinner. And as I walked through Washington Square Park—and it's very light—a big black guy (maybe six three or so, and, as I tell people, every time I tell the story he gets bigger) stops me and says, "Give me a quarter, man."

I say, "No."

At that he picks up his fists and threatens me. He says, "Give me a quarter or I'm going to beat the shit out of you."

I say to myself, This is intolerable. Then I did something irrational. I said to him, "No, I'm Congressman Koch and I'm going to have you arrested." Well, he's really shocked. He puts his fists down, so to speak, and he walks away. I look around and there's no cop in Washington Square Park. I say to myself—it's now about six-ten or so—I could walk away from this, but if I do, I'll never forgive myself; here's this sonofabitch who threatened me—imagine what he does to other people. I see him go over to two other guys, ask for quarters, and I see that they give him quarters because they're afraid. I say to myself, I'm not going to leave; I'm going to follow him; I'm going to get him arrested.

So he walks through the Washington Arch, up Fifth Avenue, no cops around. I walk on the other side of the street following him. We go up to Eighth Street; he turns right, across to Broadway. At that point a patrol car comes down Eighth Street. I step off the curb. I stop the car, I say, "I'm Congressman Koch."

The patrolman says, "I know who you are."

I say, "I've just been hassled in the park, and I want to have the guy arrested."

He says, "Do you know how long that will take?"

I say, "I don't care. I'm supposed to be at a dinner at six-thirty, but I don't care."

He says, "All right, get in." I get in the car, we drive down Eighth Street. There's the guy talking with two other guys, the three of them standing there. We get out of the car, walk toward them, and the guy says, "I didn't do it."

I say, "That's him."

The cop says, "Okay, come on." He takes us down to the Sixth Precinct and they're very nice to me. They really want to get me through in quick time.

I say, "Listen, I've got this dinner at six-thirty that I am supposed to be a dais guest at."

"Okay." They book him. It takes forty minutes to book him. At that moment it looked like half of the

cops at the Sixth Precinct were dressed as gypsies—
they were in disguise, as decoys, you know. This was a
funny place to be in. Meanwhile, this guy, who was
obstreperous and probably somewhat under the influ-
ence of liquor, begins to yell. The cop who's taking the
information from him—he's dressed like a gypsy—says
to him, "You keep that up and I'm going to take you
into the back room."

Now, what was interesting was my own mental reaction. Here I am, a civil libertarian, yet I'm so angry I
say to myself, You know, if he does, I'm not going to
stop him.

They book him. They drive me down to 100 Centre
Street, because now he has to go to night court. They're
rushing me through this thing. The cop says to me at
the desk, "Listen, I'll put this on the police wire so that
the press will know about it."

I said, "No, I don't want to do that."

He repeated, "I should put it on the wire."

I didn't say no the second time.

He puts it on the wire: "Congressman Koch arrests
panhandler who threatens him in the park."

So we get to 100 Centre Street and now the guy had
to be booked again by the assistant DA. We go up to
the complaint room, and they recognize me. I say,
"Listen, I hope you can rush this thing through a
little," because it's about seven-fifteen now.

He says, "Oh, yes, we'll do it. But what's the
story?"

I tell him the story.

The assistant district attorney says, "Well, let's book him for robbery."

So I said, "Listen, I don't want to make a federal case out of this thing. He threatened me. Let it go at that."

He said, "No, we should book him."

I said, "No, I don't want him booked for robbery. In the first place, robbery is the forcible taking of money."

It takes another forty minutes to book him there. They have the same questions they had at the Sixth Precinct, the same card, I'm sure, the same business, and I have to sit there and they're rushing me through. I'm thinking to myself, If they weren't rushing this, when would I get out of here?

So now it's about eight o'clock, and we go upstairs and there's another assistant DA. He says to me, "Congressman, it's a waste of your time. Why don't you just drop it?"

I say, "No, I'm not going to drop it."

He comes back a little later and he says, "Listen, the guy's agreed to plead guilty to harassment."

I say, "That's okay." Harassment isn't even a criminal offense. There are three things: offense, misdemeanor, felony. Harassment is like spitting on the sidewalk. You can be fined for it, but you get no criminal record.

So then I say to him, "Okay, I want to say something to the judge. I want to make a statement."

The assistant DA says, "You can't. The judge doesn't take statements."

I say, "You tell the judge that Congressman Koch wants to make a statement."

The assistant DA says, "Your Honor, Congressman Koch wants to make a statement."

Says the judge, "By all means."

So I say to the judge, "Your Honor, I don't know why I'm here. I'm crazy to be here. I have to be at a dinner, and the dinner's probably over by now. What is the use in my taking on a guy like this over a quarter? But he threatened me. And if he does it to me, what does he do to women and children? This whole park can't be used anymore, and people are so fed up—and that's why I'm here. I just want you to know."

"Oh yes, Congressman, the whole city is like that. It is just awful." And then he looks in the direction of this defendant and he says, "I want you to know if you ever come into my court again . . ."

I thought, Ah, the usual, nothing with nothing. But then he did something remarkable. He said, "I'm going to fine you fifty dollars." I thought that was not bad. I expected that the defendant would pay it in quarters; but to be fined fifty dollars is not bad for that offense.

The Legal Aid counsel representing him said, "Your Honor, my client is employed and he lives at so-and-so. He's a little short. Could we have time to pay the fine?"

Says the judge, "How about three weeks?"

Says counsel, "That will be fine, Your Honor."

We leave. The defendant and I leave together. We

leave the courtroom together. He sort of smiles at me, this defendant. I couldn't figure out why, but he smiles.

Three weeks later—because I'm a very persistent person; I've got a stick-to-itiveness that baffles people— to the day, I send a letter to the court clerk: "On such and such a day the following incident occurred. The fine was $50. Has it been paid?" I get no response. I wait a week and I send a letter to David Ross, who was the administrative judge. I happened to know him; he was majority leader of the City Council when I was there. "Dear David," I wrote, "I am shocked that a letter I sent to the clerk, a copy of which I am enclosing, has not been responded to. I'd appreciate your looking into this matter."

A couple of days later there's a letter from the clerk: "Sorry that we didn't respond to your first letter, Congressman, but we were hoping that he would come in and pay. We have found out that the name he gave us was a false one; and so we have issued a warrant for his arrest." I mean it's insane, right? And I thought to myself, You don't know his name. You don't know where he lives. He knows my name, he knows where I live, and it's very unpleasant when you think about it.

Okay. I put that story into *The Congressional Record* and it went out all over the country. The papers picked it up, and *The Wall Street Journal* did a huge story on it, just taking my story right out of *The Congressional Record*, and I got mail from all around the country saying, How nice it was, really nice, that you did this.

And then I had a different reaction from a guy like

Jack Newfield at *The Village Voice*. Jack Newfield, I was told, said to people, "I'll never forgive Ed Koch for arresting that poor guy." This poor panhandler who threatened to beat the shit out of me. People like Jack Newfield found it offensive that I would do that to this poor guy. This poor nine-foot-tall guy.

Now, as a result of pressure from me and from the community we worked it out several years later that the Sixth Precinct would keep a car parked at the corner of Thompson Street and Washington Square South as a sort of mobile headquarters, and that cops would walk through the park. And that was fine. But the cops stopped doing that. On a couple of occasions there were just no cops in the park and it became, once again, intimidating.

For instance, one time in 1976 I walked through the park and suddenly I saw a woman, very unusual-looking, a turban and rather strange clothes, and she was saying to anybody who walked by, "Nickel bags and loose joints—nickel bags and loose joints." That means heroin and marijuana. I'm really offended by this. I mean what the hell's happening to Washington Square Park? It's now the center of drug traffic?

So I go to a phone at the corner of Washington Place and Washington Square West, and I call 911, and I say, "This is Congressman Koch, and I am standing at the corner of Washington Place and Washington Square West, and I am at this very moment observing a woman in a turban, a black lady, in rather distinctive clothes, who is saying, 'Nickel bags and loose joints,' and she is obviously selling dope. Don't you think you might send somebody over, maybe an undercover person, and do a little arresting?''

So 911 says, "Just a moment," and he's evidently trying to locate the address, and he comes back and says, "There is no such corner."

So I say, "Listen, I am not only standing at the corner of Washington Place and Washington Square West, I am looking at a street sign that says Washington Place and Washington Square West."

"Just a moment." I could hear the machine whirring. "Oh yes, we found it, we'll take care of it."

So I wait fifteen or twenty minutes, nobody comes, and then I take off. I mean there's a limit to how much time I can spend on this crap. In any event that was the incident, and I write a letter to Captain Fortune at the Sixth Precinct and I say, "I'm just really angry that this can go on. It's driving the decent people out of the park. You've got to do something."

The letter goes unanswered.

Then on Thanksgiving Day I'm walking through Washington Square Park. I leave my house about three o'clock in the afternoon. I have a dinner engagement and I just want to get some air before I go to dinner. I walk over through the park and over to the corner of Sixth Avenue and Eighth Street. There may be fifteen or twenty people on the street, which is not a lot of people for that area except it's a very quiet day, Thanksgiving Day, and there at the corner of Sixth Avenue and Greenwich Avenue is a middle-aged guy naked, pissing into the street. Well, even in the Village, that's unusual. I walk across the street and I say to the florist at the corner, "How long has this been going on?"

He says, "Oh, since about eight o'clock this morning."

I say, "What about the cops?"

He says, "Haven't seen one for days."

At that moment an elderly man, very well dressed, comes over and he looks at this guy who's still pissing, and he says, "One of your constituents, Congressman?"

I say to him, "You know how to hurt a guy."

So I go over to the phone there and I call the Sixth Precinct, and I say, "This is Congressman Koch. I'm standing at the corner of Sixth Avenue and Greenwich Avenue. There's a guy pissing in the street. He's naked. Just a moment, he's on his knees praying. Don't you think you should send a patrol car here and take him to Bellevue?"

The cop at the other end says, "We are not doctors. We can't decide whether somebody belongs in Bellevue."

I say, "I didn't suggest you should decide how many days he stays there. Just that you take him there so a doctor can look at him."

"What did you say your name was?"

"Koch, K-O-C-H."

"Will you still be there when we come?"

"Oh," I said, "indeed I will."

Okay. About seven minutes later a patrol car arrives. There are two cops in it, very mod-looking, tall, mustaches, long hair. They get out of the car. This guy is still on his knees praying in the street. His pants are now around his ankles. He's otherwise naked, and holding a bottle in his hand, a wine bottle, and praying to the sun. The cops go over and they jerk him to his feet. I say to myself, Well, they're not saints.

A lady observing all this yells out, "Don't you dare hurt him!"

Says the cop to her, "Want to take him home for dinner, lady?"

This could happen only in the Village; I mean it's terrific. So they pick up his trousers and wrap them around him and throw him into the back of the car. I go over and I say, "Are you taking him to Bellevue?"

The cop says very curtly, "Don't worry about it. We'll take care of him."

I say, "I didn't ask you that. I'm Congressman Koch. I'm the guy who called you. Are you taking him to Bellevue?"

The cop says, again somewhat curtly, "We're going to take him to a hospital and dry him out. Don't worry about it." Less curtly than the first response, but still not very friendly.

Well, I am annoyed. I write another letter to Captain Fortune. (The mail on this matter I would send to every member of the Community Board. And they loved getting it, believe me.) So I write to Captain Fortune: "It's very distressing to me that a letter that I sent you on [whatever the date of that first letter was] has still not been responded to. And it's obvious to me that I have to pursue this matter not with you but with [Police] Commissioner Codd, who's also going to get copies of this mail." And then I go on and describe this situation with this guy on Thanksgiving Day.

Well, that gets them all upset, and the captain calls up and he's very sorry that the mail has not been answered, and they're trying their best, and the cops had been used for the Thanksgiving Day parade, but in the future he will make certain that even if it means that the cops can't take a day off if Washington Square Park and the other posts would be unmanned, they will not take their day off. You can imagine what it does for my relationship with the cops when they are told, "If you don't get a day off, blame Koch."

Then I got a letter from Codd saying, "This whole matter will now be the subject of investigation."

And then I get a letter from Captain Fortune that he's now asked for undercover people and he's going to make sure that the clean sweep of Washington Square Park will continue. That means that they will pick up everybody who, as he describes it, is "disheveled."

I say to myself, This guy wants to make me look like a fascist or at least entrap me that way, because you can't pick up everybody just because you don't happen to like the way he looks. You can't even pick people up who are drunk. It has to be not only that they are drunk but that they are committing some kind of criminal act harassing other people or are a danger to themselves. Public intoxication is not a crime. The Supreme Court has said that. So I write back saying: "Just in case anybody sees our correspondence, I want them to know that I do not think the police should pick people up simply because they are disheveled or you don't like their looks—only if they commit a crime. I am sure that's what you mean, too.''

And he writes back, ''Oh yes, that's definitely what I mean,'' and so they put the cop back into the park.

4

Party Loyalty

JOHN LINDSAY WAS ELECTED TO THE CONGRESS from New York's East Side Silk Stocking District in 1958. Most of the chroniclers—including Bill Buckley, Ed Costikyan and me—agree that Lindsay did not distinguish himself in Washington as a drafter of outstanding legislation. Buckley's study indicates that Lindsay's congressional record was noteworthy only for the regularity with which Lindsay, a Republican, voted with the Democrats. The consensus on Lindsay the Congressman seems to be that he distinguished himself less as an effective public servant than as a charming candidate, a charge Lindsay once leveled at John F. Kennedy.

Nevertheless, in 1965 when Lindsay ran for the mayoralty he was able to marshal not only the support of the Republican Party but also that of the Liberal Party and of many reform Democrats who would not support the clubhouse candidacy of City Comptroller Abraham Beame. As we got closer to the election it was clear the Village was supportive of Lindsay. The membership of the VID was basically for him. And I was supportive of him, for mayor.

The weekend before the election I was called by Henry Stern, who was an important member of the Liberal Party. He said he wanted to advise me that he thought I should come out for Lindsay. That's a very grave step for a Democratic district leader to take. I thought about it and I said, "You're right, I'll do it."

Over the weekend I met with Henry Stern; and in my apartment at 14 Washington Place we hammered out the statement that I would use the next day, Monday, the day before the election. It's my recollection that during the preceding week, the week before the election, two polls were released. The *Daily News* poll showed that Lindsay would lose, and the *Herald Tribune* poll showed that he would win by about one percent.

Having made the decision, I go to bed Sunday night and try to sleep. Oh, on Sunday we had sent out telegrams that there would be a press conference at my law office on Monday at 10 A.M. And I can't sleep Sunday night. I am tossing, I am turning, I am convinced that I have destroyed my political career, because one does not cross party lines with impunity. Very realistically, I do not sleep all of Sunday night.

At 6 A.M. I get out of bed in a cold sweat and I

decide that I really ought to talk to my friend Dan Wolf, who was then the editor of *The Village Voice* and who I knew got into the office early because on very many other occasions I would meet him for breakfast at seven o'clock in the morning.

So I get dressed and I walk over to Christopher Street, where they had their offices in a little corner building at Seventh Avenue South (since torn down), and I see him in the window. I get into the phone booth across the street and I call their private, off-the-board number. Dan answers and I say, "Dan, I'm downstairs. Can I come up?" He looks out the window and he sees me and says, "Sure, I'll be right down." He comes downstairs and opens the door; I go upstairs. I'm a wreck. I've never been such a wreck.

He says to me, "What's up?"

I say, "Dan, I've decided to come out for Lindsay and I've called a press conference for ten A.M. in my office and I feel that I'm going to be destroyed. It's the end of my political career and I'm really quite distraught."

He says, "Look, you are not liked in the Democratic Party. They'll never like you. You are a maverick. They hate you. If they could destroy you they would, whether you come out for Lindsay or not. Nothing you can do will make them angrier than they are and have been since you beat De Sapio." That was the thrust of his statement to me. "So don't worry about it. In fact, it can be good for you."

I thought maybe he was trying to make me feel good, but the truth is that the die was cast. The telegrams had been sent out the previous night. So the press all knew. But then he said, "Have you told Carol?" Carol Greitzer.

I said, "No."

"That's a mistake," he said. "You've got to tell her because if you don't tell her, when you make your statement the press will call her, and she will not have been alerted, and she's apt to attack you because you didn't fill her in before. So at least tell her."

I hadn't thought of that, because I was sure she would not be supportive of the endorsement, and she's a very difficult person to deal with. I like Carol, and we are very close friends politically, and we like each other on a personal basis, but she is very difficult to deal with.

So I said, "That's a good idea."

But Carol usually takes her phone off the hook at night. You can't really get to her until she puts the phone back on the hook, which sometimes isn't until the afternoon.

I go to my office—it was then at 52 Wall Street—and I keep calling and calling and keep getting the busy signal because the phone is off the hook. But finally, at about 9:30 A.M., the phone rings through. And it's Carol, and so help me I spoke to her like this: "Carol, this is Ed. I'm coming out for Lindsay this morning and there's nothing you can do to stop me." Because I was sure she would be opposed and try to harangue me and so forth, and threaten me maybe and who knows what?

She says, "Why didn't you tell me before? I might have done it with you."

I say, "It's not too late. The press conference is at ten A.M."

She says, "I'm not dressed and my hair isn't done."

I say, "I will hold them here until eleven. We'll have the press conference at eleven A.M. Put something on and come down here." I must say parenthetically that I had told Marty Berger—the president of the VID—the night before and he had agreed to the endorsement. I'm the male district leader and I'm on the phone to the female district leader and she says, "Okay, I'll come down." I was ecstatic.

Well, I had never had such a big press conference in all my life. It was a small office, maybe twelve by fifteen, and the place was swarming with television and press, because they knew, based on the statement that we sent out, what the likelihood was. It was that kind of year. They smelled it.

Well, Carol comes in and Marty Berger is there and we had a press conference that was just terrific, the best one I'd ever had. The formal statement was done by Henry Stern, a lovely statement, one page. But then, we're pretty good. I mean Carol and I are pretty good with the press, and Marty Berger isn't bad. We did a bang-up job.

Now, on Tuesday, in the *Daily News*, the banner headline on the front page, the biggest headline I had ever been involved in, read: "LBJ AND HUMPHREY PUSH BEAME; REFORM DEM KOCH BACKS LINDSAY." Same-size type. I mean crazy . . .

Well, I can only tell you that Marvin Gersten, one of

Lindsay's campaign people, said my endorsement made it possible for Lindsay to win. I don't say I believe that, but it's very complimentary. Gersten said he was in Brooklyn that Monday afternoon on the boardwalk and that's all people were talking about: "That Koch who beat Carmine De Sapio came out for Lindsay. A Democratic district leader."

Later on that day I got a call from Bob Price, Lindsay's campaign manager: Would Carol and I and Marty Berger come to Republican headquarters to attend a TV marathon that Lindsay is holding? I thought, Look, I'm in it, I might as well do as much as I can.

I get there with Carol, maybe at seven or eight o'clock at night, and I look at this group of people assembled to help Lindsay, and all I can say to myself is, These are terrible people. I wouldn't associate with these people. These are all the richies, all the people who are dilettantes. These are not the people who would ever be supportive of me. I don't like them politically, and I don't like them socially. What the hell am I doing here? But I'm there. People are going on television. Bob Price says, "We'll put you on, too, and you'll make a statement for Lindsay."

I said to myself, I'm not going on television in this milieu. It's like they took out a trained monkey they're going to parade around on stage. And I'm the monkey.

"Not me," I said to Price. "No, I'm leaving. I'm not going on television where you bring me on stage like a trained monkey. Not me."

He said, "Suit yourself." And I left. But Price never forgot what I did for Lindsay, particularly since Carol and I were then placed on trial by Tammany Hall.

J. Raymond Jones held the trial at the Commodore Hotel. The purpose of the proceeding was to get Carol and me to apologize, or to resign from the party, or to resign our district leadership, or do something to atone, or else suffer the consequences of their kangaroo court.

We were asked beforehand to recant, but we would not apologize and we would not resign. We said, "We want the trial." Stanley Geller was our lawyer. He demanded specifications, and that went on for weeks. He demanded . . . God knows what he demanded under the election law before they could actually hold the hearing.

It was funny when you think of it. J. Raymond Jones was the judge. Mitch Bloom, a district leader who is not exactly a model of propriety, and who happened to have a broken leg in a cast at the time, was there. Louis Grossman, the Tammany Hall lawyer, was the opposing counsel.

Now, Stanley is a very good lawyer. He had represented me in a trial when Carmine De Sapio sought to set aside the '63 election. That went on for a month. All my life I was in court with these guys—over crap!

Geller made a motion to dismiss the case on God knows what grounds. I don't remember the technical aspects of it. But suddenly the place became pandemonium. Everyone is yelling and screaming, and Mitch

Bloom, who is walking around with a cane and with this cast, begins to yell and sort of approach Stanley, shouting, "Throw him out! Throw him out!"

And Geller says, "If you take one more step in my direction, I'm going to break your other leg."

When you think about it, grown men, political people, lawyers—it's a joke.

Well, J. Raymond Jones decided, based on the advice given him by other district leaders, that if they removed us, as they might have, and there was another election, we'd cream them, because we were going to run again. The fact is we were heroes, Carol and I. And here we are being tortured by Tammany Hall. What could be nicer?

So they decided that it's not to their advantage to remove us as district leaders. Instead, they decide that they will reprimand us and censure us and also subsequently pass a new rule: that if you endorse a candidate other than someone in the party, and you are a district leader, you can be removed by a mere majority vote. It became known as "the Koch-Greitzer Rule."

I couldn't stop them, and I didn't do anything, and they didn't ask my permission to do this. Then they dropped the charges. So we walk out, J. Raymond Jones, who was a lion of a man, and the rest of us. He had a head that was like an Olmec statue. That's the closest approximation I can think of, an incredibly powerful personality, and a wonderful West Indian sound in his voice.

So we come out, and he's interviewed on television.

I think it was Gabe Pressman. They don't invite me, but I just stand next to him when they're having this interview. And he's coming on very strong. "Yes, we have censured them. We've told them that if they ever do this again, they are going to be removed."

And then Gabe Pressman shoves the mike into my face and says, "Isn't it a fact now, Mr. Koch, that you've been censured and you'll never do it again?"

I say, "No, that's not a fact. Under the same circumstances, we'd do it again!"

•   •   •

At the end of 1965, when John Lindsay was sworn in as mayor, he resigned his congressional seat. A month later Ted Kupferman, a Republican, resigned his Second Councilmanic District seat to run for the Silk Stocking congressional seat vacated by Lindsay. Following Kupferman's resignation from the City Council, the Council appointed Woodward Kingman, a Republican, to fill Kupferman's seat on an interim basis. In November 1966, in the general election, I opposed Kingman—who, astonishingly, had Lindsay's support.

Lindsay's problem, that he was ideologically more Democrat than Republican, was already becoming sticky for him. Moreover, in the race for the Council seat his problem set him at odds with my problem—that I had crossed party lines to endorse him. Our relationship had only begun to cool.

The Second Councilmanic District was made up of most of Manhattan's East Side and some of Greenwich

Village. It had been a Republican district since the 1920s. I was strong in parts of it because I had built up a record on community issues, but only in the area of my district leadership, not uptown. It was in this area, the Upper East Side, that Lindsay could have been helpful. Always the optimist, I went to work at the subway stops uptown.

Early on in the race it became evident I would be able to count on my unlikely-seeming downtown coalition of the early-rising Italians in the South Village and the late-sleeping liberals of the West Village. Under the leadership of Dina Nolan, we had opened a storefront on MacDougal Street called Independent Citizens for Koch. From that South Village headquarters the word of my effectiveness in solving community problems continued to spread among the Italian families who lived in the neighborhood.

I tell you, the Italians are far better than the liberals when it comes to understanding. That year, as it happened, the Independent Civilian Police Complaint Board referendum was on the ballot and I supported its retention. I thought the prior board, which was made up of police personnel, never did anything to deal with police brutality. And I had in fact represented some people, in a pro-bono way, who had been assaulted by cops unfairly. It became the major issue in the city and the district, notwithstanding the fact that I had hoped *I* would be the major issue in that campaign. I wasn't—it was the referendum on the Independent Civilian Police Complaint Board.

Now, the liberals were for it; the moderates and conservatives all across town were opposed to it. And it lost. That is to say, the revocation of the Independent Civilian Police Complaint Board won.

Well, for a period of a year or more after I became district leader the Italians had chosen to forget about my strong civil-rights stands. At first we had yelled and screamed at one another, they primarily at me, and then—as reasonable people are wont to do when they sit down over a table every Saturday and have coffee— they stopped screaming after the first six months. Then they started worrying about if you have a cold, how about a little glass of tea? We became very good friends.

When I ran for the City Council, therefore, they said, "We would like to open a storefront for you. We can't go and work at the VID, because they're a bunch of Communists." That was their feeling. "But we'd like to have a separate operation for you here in the South Village." There are ten Village election districts that are Italian, all of them south of Washington Square Park.

I thought, Isn't that wonderful?

So they opened up the storefront on MacDougal Street for me: Independent Citizens for Koch. Dina Nolan, who is a wonderful woman whom I truly love— she's sort of an Anna Magnani; she's Italian, and her husband was Irish—ran this operation. She was a Republican, but she was very appreciative of what I had done. And Dina says—she'll say it today—in 1960 she hated my guts because I was for keeping Washington Square Park open for folk singers, and the Italians were against it, and they thought I was terrible, and I probably was. I didn't appreciate some of the problems that they saw then, namely two: the decay of morality, and safety in the park. They were too reactionary, it's true, but there was some merit in their position, which I didn't see at all. And they, on the other hand, saw no merit in my position. I had formed the Right to Sing Committee. That was in 1960. It was a terrific name, right?

Dina had been a captain in MacNeil Mitchell's club. He was the Republican state senator for that district; he was later succeeded by Roy Goodman, but at that time Mac was a very powerful man. And when she came to work for me on a volunteer basis—she didn't get a single dollar from me, we didn't pay anybody—MacNeil Mitchell called her up and said he was very upset that she was working for me, a Democrat, and would she please come back to the club. And he offered her a thousand dollars.

Well, this was a woman of modest circumstances. But what she said was, "What does he think I am? A whore?" She was incensed that he would think he could buy her back.

The Independent Citizens for Koch won all ten of the election districts that were Italian, and you have to contrast that with the election the year before. Then another Democrat was running for the City Council seat, an Italian named Bob Ferrari, and he won only one of those districts in the general election. Italians supposedly vote Democratic in the primary and Republican in the general election. He had won only one of the Italian districts. I won all ten.

Now, the reason I tell the story is this: To get on the ballot in the primary, you have to have signatures. Your people have to climb stairs—these tenements are five-, six-, seven-story walkups. Wally Popolizio is highly regarded in the Village—he's lived there all his life, and his father was like ninety-two years old and used to be the iceman (he died at age one hundred), and Wally is a very successful lawyer. So they said to me, Dina and Wally and Nick Marucci, who is now dead, "Listen, why do you have to be for the Independent Civilian Police Complaint Board?"

I said, "Because I believe in it."

"Well, why can't you just shut up?"

I said, "No, because that would not be me. You don't have to be for the board, but I have to be for the board, and I have to say the same in the North Village and the South Village. I can't have two stories." They sort of shook their heads like I was a nut.

Wally told this story: He would go to the tenements and knock on the doors to get signatures to put me on the ballot, and he came to this elderly Italian lady's apartment, six flights up, knocked on the door.

"Who's there?" she said.

"It's Wally, Wally Popolizio. You remember me. I used to deliver ice," because he used to deliver ice as his father's son on the truck.

"Oh, yes, Wally, how are you?" And she invites him in.

He says to her, "I'd appreciate your signing this petition for my friend Ed Koch who's running for the City Council."

She says, "How does he feel about the Independent Civilian Police Complaint Board?" Because that was the issue. Every Italian I met was opposed to the board.

Wally says, "Listen, on community matters Ed is great. On the Independent Civilian Police Complaint Board, he's a little crazy." She signed. Now, you couldn't get a liberal to do something like that for you, not at all. They would walk away from you, indeed denounce you, on any major issue where you did not toe the official liberal position. The liberals couldn't tolerate that difference of opinion for what in that community was a fundamental issue.

•   •   •

That was the Independent Civilian Police Complaint Board. Then there were the posters. Woody Kingman's people were tearing down my posters. The night before the election, Tony Piazza and his wife, Mary, and Wally Popolizio were riding up Third Avenue putting up my posters on every corner—this was at about two o'clock in the morning—when they detected a car with no lights following them and stopping at each corner and tearing down the posters.

So, as Tony related it to me, they all got out of their car, and Mary was first, and they ran back to where this guy was tearing down the posters. It was Woody Kingman's assistant campaign manager. He was stuffing one of my posters into a trash basket or something, and Mary went over to him and said, "Stop it." So he pushed her.

Well, Tony Piazza is a very tough guy and a loving husband. At that point he arrived and started to swing at this guy. But Mary said, "No, don't touch him. He's mine." And *she* hit him. Some wonderful relationships came out of that campaign—friendships I will always treasure.

So the next day is the election, and after the polls close I'm up at the VID and we're waiting and we don't know whether I've won or not, but I keep getting these calls from MacDougal Street, Dina Nolan: "Why don't you come down? We've won! We've won!"

I said, "Dina, we haven't won. We haven't gotten all the results."

She said, "You've won, you've won." I had won all ten election districts in the South Village, but there were 235 election districts in the whole district and we hadn't heard from uptown, where I was weakest, which would be the Upper East Side, where the Republicans lived. But ultimately I take a cab down when the votes are all in and I know I've won. I won by 2,500 votes.

So I get into the cab and I go down Bleecker Street, and as we approach MacDougal off Sixth Avenue, between Sixth and MacDougal, the cab has to stop because there's an enormous crowd on the street—hundreds of people. I can't figure out why. And they're carrying candles. The cabbie says, "We can't go any further," so I get out, thinking, God knows what's happened down here. And they are my people. It's Dina Nolan and Wally Popolizio and all these others, and they're crying—grown men crying, including me. Joy. Tears of joy. And they take me into our MacDougal Street headquarters, and Tom Hoving, Lindsay's Parks Commissioner, came down, and he did a sort of jig on one of the tables. They lifted him up. And then they lifted me up.

It was a night like no other I'll ever go through—just sheer joy and love and affection came from those people. They had made the difference in the South Village. I'll never forget it as long as I live.

• • •

So I'm elected to the Council, and a couple of months go by. I'm an independent person—always have been—and I make some criticism of the Lindsay budget. I can't even remember: there may have been some legislation on the floor that he was supportive of and that I was not. But while a meeting was going on in the City Council, the sergeant-at-arms called me and said, "There's a phone call for you, Councilman, and it's from Commissioner Hoving."

So I go out and take the phone call, and Hoving says something like "Listen, Ed, the Mayor is very upset that you're sniping at him and you're attacking this and you're attacking that, and he wants you to stop it."

I'm furious. I say to him, "Listen, Tom, I'm not the

Mayor's man on the City Council. I'm not even your man. I am my own man on this Council, and I'll vote the way I want to vote." I was furious that they should think they could intimidate me or tell me how to vote.

Well, that was the beginning of the end of our cordial relations. Now to skip ahead to 1968: I am running for Congress against Whitney North Seymour, Jr., who's the very posh candidate of the Republicans. He and I had both won our respective primaries. And on a radio program, WRVR, off the air, he said in response to a question, "Yes, the Mayor is going to endorse me shortly."

I am horrified. I need Lindsay's endorsement on the East Side of Manhattan in the Silk Stocking District: they loved him. I'm horrified. I thought, My God, this means I'll lose, and how can he do this to me, I who crossed party lines for him?

So I call up Bob Sweet, who was then the Deputy Mayor and is now a federal judge, and I say, "I'd like to have a meeting with the Mayor."

He says, "I'll see what I can do."

A few days later he calls me up to ask me to come in and see him—Bob Sweet, that is. I come in and Bob says, "What do you want to see the Mayor about?" They really knew.

I say, "I'll take that up with the Mayor."

"No," says Bob Sweet, "you'll have to take that up with me. I have to know in advance what it is you want to discuss with him."

I say, "Oh no. Are you telling me that I, a city

councilman, have to clear with you what it is that I want to take up with the Mayor? Is that your statement to me?''

He says, "Yes.''

I say, "I certainly am not going to discuss it with you." And I get up from the chair.

He says, "Are you going to have a press conference?''

I say, "No, not immediately." And I leave.

A half hour later there's a call at my law office: Bob Sweet. "Ed, you can have your appointment with the Mayor. It's set up for next week.''

This meeting with Sweet was sometime in September: the meeting with Lindsay was to be shortly thereafter, but it was delayed because of the teachers' strike that took place in September and October. Finally they tell me the Mayor will see me. It's late October. The appointment is set for let's say 10 A.M.

I get there about 9:30—at City Hall. And the son-of-a-bitch keeps me waiting. He comes in. He keeps me waiting for an hour and takes other people. It wasn't like these other people were involved in the strike, but just an outrageous situation clearly intended to insult me, or at least I felt that way.

Finally I'm told, "Okay, the Mayor will see you." It was Harvey Rothenberg, his appointments secretary, who comes out and shows me into the Mayor's private office. I had been in there before, with Mayor Wagner, never with Lindsay. And instead of taking me over to the section of the room that has a couch and chairs where you might have an informal discussion under the picture of Fiorello La Guardia, Lindsay takes me over to the desk area, where I was to get what I call the Mussolini treatment: a very big desk, he stands behind it, I'm sitting in front of it and he's towering over me. It's an attempt to intimidate me. And this is reinforced by what he does. He doesn't let me talk. He's talking about every non sequitur he can think of. And I realize that what he wants to do is use up my time so I can't get to what I want to ask him. So I stop him and I say, "Mr. Mayor, forgive me, but I know that in a short time Harvey Rothenberg is going to come in and tell you you have another appointment. So let me tell you why I am here."

He says, "Why?"

I say, "Mr. Mayor, Mike Seymour says that you're going to endorse him, and I'm here to find out if that's true."

Well, he blanches and he says, "Yes, I am. I am going to endorse him. He's a wonderful Republican, and I have an obligation to support good Republicans."

I say, "Mr. Mayor, I did not expect that you would endorse me, but I certainly expected that you wouldn't endorse anybody who ran against me in view of what I did for you. Maybe you have forgotten about it." And I take a piece of literature which I had used in my City Council race, which showed the banner headline of the *Daily News* about Johnson and Humphrey endorsing Beame, and me backing Lindsay. I take it and I throw it on the table, and I rise in wrath, and here he really turns white like a Boy Scout. I say, "Maybe you don't remember this"—*zock* on the table. Then I say, "Mr. Mayor," very calm, "life teaches us a lot, and one should learn from one's own experience, and I have, and let me tell you what this experience has taught me: it is that one should never cross party lines except in extremis. And it'll be a long time before I ever do it again. And let me tell you one other thing, Mr. Mayor, you're looking at the guy who's going to win." Then I turned and walked out.

From that point on, I never forgave him. I attacked him unmercifully—always, I think, with reason and never on pretexts. Whereas before, if he had remained a friend and a political supporter, I might have held my fire. After that, never. When Lindsay ran for President I was on a television program and the interviewer says to me, "Congressman, will you please explain this to us? In Arizona, in Oregon, you mention the name Lindsay and they love him. In the City of New York his name is mud. How can that be?"

So I looked to heaven and a thought came to me, and I responded just this way: I said, "Well, to know him is not to love him." And that was carried just that way in the press.

That really wounded him. He was furious.

Finally, there were several additional personal reasons why over time I have not gotten along with John Lindsay. When I beat his candidate, Whitney North Seymour, Jr., in 1968, Lindsay was quoted as saying, "Koch's win is a catastrophe for the city." That is not how you make friends. Bad enough that he should have supported Seymour, but then to denounce me—the next Congressman? Dumb. Then there was his wife, Mary. She was quoted in *The Sunday Times Magazine* as having said, "Why is there antipathy between Koch and John? Jealousy. John's attractive and sexy; he's neither." Foolish. The fact is, if I was distressed at anything it is the way Lindsay was treated by the editorial writers. And that was not based on his ability but rather on his good looks and his being a WASP. He was not held accountable for having given the city away to the labor unions, to the rip-off artists who dispensed poverty monies, and for his general coziness with the richies and the powerful in this town.

Anyway, after all I had said about the way Lindsay ran the city, and after I had as mayor spent hours and hours in meetings trying to figure out ways to make right the things that Lindsay screwed up, Lindsay goes on the radio and calls me "petty" for telling people what he did to them. And then the editorial writers step in and say to me: Hey, lay off him.

It happened to be on the same day, in early December 1980, that I had had a meeting on the Yankee Stadium lease. Lindsay had budgeted $24 million to fix up the stadium for the Yankees. But it had cost $100 million or more. It was a white elephant, and we were trying to renegotiate the lease. I couldn't talk about those negotiations, but when the press came in for the morning briefing I tried to explain to them what had happened, and how I felt on that day about John Lindsay.

One of the reporters says, "When are you going to stop attacking Lindsay?"

I say, "Here is my problem. How else can you talk about what was done in the past unless you talk about who was in charge? You have to give a name to an era—you know, like the Ming Dynasty? But here's what I'll do. I am going to refer to Mayor Wagner as 'Mayor W.' And I will be 'Mayor Z.' And you can decide for yourselves who Mayors 'X' and 'Y' are."

5

The Public Persona

DURING MY PREPARATION for the 1973 mayoral race, David Brown said that my voice was way too high and too New Yorkish in tone. He suggested that I go to a voice teacher. I said okay. He found one on East Thirty-eighth Street.

I went there about ten times. I was a very good student—when I was in the studio. On each occasion, when I had practiced with her, I could do this very cultured baritone. But as soon as I left I would go right back to my old New York staccato. I thought the whole thing was ridiculous. It was like asking me to wear a toupee.

On the last occasion she said to me, "Congressman Koch, I know how confidential this matter must be, and you can rely on me. I have other students who are sensitive about this, such as Gabe Pressman." And then she named ten others.

I thought to myself, This is the pits. I said, "Bye-bye," and I never went back.

A similar thing happened to me before the 1978 St. Patrick's Day parade. You know, people have the best intentions . . .

A large contingent of congressmen and senators came to town for the parade. We arranged for them to view the King Tut exhibit at the Metropolitan Museum on the Friday night prior to the parade. The next morning in advance of the parade we fed them breakfast at Gracie Mansion and then took them over to Charley O's for the Irish breakfast. We were together all morning. I was wearing my Irish fisherman's knit sweater and my green jacket. Bess Myerson* met us at Charley O's. I had taken off the jacket and left it in the car. She said, "You're not going to wear that sweater, are you?"

I said, "Well, yes, I was thinking of it."

She said, "Oh no, you shouldn't." And she really started to hector me on it. It was rather interesting, very funny. But I did want to wear the sweater. My taste in clothing is not impeccable and I know it. And she was so adamant that I thought, Well, why take a chance if it might be insulting to people? She said it was too informal. So I took it off. Maureen Connelly, my press

---

*Bess had been consumer affairs commissioner under Mayor Lindsay and was an early and ardent supporter of my candidacy in 1977. Without her it could all have been different.

secretary, was there and she saw me taking the sweater off. She said, "What are you doing?"

I said, "Well, Bess said the sweater is too informal."

Maureen said, "What does she know about the Irish? The sweater is terrific!" So I put it back on and it was the hit of the day. I wear it now in every St. Patrick's Day parade, and were I not to wear it people would be disappointed. It's now a trademark. In 1985, ten city commissioners who are Irish wore similar sweaters and marched with me.

After you get a reputation for doing these unusual things it gets easier to do them.

I like campaigning, and I always have. That, for one, makes me different from most campaigners. And it shows. I am often ahead of schedule. There is another reason for that: I do not believe that the individual handshake—which politicians traditionally believe is magic—has any applicability to votes or non-votes. What is important is that you are there and that people know you are there seeking their support. The touching of the flesh is vastly overrated, and it slows you down. That doesn't mean that I don't shake hands; I do. But it is far more important to establish voice contact by just yelling "Hi!" and getting people to respond, which they invariably do. The key is to convey energy in voice and body movement, particularly the raising of your arms. Hands high and thumbs up have become my trademark.

Now, when I ran for reelection in 1981 I began doing something a little different. It is kind of nice and kind of foolish and kind of New Yorkish. And it is special to me. No one else could get away with it. It is like Kenyatta with the Mau Mau. What I said was (this was during the primary), "Now everybody raise your right hand and repeat after me: I (state your name) solemnly swear that on September tenth I will rush to the polls and vote for Ed Koch."

Over the first weekend in August first David Garth and then Maureen Connelly went campaigning with me to see how the response was. I was in the Rockaways at the swimming pools, on the Coney Island boardwalk, at the Bronx beach clubs and on street corners in between. And they saw the tremendous response that was there. They like to frighten me by saying that their poll is lower than some other poll. They always like to say that I will turn people off with my directness and that I should soften up and serve up some treacle once in a while. Well, now on that weekend I probably saw five thousand people: Jews, Italians, Blacks, Irish, Hispanics, you name it. And they all responded with interest and with candor, and almost to the last soul they would raise their hands and take the oath. I would say, "Now, some people say I am going to win and why campaign? I say, this is not going to be easy and I am taking nothing for granted, because I know that the people who hate me will come out and the ones who think I have done a good job won't necessarily vote in the primary, because they won't think it is necessary." And then I would give the oath. And it was extraordinary to me that people would actually swear to vote for me.

But there are more ways than voice coaching and dressing right and campaigning right to win. The single best is involvement, emotionally and physically, in the most controversial of issues.

•   •   •

Nineteen sixty-four was the year of the big drive to register black voters in the South. And also the year of the killing of those three kids, Schwerner, Chaney and Goodman. Something called the Lawyers' Constitutional Defense Committee had been formed nationally, and they were looking for lawyers to go south and help black people register.

I decided I would take eight days off from my law practice and district-leadership responsibilities—my vacation, so to speak—and go down there. It was August.

I called up—it was the American Civil Liberties Union that was running the drive—and I said, "I'd like to go." They said, "Fine."

Henry Stern, a good friend of mine, later a city councilman and now parks commissioner appointed by me, said he'd like to go, too. And I get the call back that they're going to send me to Tennessee. So I mentioned it to Dan Wolf, and Dan said, "You can't go to Tennessee. You've got to go to a place like Mississippi. You go to Tennessee, nobody's going to think it means anything."

So I called up Henry Schwarzschild, who was running it, and I said, "I don't want to go to Tennessee. I want to go to Mississippi."

He says, "Why?"

I say, "Because I want to go to a place that's dangerous, and I want to be more involved."

He says, "Tennessee is more dangerous. The area that we're sending you to is more dangerous than Mississippi."

I say, "But no one will believe it. I've got to go to Mississippi."

I went to Jackson, Mississippi. And Marian Wright, who's now the wife of Peter Edelman, was in charge of the project down there. She was a Southern woman. Peter Edelman was a Kennedy guy. He's white, Jewish; she's black.

They were suspicious of me. Here's this guy: he's a district leader and he's running for reelection and he's probably just doing this for the headlines and he's not going to do anything anyway. But I'm a very hard worker. No matter what I do I always work very hard, and I really was committed to this cause emotionally.

They sent me with a young Jewish kid named Perlman to go from Jackson to Laurel, Mississippi, to help a group of college kids—eighteen to twenty, half were white, half black—who were in Laurel registering black voters. We went there in a car. It was about two hours out of Jackson before we found where these people were. They had their office in a trailer truck and they'd been living there for the summer. The day before I got there they had gone down to Kress's soda fountain in Laurel to integrate it—blacks and whites demanding service together at the soda fountain. They were assaulted, and then typically they had been charged with assault and other crimes. My job was to represent them.

I go into the courthouse; I'm waiting for the case to begin. I look outside the court and I see a white farmer go over to one of these kids and hit him. I was so shocked I didn't know what to do. This was a foreign milieu to me. So I go over to a sheriff and I say, "That man hit him. Do something." He looks at me as though I'm crazy, and does nothing.

These kids are arraigned and the trial is set for the next day. We file countercharges: these kids against the locals in cross-complaints of assault. The technicalities are taken care of, and I had been told before leaving Jackson that I should pick up some transcripts from earlier trials that are in the Laurel County Clerk's Office across the street. So after we had finished with the arraignment I say to Perlman, "Let's go across the street and get the papers."

When we get outside and start walking across the street, suddenly this group of people, white Southern farmers, start following us and ominously clapping their hands, about ten or fifteen of them. Perlman says to me, "We're in trouble." He had been beaten up in Hattiesburg on an earlier occasion.

I say, "What should we do?"

He says, "Let's make a quick turnabout and try to get back into the courthouse." I'm scared; I never had this happen to me before. So as we're walking he says,

"One, two, three," and we spin around and start walking through these people, who are so surprised by the sharp turn they let us through.

We get inside and whom should I see but the prosecutor, whom I had met that morning upstairs at the arraignment hearing. And I say to him, "There's a crowd out there and they want to assault us, and you have to help us."

He says, "I can't do anything."

I say, "I'm an officer of this court"—which in retrospect was a ridiculous statement—"and I demand that you protect me as an officer of this court."

The guy looks at me like I'm crazy.

Then I say, "At least get me to a phone."

He says, "All right, I'll get you to a phone."

He takes me into the clerk's office and says, "Let him use the phone." What I do is, I call the FBI. They had an FBI office in Laurel. I had the number and I call them up, and the voice at the other end says, "Federal Bureau of Investigation, Robert E. Lee speaking." So help me, that was his name. That was the name of the agent in charge—with the thickest Southern accent imaginable.

So I said to him, "This is Ed Koch; I'm here as an attorney, and there's a crowd outside and they're building up, and I think we're going to be in trouble. Come over and help us."

And he says in his best Southern drawl, "Well, we're just an investigatory agency. We cannot intervene in these matters, but I'd like to have the facts."

I say, "There's a crowd out there and we're going to get killed."

"Well, we'd like to have all the facts. How many people are out there and will you please spell your name?"

I say, "Listen, my name is Koch, K-O-C-H, and I've got to get off this phone, because I've got to get out of here, because I'm going to get killed. I'll give you my itinerary so that'll make it easier for you to find the bodies. We're going back to Jackson if we get out of this building." And I hang up.

The prosecutor is still waiting, and he says, "Come with me." He takes us to a side door, and we slip out and get into the car and take off.

Okay, I've got to come back the following day because I've got to help these kids. I'm frightened, but it's my job. So I go back the next day and pick them up at this trailer and we go to the courthouse. We get upstairs and the sheriff says we can go into the courtroom. We had a number of people who were with us, a lot of local blacks who were supportive.

And the sheriff says, "Okay, the niggers out." And then, "The nigger defendants on the other side of the room." It was a segregated courtroom.

So when the judge takes his position on the bench, I say, "Your Honor, I want to make a protest. The sheriff has ordered the Negro members of the public out of the courtroom and has directed the Negro defendants to the other side of the courtroom and I protest. This cannot be allowed."

So the judge says, "Okay, tell him not to do it."

I say, "Your Honor, I can't tell the sheriff what to do and what not to do."

So he says to the sheriff, "Let them back in." And they bring them back in. I felt really terrific about that.

This is what they call a court not of record. They made no transcripts of what took place. Like a justice of the peace. We don't have that in New York City, but they had it there. And what was also interesting was that they allowed me, as a non-Mississippi lawyer, to defend. You couldn't do that in New York. A Mississippi lawyer couldn't go to New York and defend someone except with enormous processing in advance and so forth. In that respect, Mississippi was more liberal.

Anyway, we try all the assault cases and we lose them all. But in every case, I was convinced that the judge was aware that we were right and the prosecution was wrong, so he gave everybody suspended sentences. I took it as a victory.

I also marched into Montgomery, Alabama, with the Reverend Martin Luther King, Jr., but that's another story. In 1965 Henry Stern and I went on that march. That brings me to another issue.

Let me tell you why I think I'm a successful politician. People, strangely enough—I always found it curious in the Congress—thought of me as being solidly seated in my New York City constituency, like a Southern congressman. That's the way a lot of people saw it. And I always took a good deal of pleasure in it, notwithstanding the fact I always said, "Oh, no, no, no." The truth is, I turned my congressional district around so that a seat I won originally with 51 percent of the vote in my first election I won with 75 percent of the vote in my fourth and fifth terms.

Now, how does that happen? You have to establish a reputation. You have to speak candidly. People have to be convinced of your intellectual and fiscal honesty. There are a lot of people who think they are smarter than I am, but I'm still pretty smart. I'm no genius, but I know how to employ the services of geniuses. And even those who think they're smarter than I am came to a certain conclusion, which was that I have a superb gut reaction to issues, that either I have been able in a prescient way to foretell what would become of an issue or, when the issue presented itself, I was able to know what was right even if it was controversial and even if at the time people would say, "It's bad news for a public official; don't get involved—it's controversial." And I like to say to people that at one time or another in my constituency everybody has been angry with me on an issue that they were involved in. But when they look at all the issues I'm involved in, they find that overwhelmingly they are in accord with me.

So, finally, you have to have a gut that tells you which way to move and you have to have the guts to follow your intuition.

The issue that aroused the most fear among my supporters when I got into it was that of amnesty for Vietnam draft resisters. I was the only member of Congress up to that time, December 1969, to have gone to Canada and talked to draft resisters. I went to Ottawa, Toronto and Montreal. I went up there with David Brown, who was then my counsel and administrative assistant. We spent two days there, talked in that period of time to about forty American draft resisters and several deserters. I came back and I held a press conference at 26 Federal Plaza on New Year's Day; and, by chance, there was an enormous snowstorm, so that only one reporter came. I thought it would be the biggest thing I'd ever been involved in. "Here I am— I'm back from Canada, fellas. I want to tell you about the draft resisters." One person came. He was the AP reporter, and when he walked in he takes off his coat, and he's loaded with ice—he's an icicle—he says to me, "Your middle name must be Lucky." He was the only reporter there. So I hold this exclusive press conference for the AP reporter. But the issue was so important it got coverage all over the country.

I said that we had to find a way to permit the draft resisters to return home without punitive action. At that time I was not talking about the deserters. There weren't very many deserters involved, anyway. My recollection is that the figure on deserters both at that time and later was about 8 percent of the young U.S. male emigrés to Canada. And I must say frankly, I didn't have the same feeling about deserters that I did about draft resisters. It's an irrational feeling, because you can make out the same kind of case for a deserter that you can for a draft resister. Indeed, maybe a better one, because the draft resisters in the main were middle-class college students who knew what they were doing and who did it either because of philosophical reasons concerning the war or because they just didn't want to expose themselves to danger, and it was all pretty much thought out, whereas the deserter, in many of those cases, was some poor kid who really didn't know anything about the cause of nonviolence or why we shouldn't be in Vietnam who goes to Vietnam and suddenly is aware of it—or hasn't yet gone and becomes aware of it. I'm not for a moment suggesting that there aren't cases of cowardice, which are to be condemned. But the draft resister may not deserve as much credit as the deserter who comes to the philosophical conclusion somewhat later, because I've met some of them. I know that some of the deserters really had a change of mind and heart based on what they saw and what they were doing, and deserted.

I said then what I have just said here, and there was a storm of protest, of mail denouncing me. The mail went something like this: Generally it would open by saying, "Go back to Israel." A lot of anti-Semitic mail. Then "coward"—that kind of mail—and "un-American." And it ran overwhelmingly, more than 60 percent, denunciatory. And that came from my district as well as the rest of the country.

But within a few weeks, because I didn't retreat from my position, there was a change. My friends and supporters were scared to death I would not be reelected. I have never been frightened about that on anything I've ever done. Within a few weeks the mail began to change and became 60 to 40 percent supporting me, at least in the district. Today, of course, if would be 98 percent, and those who said no then would tell you they didn't say no—they said yes. That's the way things are. People forget their positions. They don't want to be left behind.

But I had a little experience at the time that convinced me you don't have to please them all the time. I'm walking along the street very close to my home and I meet a woman whom I knew as a result of her being on the rent commission and my being a practicing lawyer, and so I'd known her over the years. This was in 1970. And we meet on Eighth Street right in front of the Art Theatre, and she says, "Mr. Koch"—she was very formal—"I want to talk to you," in that tone. So I say to her, "How are you?" She says, "I'm very good." I say, "How am I doing?" I've often used that expression. She says, "Well, I like everything you're doing except what you're trying to do for those yellowbellies." And then she began to cry bitter tears. And she said, "My grandson is in Vietnam and his life is in danger and you're helping these draft dodgers." So I said to her, "I hope and pray that your grandson is alive and safe and comes home well. But I also want to do something for the sons of other people who didn't go and who are criminals now. Think about their mothers and their fathers, even if you don't agree. I hope you understand that I'm doing the best I know how." So she says, "Well, I like everything else you're doing." And that's sweet, you see. It really is.

Now, I think you can duplicate that with so many people in New York who have been angry with me on some issue, but when they look at my record they find they like in general what I'm doing. The only thing I want to avoid is getting all these people who dislike me on various issues in the same room where they can join forces.

Now, getting back to the basic question of why I increased my majorities: people are very responsive—and most politicians simply do not recognize that—to honest, intellectual honesty, and a lack of fear of getting involved in controversial issues. For instance, I do not accept the liberal distinction made between fascism and Communism and the one-party regimes occurring in Third World countries. It distresses me that we impose a level of morality on the right-wing states where fascism reigns and if they don't meet it we attack them, but when the left-wing states where Communism reigns go for a lower standard and repress human rights, the liberals (not I) accept it and find reasons to understand. And for the Third World they accept an even lower standard and rarely condemn the repression. I've said it repeatedly, "I believe in only one standard. Either it's right or it's wrong. If it's right, then everybody has to be condemned if they're not doing it. I'm talking about standards of morality." And I've said, "I happen to be one of those who believe in tyrannicide. It's not a liberal position. The liberal position is you must never kill and it's wrong for the government to be involved in tyrannicide." I've said, "Wouldn't we be better off today if Adolf Hitler and Joe Stalin had been assassinated before they each had killed more than fifty million people?''

Also, I'm *for* the death penalty.

When I ran for reelection to Congress in 1972, I appeared before a group of the League of Women Voters, and they were asking candidates their positions on substantive matters, and the last question was, ''What is your position on the death penalty?'' They asked all these candidates who were there. And all of these liberal reformers from the East Side—Tony Olivieri and a number of others—got up and said they were opposed to it. Then I got up and said, ''I'm for it. I am for the death penalty in certain limited cases—where you have killing involving torture, the Manson kind of killing; where you have skyjacking and the deaths of passengers; where you have police officers or prison guards killed; where you have an assassin for hire and someone is killed; where you have kidnapping with the death of the victim. There are a certain limited number of cases where I believe that the penalty of death is warranted.''

I'm not suggesting that it necessarily is going to have a deterrent effect. I think it will. You can make arguments on both sides. They can show you statistics that demonstrate that if you remove the death penalty it doesn't make any difference or that if you keep the death penalty it doesn't make any difference, people kill anyway. Well, maybe they do, but the people who have been executed for crimes of murder certainly will not. Still, these are the exceptions. I'm not for the death penalty in crimes of passion. Many killings involve husbands and wives. I'm not for killing the husbands and wives who kill each other. I'm not even for keeping them (those who commit so-called crimes of passion) in jail too long—maybe seven years is enough.

But this is a position you'll rarely get from a liberal. They're afraid of it. Half of them believe what I'm saying. The other half may not believe it. But the half that does believe it is afraid to say it. I'm not afraid to say it.

At that time I used to debate a lot with Martin Abend on Channel 5 and I enjoyed it immensely. I started it in August of 1975. It came about because one day his office called and said, "Can Congressman Koch come up and debate with Dr. Abend this evening?" And my office got in touch with me and I said, "Sure."

So I go up there and he says, "Gee, you are a brave man."

I say, "Why?"

He said, "Well, we've been trying to get somebody all day to come up and debate with me who would take the position that the increases in congressional salaries just awarded were justified. You're the only one willing to do that." Well, of course, they hadn't told me the subject of the debate.

But I said to him, "Of course," because I happened to believe that the raises were justified.

Obviously it's not a politically helpful position to take, but I debated with him anyway. And they liked me. They liked me plus the fact I had a pretty good style. It was a different style from my usual. It's a style that I only employed with Martin Abend. By that I mean he is a very outrageous guy in his debating style. It's filled with histrionics. It's filled with club-him-to-death-type rhetoric. It's crazy to listen to him. He's a screamer. And the people who had been debating with him were screamers. So they screamed as loud as they could, and they both came out looking ridiculous, except Abend generally came out better because he's clever about it. So I decided that the way to debate with Abend is almost monotone. I get the issue, I look at the camera, I make very flat kinds of statements—but in counterpoint to Abend, who's a screamer, and me very low-keyed and simple in exposition; it comes out terrific, I must say.

The fact of the matter is, the people who were very supportive of liberal positions loved it. I always espoused the liberal position, not only because I believe in reasonable, rational, liberal positions, but also because Abend is on the right, and they have to have someone on the left because this program is intended to be a clash: never grays—it's always blacks and whites in terms of issues.

Some of the people who supported me would say, "Why aren't you yelling? Why aren't you screaming? Why aren't you more emotional?"

I would say, "Well, there are a couple of reasons why. The first one is I wouldn't be effective. Nobody could hear what I was saying. And secondly, what happens is this: there are many people who catch that show on a Friday night—about 500,000 to 750,000 on a Friday night—and I am always on on a Friday and sometimes on a Sunday too. The mail that I get, as opposed to the mail that Abend gets when he's debating with others like Sidney Offit or maybe even Ted Sorensen, is terrific.'' Sorensen, incidentally, has a different style, too—his is low-keyed, too, but it is the kind that is insulting to his adversary; people don't like it. I mean he was arrogant; he put Abend down. Whereas I always tried to blend in some humor.

One of the first Abend programs related to pornography. And they always try to work the evening's issue in with the news. That night at Forty-second Street, Lindsay was closing down the porno shops, which they were doing in those days like every Thursday: suddenly someone wants to get a little news and they want to do something, so they'll close down the porno shops, and generally there was nothing they could really do, because if it were hard-core pornography, then you could go into court and do something about it, but if it's just salacious and doesn't meet the hard-core standards imposed by the U.S. Supreme Court, the city was really at a loss to do something. I think there should be changes in the law, but that's another matter. Anyway, Abend comes on very strong: ''Pornography! It does this and it does that,'' really tough and puritanical. And then me. And you have to understand, each of us has a minute and fifteen seconds to talk. My opening line (this was a classic) was exactly this: ''Pornography, it ain't all bad.''

What, you may ask, has all this to do with self-promotion? The Abend debates are always on prostitution and gun control and crime, with Abend always saying that we treat people too leniently in various areas, whereas gun control means arming the criminals and taking guns away from the decent people. There may be six issues and you debate them over and over again *ad nauseam*. But it's okay. It was, up to that time, the best publicity I had ever had in my active political life. I would walk down the street, and it was amazing how many people would stop me, and it would be because they'd seen me on the Abend show.

After one appearance, a black lady, late-middle-aged, in her sixties maybe, smiles, obviously recognizes me, and she comes over to me and she says, "You're Congressman Koch. I know you."

I said, "Yes."

She says, "I see you on the Abend show all the time."

I say, "How am I doing?"

She says, "I'm with you! I'm law and order." And a big smile.

I'm walking up Fifth Avenue at Fifty-seventh Street on a Saturday afternoon. A guy comes over to me, well dressed. He says, "Excuse me, Congressman, but you are Congressman Koch, aren't you?"

I say, "Yes."

He says, "I see you on the Abend show." They always say that. That's how they refer to the news, as the Abend show. "I see you on the Abend show."

I say, "How'm I doing?"

He said, "Well, first let me tell you where I am politically." We're walking up Fifth Avenue. He says, "So far as I am concerned, anyone who is a member of the John Birch Society is a Communist. Now that you know that, I also want to tell you: I like your style." That's very complimentary, from an arch-right-winger.

Another case: I'm handing out Equal Rights Amendment literature at Sixth Avenue and Eighth Street shortly before the ERA debacle on Election Day, and a woman comes over and she says, "Oh, Congressman, I'm so pleased to see you. I'm so proud that you're my Congressman. I really like you." A late-middle-aged woman, white.

I say, "Oh, isn't that nice?"

She says, "Oh yes, I see you on the Abend show all the time."

I say, "How am I doing?"

She says, "Wonderful, wonderful. But let me ask you a question."

"Yes?"

"Why are you debating with that *mashugana?*"

In the last analysis, the Abend show was my best opportunity to work in a little good humor. We were talking on one occasion about the Attica prison and Abend says, "They treat them too good up there. Do you know they give them mattresses and food?"—the prisoners. And I opened up by saying, "Tonight Dr. Abend sounds like Attila the Hun rather than his usual reasonable self." And he has to break up because it's such a funny kind of description of him. The best publicity is free.

•   •   •

And also the worst. I'm thinking of an interview that appeared in the *Soho Weekly News* after the 1977 mayoral campaign. Thank God it appeared *after* the election; otherwise it would have been devastating. People don't always know what they are saying.

My father, Louis Koch (who died at age 87), wanted to be involved in the campaign, and it was nice to have him. He walked around—and people like to see the candidate's father. He was visiting with my stepbrother in Scarsdale, having come up from Florida for the campaign, so that day he was picked up by car and one of our advance men went with him. It was my father, my stepmother Rose, the advance man and a reporter. The advance man aged ten years during the car ride.

A brief rendering of that car ride from Scarsdale to Far Rockaway:

Reporter to my father: "What do you think are the problems your son will have to face?"

"The problems. You talk about the colored people. They're on relief, they don't want to work. They don't want to work." Then he says, "You know, when I was a young man I would go to Harlem at two A.M. and it was perfectly safe. I would look around and I would see people and I would say, 'Hi, boy.' " Now, you have to understand, this never happened. I don't think my father had ever been in Harlem in his life.

The next question was, "Have you ever thought of running for office?"

"Yes," he says.

"Where?"

"Well, I was thinking of mayor of my hometown in Florida."

"What is the Mayor there like?"

"He is Italian—a racketeer," says my father.

And my stepmother is asked, "What did you do when you were younger, Mrs. Koch?"

"Well," she says, "I was a milliner. I used to make these wonderful, beautiful hats. I made them for Gloria Swanson and for Adolf Hitler's girlfriend—a very nice girl."

I mean it was . . . I read this and I thought to myself: This can't be real. These things never happened. This is fantasy.

In the City of New York, in terms of ethnic politics, once you have alienated the blacks, the Italians and the Jews, then there is only about 50 percent of the city left to go.*

---

*In my father's defense, he was prescient on the issue of Sunrise, Florida, Mayor John Lomelo. On June 28, 1985, Lomelo was convicted of conspiracy to commit extortion, conspiracy to defraud, and mail fraud, and he was sentenced to seven years in federal prison; he has appealed that conviction.

6

Coalition Building

WHEN YOU ARE RUNNING for a new office, you will generally find that funds and support are scarce, at least early on. There will be people who will offer to help and some of these people will be untested, at least by you. Beware of people who offer to help when there is no rational basis for their offer.

When I was first running for Congress, John DeLury, the legendary president of the Uniformed Sanitationmen's Association, called me up and offered to help. He lived on Christopher Street, in my district, but I couldn't figure out why he would be for me. He said, "Ed, my union members will put up your signs."

I was delighted, and I had all our signs delivered to him. A week went by, two weeks, three weeks, and I called up: "John, where are the signs? I am walking in the district every day and I haven't seen any."

"Yes, well, we're going to put them up," he said.

Another week went by, it's getting close to the election, still no signs. I am thinking he has all my signs and they are locked up somewhere. I needed those signs on lampposts. I called him again: "John, please let me have my signs back. I have to get them up if I have to put them up myself."

Ultimately, he gave me my signs back, and with herculean efforts by my real supporters we got them up before the election. It is still a mystery to me why he did what he did. But I am grateful to him that at least he let me have my signs back. Sometimes you have to take chances, but it is devastating if you allow your opposition to get your materiel away from you.

•   •   •

There are other things you can do to make a presence that cost little or nothing and that can provide enormous goodwill to you.

I love parades. A lot of people don't like parades because they find them jejune or the excitement threatening. But I like to march in them, not just to review them. Now, it happens that in 1976 at the Columbus Day parade I was interviewed by Mary Breasted of *The New York Times*. She said, "What are you doing here?" and I said, "Well, today I'm Italian; last week I was Polish, and two weeks before I was Ukrainian. But every day I'm Jewish. I love the parades. I go to all of them.'' It was the quote of the day, and it was a very nice quote.

The fact of the matter is that the City of New York is utterly polyglot in its ethnicity—and I love it that way. I relate to these people. I'm one of the few people who's Jewish who marches in the Ukrainian Day parade, or the Polish Day parade. I've marched for years at the head of the Ukrainian Day parade. I can't say I'm a grand marshal, but I'm at the head of the parade with the grand marshal and I march in the rain with them. And they have been so unlucky—almost every time they march it rains. And I march with them in the rain and I love it.

I said to the grand marshal on the first occasion that I marched, ''You know, if this were the old country this wouldn't be a parade, it would be a pogrom. I wouldn't be walking down Fifth Avenue; I would be running down Fifth Avenue and you would be running after me. But this is not the old country; this is the new country; and we will all be walking together.''

He laughed and I laughed. I love parades.

●　　　　　●　　　　　●

But, believe me, I know more about parades than just how to march in them. Let me tell you the story about the 1974 Gay Pride parade.

The Stonewall Inn was a private homosexual club on Christopher Street near Sheridan Square. At that time it was not legal to have gay bars. Therefore the ones that existed were subject to police extortion, and either they were Mafia-owned or the mob had a piece of them—at least that was their reputation.

So in the summer of 1969 the Stonewall was invaded by the police. A private club—they came in, and the gays fought back. I mean it was like the Warsaw Ghetto with the Jews rising up. And the gays date their movement, in terms of strength and pride and so forth, from that event. They celebrate annually with a parade that begins at Sheridan Square on the anniversary of the Stonewall uprising.

Now, in 1974 the parade's sponsors are negotiating for permits. They want to march up Sixth Avenue, and they want to form on the block of Christopher Street west of Seventh Avenue South. It happens there is a church there, and the pastor of that church is the chaplain of the Fire Department, and the Fire Department personnel were very anti-gay. You may remember Michael Maye, the former president of the Uniformed Firefighters' Association, who allegedly beat up a gay-rights demonstrator at an Inner Circle dinner at the Hilton Hotel. (A criminal court judge acquitted Maye of the charges.)

So the pastor protests that he does not want to have a parade form in front of his church on a Sunday morning at ten o'clock, and he pulls out an administrative ordinance that says you can't do that—you have to be so many feet away from a church if you're going to engage in a parade on Sunday. But there wasn't any question in my mind, when the gays raised this with me, that it was harassment on the part of the church.

So they had a meeting, which I set up for them. They invited every major public official in the city. I'm the only one who went. It was at the Parks Department—a very funny scene. There are about ten gays, the deputy parks commissioner and the counsel for the Parks Department, an elderly civil servant who was very jittery as he was sitting in this room with these gays. And they—the gays—know how to harass. They've had a lot of experience being harassed, so they know how to harass.

The Parks Department and the Police Department are there, and there are two issues. One is the Police Department's issuing a permit to start the march on Christopher Street; the other is the Parks Department's wanting a bond to be posted because the parade ends in Central Park. The gays wanted to form on Christopher Street; and they didn't want to post a bond. They wanted the public officials to come and support their application.

So I go. And Doug Ireland, a gay-rights activist, is there, with the two leaders of the gay parade. One is a lesbian, a very powerful woman—I think she could break your arm if you shook hands with her—and the other is a very difficult guy, very argumentative and hostile. He was awful, made my job as the negotiator very hard, because I became the chief negotiator for them.

There's Alexander Wirin, who was the deputy administrator of the Parks Department—he's looking around the room; he'd like to escape. First we handle the police. An inspector was there, and he said, "We want to be cooperative, but the fact is that the minister has an ordinance here which he's brought to our attention that says you cannot form in front of a church."

I said, "That's a very reasonable ordinance." It says you can't form two hundred yards in front, two hundred yards in the back—something like that. "I think that's reasonable. They should just be on either side of that and they certainly should make sure that they don't engage in any noise and aren't disruptive. But he doesn't have the right to bar them from Christopher Street."

"Well," he says, "I have another ordinance here which says that you can't begin a parade on Sunday until one o'clock in the afternoon."

I say, "Let me see that ordinance." He shows me the ordinance. I say, "Do you know what this means? It means that next week when they have the Salute to Israel parade, if you enforce this ordinance against the gays, then you're going to enforce it against the Jews. Are you? Are you going to stop that parade next week? Because if you don't, we will take you to court, because the law is going to be enforced against everybody, equally."

Well, he gets a little flustered. He says, "Why don't you have somebody sue me and then we'll give you the permit."

I say, "They don't have to sue you to get a permit.

That's not the way this is going to be handled. Make that minister sue you not to give that permit." That was the thrust of my argument to him.

So the police guy collapses. He says, "Okay, you can have the permit."

Turning now to the gays, I say, "The minister doesn't want you in front of his church. Why can't you form on the east side of Seventh Avenue? Why can't you form in front of the Stonewall?"

Says the head of the parade to me, "Oh, we can't do that. No, no, no. Don't you understand? We have to form elsewhere, and then when we pass the Stonewall, we must pay tribute to the Stonewall. We can't form in front of the Stonewall, because then we can't lower the colors . . ." or whatever. I mean it's a joke, a real joke.

So I say, "I understand that. Why don't you form, then, on West Fourth Street?" Because there's a little park at West Fourth and Christopher, and they could form on that side. And everybody else except this guy who's the head of the parade says, "Brilliant!" So it was tentatively agreed—that they would form there and then they would be able to walk into Christopher Street and lower the colors in front of the Stonewall.

Then we got to the Parks Department. Oh, at that point I think Doug Ireland comes in. Doug Ireland says, "I'm here on behalf of Assembly Speaker Steingut." The question is whether Speaker Steingut knows he's there. And then others come in: "I'm here on behalf of Borough President Robert Abrams." . . .

But I'm the only public official who's actually there,

because people run away from it. It's an issue that can cause you embarrassment, and if you can avoid it, you avoid it. But I decided I'm going to do what's right, and I've never suffered as a result of it. I mean I don't want to sound like I'm a martyr type here, because I'm not, but I have always found that when I have done what I thought was morally right, I have never suffered, never, not on any issue no matter how controversial, no matter how difficult. I've never suffered. And so I'm going to continue with that approach.

Now Wirin says, "I think they have to file a bond." Maybe he wanted a $3,000 bond. The gays had never been in Central Park before. This was the first time they were going to end up in Central Park. He said, "You know, we've had parades, and we're charging everybody now. The Puerto Ricans did a lot of damage, and we're charging them."

I say, "Now, look, it happens that the gays have paraded up Sixth Avenue regularly, and they have never been charged with any damage. So if next time they cause damage, then you should ask them for a bond. But you should take it on faith, since they haven't had any problem up to now, that they will not do any damage. And that's what I'm urging you to do."

And Wirin, who wants to get out of this room as quickly as he can, says, "Okay, let's do it that way."

His counsel begins to object, and I say, "Who asked you? If the deputy administrator says it's okay, why are you telling him it's not?" So that ended it. And that's the way it was left.

•   •   •

Let's skip ahead to the summer of 1985 when I marched at the head of the Gay Pride parade as the Mayor who marches when he can in all the Fifth Avenue parades (it's now legally on Fifth Avenue). The parade occurred only days after the Court of Appeals ruling that I needed legislative authority to issue Executive Order 50, which prohibited those who contract with the City of New York to discriminate against individuals on the basis of their sexual orientation. I delivered the following extemporaneous, unprepared speech at the conclusion of a two-mile walk ending up on West Street at Christopher Street in Greenwich Village, next to the Hudson River.

"I want you to know the following. The Court of Appeals issued a decision, which I respectfully disagree with. I happen to believe that it is wrong to discriminate against individuals based on their race, their religion, their sex, or their sexual orientation. The Court of Appeals said that while they think my executive order was laudatory—that is to say, had a good motive—that they did not believe that I had the authority to do it without legislative authority. Again, I think they're wrong, but let's get the legislative authority. I believe that every decent human being who had fought the good fight to prevent discrimination against blacks, against Hispanics, against women, against Jews, and Italians, and every other group that's been discriminated against, that every single person who believes in human rights should stand up for the human rights of gay men and lesbians. It is not the role, the prerogative, of government or of an employer to ask you what your sexuality is. It is not their business. The only criterion for jobs, the only criterion, is: can you do the job? That's it. And that's what the gay rights legislation is all about. It does not ask for special treatment. It does not ask for anything other than freedom from discrimination.

"Now let me turn to a very serious matter that everybody—gay or straight—has to be concerned about, and that is the catastrophic disease of AIDS. At this particular moment, our hospitals treat AIDS patients, and we have the resources to provide home health care and to make sure that they are legally protected from their landlords, and other discrimination. On July first, this coming week, we will be opening a special clinic for those who don't want to go to the regular hospital clinics, or who feel somehow inhibited from doing that; who want absolute confidentiality—as would be the case in a hospital setting, and will certainly be the case in this clinic setting—absolute confidentiality whether you actually have the disease or you are afraid or you just want information. That clinic opens this week.

"Let me conclude by saying this to you. You know, it was in 1939 when the City of New York first, after many, many years of trying, passed a civil-rights bill which prohibited discrimination against our black citizens in public housing. Nineteen thirty-nine. That same kind of emotion that prevents discrimination by law against blacks, and Jews, and women, and Hispanics, and all other persecuted minorities—that must apply to gay men and lesbian women. There is not a single public official, to the best of my knowledge, in this whole country, who has voted for gay rights and then lost because of it. Not one. And so I say to those who are afraid to stand up for human rights because they fear the political consequences; have no fear. Your fears are unwarranted. But even if you believe, even if you believe that it is politically wise not to do it, as a matter of conscience, stand up and be counted. Take care, and God bless.''

•   •   •

Nineteen sixty-nine was a year of liberation including radicalism and terrorism. There was Woodstock. There was the Stonewall. There were the Weathermen. And there was Sam Melville—the radical leftist bomber who specialized in bombing Chase Manhattan banks.

There was a riot at the Federal House of Detention for men on Wall Street. I went there because I really wanted to know what had happened. It was my first visit to a jail as a congressman. The guards had quelled the riot with tear gas. There's nothing wrong with tear gas to quell riots, but I wanted to know what had happened, and so I went in there.

It's an old building; it has since been turned into a residential co-op. The warden took me around. I said, ''I want to see the maximum-security section,'' whatever that means. I didn't know. So he takes me into this room, large room, and on all sides of it were cells. And I go over and I talk to a couple of the prisoners; and

122

they're explaining that they're being tortured with tear gas, and they're not getting their food. I must say, I discounted their claims. But it was immediately after a riot, and the food was handed under the bars close to the floor. They were the rioters. They were not getting the regular treatment.

And as I'm in that room, suddenly I hear a voice and see an arm reach out of a cell, and the voice says, "Congressman, can I have a word with you?"

I say to the warden, "Can I go over there?"

He says, "Sure."

So I walk over, and this guy—there are now three in the cell—a white guy, says, "Congressman, I really have a lot of complaints. We really are not being treated fairly. They keep six people in this cell and the cell was only built for one. They don't let us shower more than once a week, and they don't let us exercise at all."

So I say, "What are you in here for?"

He says, "Bombing."

I say, "What's your name?"

He says, "Melville."

I say, "I know you. You're in the posters: 'Free the Village One.' You're him." The radical groups had taken on his cause. He had been arrested for bombing.

I say, "I'll see what I can do." And I go to the warden and I say, "Why can't he shower every day? Why can't he exercise?"

He says, "Well, we have to protect him from the other prisoners. They don't like bombers."

Ridiculous. So I write to Norman Carlson, the federal prison director, whom I did not know at that time. He's since gotten a lot of correspondence from me. I became the biggest recipient of prison mail in the country, I think, because word quickly spread: "Koch answers prison mail and takes on causes." So I wrote to him and explained that I'd been there and I think it's an outrage that these prisoners cannot shower, cannot exercise.

I get back a letter, maybe two weeks later, from Sam Melville. The letter reads as follows: "Dear Congressman, There is a new adage in the prison: 'It takes a visit from the brass to get the warden off his ass.'" And then he says, "We're now allowed to shower every day, and we are allowed to exercise, and we want to thank you. And now I'd like to talk to you about the library here," and he goes into that. And then there's a postscript, and the postscript was hilarious. It said: "I'm sorry about the bombings in your district. I will try to have them moved elsewhere."

Sam Melville was ultimately killed in the Attica prison riot.

•   •   •

In the course of my 1973 campaign for mayor, Herb Rickman* suggested to me that I make an appointment with the Lubavitcher Rebbe in the Crown Heights section of Brooklyn. The Lubavitcher group is the largest single group of Hasidic Jews in the City of New York. The estimate is there are as many as thirty

*Herb later became my special assistant in City Hall who handled ethnic politics.

thousand members active in the Lubavitcher, and allegedly they all vote monolithically according to the instructions of the Rebbe. He is a very learned man. So I called him up.

The word comes back that the Rebbe, because he works so hard and prays so hard—he is praying all day long—starts his business appointments at 11 P.M., and he goes through the night with his appointments until 4 or 5 A.M.

It is considered to be a great honor to be given an early appointment. I was shocked when they told me my appointment was for midnight. So I was very prompt: I got there about 11:15 P.M. And I wait. The appointment is for a half hour.

While I am waiting a young rabbi, Rabbi Gruner, who might be described in this instance as the papal chamberlain, keeps me busy. This is what he does with all those who are waiting for appointments. He tells me of the love and affection of all the world for the Rebbe. He tells me how people come from every walk of life—not just people who are in politics and running for office—to the Rebbe for advice and for blessings. He tells me how a great surgeon had come to see the Rebbe. And when the surgeon came out of the Rebbe's room the surgeon said that the Rebbe must be an extraordinary person because he knew all about the newest surgical operation. They had discussed some operation that the surgeon had just performed and the Rebbe understood it.

Rabbi Gruner said, "And then there was a poet. And

when the poet came out the poet said, 'The Rebbe is a genius. The Rebbe read his poem to me, and it was extraordinarily beautiful.' "

I am getting more anxious by the minute as I hear these stories.

Then he says, "Then there was a judge who came. And the judge discussed his opinions with the Rebbe. And when he came out of the room he said, 'This man is a brilliant jurist. He understood the problems. And his advice was very important.' "

Finally comes my time to go into the room. I am alone with the Rebbe. The Rebbe is sitting behind a desk. He appears to me three feet tall and wearing a two-foot-tall hat. And I begin to talk to him. He is a lovely-looking man: cherubic face, well-manicured beard, dancing eyes. But he doesn't say anything to me. And I talk. First I talk about the fact that I am running. He doesn't say a word. Then I leave pregnant pauses where he can jump in. He doesn't say anything. This goes on for about a half hour. And I am praying they will come in and drag me out, because it is very lonely in there. Finally the door opens and with great relief I leave. In thirty minutes the Rebbe has not said a single word to me.

I come out. The people—Rabbi Gruner and all the students, there were a thousand students praying in the synagogue in this building—all come running up to me. They say to me, "What did he say? What did he say?"

You have to say something. So I take the palm of my hand and I sock my forehead and I say, "My God, what that man knows about politics!"

•   •   •

I have always felt very supportive of civil rights. All people ought to have an equal opportunity to apply for jobs, or housing, or medical care, etc., without regard to race, sex, sexual orientation, religion, national origin, the usual items that we now talk about; and that comes out of an awareness of being Jewish, I think, and having been aware of oppression. I don't remember ever having been personally subjected to anti-Semitism in employment, in college, in social relationships. And I don't happen to be an observant Jew, but I'm very conscious of my Jewish heritage and upbringing and very proud of it. I can't tell you how much I enjoyed being a member of Congress from the most powerful district in the country with all the non-Jewish wealth and power represented by David Rockefeller. I used to think to myself, That's a great situation. And it was.

Eleven months after I entered Congress in January 1969 I read in *The New York Times* an article by Tad Szulc which said that David Rockefeller and John J. McCloy, each of the Chase Manhattan Bank, and Robert Anderson, the former Secretary of the Treasury and then director of Dresser Industries, Inc., had been to see President Nixon. They were quoted as having urged that he change the policy of the United States at the expense of Israel to make it more favorable to the Arabs.*

*See *The New York Times*, Dec. 12, 1969, page 1.

Well, I was incensed at that, and so I wrote a letter to David Rockefeller and said, "I've read the story, in *The New York Times*. I know that sometimes reporters are not accurate. I'm writing to you to find out whether or not that conversation took place, and if it did, you will be hearing further from me on this subject." And then I went out on the floor of the House of Representatives and I read the letter. I had the letter read into *The Congressional Record.* I had already started my procedure of handing out literature at the subways, which I did every day I was in New York. Anyway, I reprinted the letter and at the bottom I said, "Why not write to David Rockefeller at 1 Chase Manhattan Plaza and tell him what you think of his statement?"

On Friday of that week I handed out a thousand copies at the subway entrance at Lexington Avenue and Sixty-eighth Street.

Jewish organizations, when they read about this White House meeting in the *Times,* raised quite a furor.

A couple of days later I get a letter from David Rockefeller in which he says that he has my letter and he wants me to know that he is for peace. He didn't respond to my question directly, but he was for peace. So I wrote back saying, "Of course you're for peace. Everybody's for peace. I assume by your not having responded to my question, that in fact the conversation took place, and I shall now pursue this matter, as others will."

Well, maybe ten days later there's a call, and it is from a guy who identifies himself as Rabbi Klapperman, who was then the president of the New York Board of Rabbis. He says he's from Long Island, he has just been to a meeting with David Rockefeller called by Jewish organizations, and after the meeting Rockefeller had told them about oil and the need to change the U.S. policy, and Klapperman said to me, "What do we know?" But in the course of this conversation, Rockefeller had also said that he had tried to get in touch with Congressman Koch, who had expressed an interest in the matter, and he would like to meet with the Congressman and had not been able to locate me.

So I said, "Well, Rabbi, that's rather strange since there's someone here at the office every day from nine until five, and we've gotten no calls."

He said, "Well, he gave me his private number. Would you mind calling him?"

I say, "Fine."

Then Rabbi Klapperman says, "You know, Congressman, David Rockefeller said something else when he referred to you. He said you were a congressman from Brooklyn. Doesn't he know you are from Manhattan?"

I responded, "Of course he knows. I'm his congressman. But so far as he's concerned, all Jewish congressmen come from Brooklyn."

So I call. Chase's Vice-President Nolan is on the other end. I said, "This is Congressman Koch."

"Oh, yes, Congressman."

I said, "I understand you've been looking for me. I find it hard to understand why you haven't found me. I'm at this telephone number, which is listed."

"Well, Mr. Rockefeller would like to set up a meeting with you."

I said, "Fine."

He said, "We would like to do that," and he gave me a date about three weeks later.

I said, "Oh no. If we're going to have a meeting, it will have to be tomorrow, because I intend to make a statement on this matter over the weekend." I think it was on a Wednesday that we had this conversation.

He said, "Well, I'll have to call you back." He called me back a few minutes later and said, "Mr. Rockefeller said it will be fine if we have a meeting tomorrow. Would you mind coming over to our office?"

I said, "No, I don't mind coming over to your office."

"Good."

So the meeting is held the next day. Now, my administrative assistant at that time was David Brown, a very able person, I would say perhaps even brilliant. He doesn't happen to be Jewish, and he went to Washington with me and stayed with me for about five and a half years and then left to become head of the New York State Commission of Investigation. In any event, I informed him about the call.

He said, "Well, what will you do when you go there?"

I said, "I'm going to tell him he'd better change his position." Well, David doesn't get as upset as I do about these matters. I said, "Come on, we'll go over there tomorrow."

He said, "Well, I don't think I want to go. You've already made up your mind." He was rather hostile on this, David was. "You've already made up your mind, and you don't really need me."

I considered him to be my counsel; he's a lawyer, a very good lawyer. I said, "David, that's no way. Whether you agree with my position or not, as my counsel you ought to sit in and monitor and guide me with your advice." I was really quite affronted by what I considered to be a cavalier stance on his part. Our relationship was an unusual relationship. I did not treat him or think of him as an employee in the usual sense. I thought of him more as a partner, and that's the way I encouraged him to think of himself. In any event, he did go with me the next day.

It just so happened that the next day there was an enormous snowstorm. Maybe I exaggerate, but it seems to me it was about two feet of snow. Well, we schlepp over to 1 Chase Manhattan Plaza covered with snow and boots and everything, go up on the elevator to the seventeenth floor, which is where David Rockefeller has his office, and out comes Vice-President Nolan, and he helps me off with my boots and my coat. I mean he couldn't have been more obliging. And at that moment after I had my boots off, out comes David Rockefeller, very genteel, and he welcomes me.

"Oh, Congressman Koch," says he, "how nice of you to come." And we walk into this really sumptuous half a floor of this building—not office but living room, beautifully furnished—and we sit down and have a little chitchat. And then David Rockefeller says, "You know, Congressman Koch, I really am a little distressed by what's taken place, because, you know, when I was at school"—and I think he said St. Paul's, but I'm not sure—"my best friends were Jewish."

I thought to myself, My God, how can he be so stupid?

I responded, "But, of course, Mr. Rockefeller, everybody knows how supportive you and your family have been of Jewish causes, and that's why I was even more doubly shocked by your statement."

He says, "You know, Congressman, I am also upset that a private conversation between me and the President should be the subject of public discussion."

I said, "Mr. Rockefeller, you are one of the ten most powerful people in the world. You don't think that a discussion that you have with the President should be the subject of public discussion?" I said, "I'm a member of Congress. I don't have half the power you have, and everything I say that bears upon the country is surely justifiably the subject of public discussion if people want to discuss it." And then I said, "Mr. Rockefeller, really what I want to know is: Did you say what the reporter said you said?"

He said, "First, Mr. Congressman, I want to make another point, which is: What also troubles me is that there is someone at the subways handing out your letter to me."

I said, "Mr. Rockefeller, not 'someone'—me. I am handing out that letter."

He looks shocked.

I say, "Now, did you make this statement?"

He says, "It's true except in one respect."

I say, "Well, what is that?"

He says, "The impression is that I made the statement because of venality and not in the public interest."

I say, "Now I understand. What you're saying is that when you advised the President to change the policy, it wasn't because of Chase Manhattan's and your oil interests, it was because you thought it was in the interests of the United States. Is that what you're saying to me? But in all other respects it was correctly reported."

"Yes," he says.

I lean forward and I say to him, "Change your position." He was clearly startled. I said, "I have to go, Mr. Rockefeller. I'll be making a statement about this on television over the weekend." He looked more startled. And then I say as I'm getting up, "Mr. Rockefeller, do you agree with those who have made the statement that Israel's military superiority in the area must be maintained?"

He says, "Who said that?"

I say, "Your brother Nelson."

Okay. Subsequent to that the Chase Manhattan went out of its way to sort of retract on that and they published big ads. There was a particularly funny one. It featured the name of a factor—that's a small institution that lends money under very special circumstances—who I think was called Schachter. They took a full-page ad saying, "Schachter Brothers, associated with Chase

Manhattan, welcomes you." It was a terrible attempt to try to indicate to the Jewish community how pro-Jewish Rockefeller and the Chase Manhattan was, with that kind of blatant ad. And then they went out of their way to retreat from their statement.

A year later I was invited to attend a cocktail party at the Museum of Modern Art—and the Rockefellers practically own that museum—to view the Gertrude Stein collection, no longer owned by her, of course, or her estate. And I go. I come in from Washington and go right from the airport to the museum—it's in my district—and as I go upstairs to the private nice rooms upstairs (there are maybe three hundred people there), David Rockefeller sees me. And it's like one enchanted evening. He's across the room in a twinkling. He runs across the room to greet me, so help me. Says he, "Mr. Congressman"—that's how he always referred to me—"I'm so pleased you're here."

I said, "I'm so pleased you invited me. I'm happy to be here."

He said, "Let me get you a drink." We go over and get a drink. Then he says, "You know, Mr. Congressman, since we were last together, you'll be pleased to know that I have gone and visited Israel." And I smile. I had heard of his trip from others. And then he says very quickly, "But of course I also visited Egypt."

So I said, "But of course, Mr. Rockefeller, one should always see both sides." And then I said, "Since we were last together, Mr. Rockefeller, you'll be pleased to know I'm now on the Banking and Currency Committee."

Isn't that a nice story? Isn't that a terrific story?

There was one little addendum, which takes us to 1973. In 1973 when I first ran for mayor I used as my symbol the flag of the City of New York; I had little replicas made up and I handed out about seventy thousand of them. But they're expensive, and I decided that I couldn't afford them anymore, and it would be nice to get some group . . . It didn't have my name on it. It was done in a very smart way. It became my symbol simply because I became identified with it. You see, few people had ever heard of a flag of the City of New York; fewer had ever seen it; and here I'm handing it out at the subways wherever I go. So then I decided—as you get closer into the election you need something with your name on it—it would be nice to have somebody else pick up this handing out of the flag or paying for it, and I started to look for private groups that might do that. I got in touch with Rockefeller and we had a meeting. This is in 1973. This was at the Park Avenue office. We're sitting at a table. There are four of us maybe—Rockefeller, another vice-president and who knows who else, and myself. I explain to him that this is the flag; it's so helpful; it gives people a feeling of identification as New Yorkers and so forth. I said, "I've been handing these out at the subways."

He said, "I much prefer your handing these flags out at the subways than that letter."

135

You have to understand that this had not been a subject of conversation for three years, but he remembered it. And I enjoyed that so much. I roared.

•   •   •

Nelson Rockefeller was another piece of work altogether.

When Robert F. Wagner was considering running again for mayor—this would have been 1973, early '73—Nelson Rockefeller, the Republican Governor, wanted him to run, and Alex Rose of the Liberal Party wanted to draft him to run. Rockefeller's sole motive was to stop Beame. He knew that no Republican could win after Lindsay, so he wanted Wagner. Bob Price, who was a very good friend of mine, still is, was a big wheel in the Republican Party, and at that time he was working for Rockefeller in some capacity, too. I like Bob Wagner, and I had said to Price, "I wish that Wagner would run. I would support him." So one day I get a call from Price saying he'd like me to come up and see Governor Rockefeller. This would be at Rockefeller's Fifty-fifth Street brownstone. I went up there, and in the room was Rockefeller, Price, Jim Cannon, who was Rockefeller's right-hand man and was later his right-hand man down in Washington—I like him—and David Brown and me.

Price says to the Governor, "Ed has said, Governor, that he would come out and support Wagner."

And Rockefeller said, "Oh, that's wonderful. That's

really good. That would be so helpful. Let's have a press conference this afternoon at four.''

I said, "No, you've got this all wrong, Governor. I will come out for Wagner when Wagner comes out for himself. I'm not running out to say we should draft Bob Wagner. But if he becomes a candidate..." (At that time he was going through the gyrations of thinking about it. It was all over the press at the time, and Alex Rose was imploring him, as was Rockefeller.) I said, "I'm not taking a position supporting him in advance of his saying he's a candidate. When he does that, then I will come out for him."

And then Rockefeller, who's been involved in all these convoluted meetings with Wagner and Alex Rose at the highest level—I hadn't been involved in them at all—says to me, "Do you think he'll run?"

I said, "How the hell do I know?" But in my head I'm saying to myself, Here's the guy who's the governor of the state. He's going through all the convolutions, and he's got all the power, and he's doing all the operations, and he's asking me whether Wagner's going to run? We are in a hell of a state. And, of course, Wagner finally decided not to run.

Later I told Nelson Rockefeller the story about his brother David and the advice he had given the White House. Maybe it was a year or two after it had taken place and Nelson Rockefeller had come down to Washington to address the New York congressional delegation. When he did that, he would always have a party at one of the nice hotels in Washington, a dinner, a nice party. And that particular night he was flying back to New York, and I had to get back to New York, so I said to him, "Governor, can I go back on the plane with you?" He had brought down the Albany legislative leaders and he was taking them back that night. "It will save me thirty-two bucks."

So we went back on the plane, and just by chance he sits down next to me. It's a small plane, a nice little plane, about twelve seats, and for an hour or so he and I are talking together. Eventually I tell him the story about his brother. The strange thing about his reaction was that it was as though I were talking about some stranger, because his reaction when I tell him this story was, "That's just like those guys." It was as if they don't know what's happening and they're out of touch, and they are so naive that his brother David feels that it's wrong to have his conversations the subject of discussion in the public arena.

The last conversation I had with Nelson Rockefeller and his wife, Happy, was when he was Vice-President and they had their parties for the members of Congress to see their new house in Washington, the Vice-President's mansion. It had just been opened, and they had erected a huge tent and invited members of Congress alphabetically to come, and I went. It was a rainy night. I got there maybe about nine-thirty. The invitation had read maybe seven-thirty—I got there a little late—and I went with John Krebs, a congressman, a freshman, from California. And as we walked into the tent, there was

Mrs. Rockefeller greeting people, and she came over—she knew me—and she said, "Hello, Ed, how are you?"

I said, "Oh, fine, how are you?"

She said, "Have you seen the house yet?"

I said, "No, I haven't, but I'll get some food, and then I'll come and see the house. I'm hungry."

She said, "Be sure you take a look at the bed." This is their famous bed. "And let me know what you think." Then she said, "There are some people who say that bed is meant for playing and not for sleeping."

I said, "I'll let you know."

After we had eaten, we went upstairs and we looked at the bed. I don't have to describe the bed, but the whole thing is silly—to spend $35,000 on a bed. It's a work of art, I guess, but there's something wrong with it. It's covered by I think a mink coverlet. It's rather bizarre. Then next door to it is a little room with two single beds.

So we go downstairs, and I don't have a chance to talk with her again about the bed, but I write her a letter the next day. The letter goes something like this: "Dear Happy, I'm taking the liberty of calling you 'Happy' because we've met so many times, so I hope that it will be okay with you." Then I said, "I looked at the bed. It's definitely for playing and not sleeping. Sleeping should be done in the other room. And in the eventuality that you were to move to the White House, the bed should be moved to the Museum of Modern Art. Sincerely, Ed."

Let me tell you one other Rockefeller story. You recall that after Nixon resigned, Ford selected Rockefeller for Vice-President, and Rockefeller's name was submitted to Congress under the Twenty-fifth Amendment to the Constitution. During that process, there was an effort on the part of Jim Cannon to draw up support for Rockefeller among the New York delegation, because aside from the Republicans they wanted some Democratic support from New York. It doesn't look nice not to have any New York Democrats voting for him and, after all, this isn't a general election.

Most of the Democrats from New York were opposed to him, certainly all the reformers were—whether it's on Attica (that would be Herman Badillo) or the Vietnam War and his identification with it (that would be Bella Abzug's shtick) or just the general opposition to the name and the man. But I approached the vote on the basis that the Twenty-fifth Amendment, as I saw it, required me to vote for someone who was intellectually able, who was financially honest and who was in the mainstream of the party in power, which would be the Republicans. I felt that Rockefeller qualified in these areas.

But I would not vote for him if his position on Israel was bad, and, as it happened, they released the testimony when he was interviewed by the Senate and, uncharacteristically, he had made two stupid statements. One related to Palestine, and he had a line in there that went something like "They [the Jews] took their [the Arabs'] land away," and also language that indicated he thought Israel should negotiate with the Palestine Liberation Organization.

So when Cannon came to see me, I said, "I'm telling you now I'm not voting for Rockefeller." And up until that moment I had been very helpful to him, telling him what I thought he should do and contacting people. I said, "I'm not voting for him."

He said, "Why?"

I said, "Why? Have you seen that statement that he made before the Senate committee?" I had gotten a copy of it.

He said, "Yes, he was tired."

I said, "I want to tell you now that unless that is amended, I will not vote for him."

Well, for whatever reason, they considered me to be a key guy and they wanted me to vote for him—because I'm Jewish and I was secretary of the delegation and I represent the East Side of Manhattan and I had been friendly to him. So they were really working like dogs to get me. "What is it you want?" said Cannon.

I said, "I want a letter changing his position. That's what I want."

"Well, would you dictate the letter to us?"

I said, "No, no, I'm not dictating a letter. I'll give you some ideas, but I'm not dictating the letter."

Presently, the letter from Rockefeller comes back: "On the history of land ownership in Palestine, I would urge a reading of . . ." and he gives me a compendium of books to read. Dopey, just dopey. He was turning it into land titles, like the board of registry in some county.

So Cannon shows me the letter and he says, "Is that all right?"

I said, "This? This makes it worse. I am not voting for him."

He said, "What do you want?"

I said, "I want a letter in which he withdraws that statement and apologizes for it and in which he says that Israel should not recognize the PLO."

He says, "What kind of language?"

I say, "I would like a line in there to this effect: 'It is in the national interest of the United States to protect the security of Israel, as well as a moral imperative.' " I always used that in all my responses to the hate mail I got on this subject.

So they bring in the second letter. In the second letter Rockefeller in effect apologizes for the statement "They took their land away," and he puts in this line that "it's in the national interest of the United States to provide for the security of Israel as well as a moral imperative." But there's nothing in there about the PLO.

I say, "The PLO, what about that?"

Cannon said, "Well, we've taken it up with Kissinger, and they just will not let us put that in."

I say, "Then I'm not voting for him."

He says, "Well, we've gone as far as we can go. We just hope you change your mind," and so forth. And that was it.

Then I think about it and think, I have pushed him as far as I can push him, and at this point I want to be able to have some entree to him, which I would lose if, after having pushed him there, I now vote against him. Almost everybody else of any consequence from the New York delegation is going to vote against him and so I decide I'm going to vote for him. This is the day of the vote, mind you. So at about four-thirty in the afternoon as I'm entering the House Chamber, there's Jim Cannon. He's standing at the chamber entrance. And I walk over to him and I say, "Jim, I have decided, notwithstanding my reservations, I'm going to vote yes." He's elated, just elated. And I do vote for Rockefeller.

That evening they had a reception at the Capitol and I went over. Rockefeller sees me and he comes over to me and he says (this is really funny), "I know what you did and you'll never regret it." Isn't that nice? I thought it was nice. But it doesn't mean shit, I want to tell you. I mean I didn't believe it meant anything, although it was nice at the moment. I said to myself, He won't remember and he won't care. That's not the stuff that most people in power are made of.

To be sure, I'm in power, a relatively modest kind of power, myself, but I believe in loyalty of a particular kind. Doubtless they have loyalties, too. But their loyalties are to their friends. I mean Rockefeller will take care of the people who work for him and are on his immediate staff—he's marvelous that way—and, I'm sure, to other friends. But in the politics we're talking about, I don't think that after that initial response of "you'll never regret it" there would be any IOU that I could have had vis-à-vis him. I just didn't believe it. Maybe I was wrong about that, and maybe philosophically, intellectually, it doesn't follow, since there was a certain loyalty that he did have.

I hope I have an intellectual commitment to keep the promises that I make on substantive issues as well as the loyalty that I pride myself on vis-à-vis people that I'm friendly with. I guess really what I'm saying is: I don't think Nelson Rockefeller had the commitment on substantive issues that he might have had.

●　　　　　　●　　　　　　●

Nonetheless, it is necessary to reach out to potential opponents in the interest of long-term coalition building, as I did successfully with the Italians who were supporting Mario Cuomo in the mayoral election of 1977. I had won the primary, but Cuomo had the Liberal line, so we had a general-election fight on our hands.

After the primary and before the runoff, Meade Esposito, the Brooklyn Democratic leader, made it clear that he was for me over Cuomo. So we set up a meeting with Meade at his home in Canarsie: David Garth, my media adviser; John LoCicero, my campaign manager; Meade; and me. We wanted to get Meade not to endorse me formally, because I was running without the endorsements of the county leaders, the banks, or the landlords. But here we had a situation where a county leader genuinely liked me. What do you do?

As luck would have it, our driver didn't know how to get there. We were driving all over the place, and we were late. And you don't want to keep the county leader waiting when the purpose of the meeting is to discuss his being helpful to you.

So Garth is beside himself. Every time the driver goes around another turn Garth turns around and slugs John, "What do you mean you don't know where he lives," and screaming at the driver. It was something!

Well, the fact is we hadn't blown it at all. When we got there, Esposito was very friendly and said, "Whatever it is that you want me to do, I will do." And we made it clear that the one thing we didn't want him to do was to endorse me in any public way. (I must say he has always been helpful to me, and he told me a thousand times after my election as mayor that the only reason he stayed in politics was because of me, and I believed him.) So, anyway, he agreed to pull strings, very discreetly. He later resigned, in 1984, even though it was not helpful to me that he do so.

But we still had to face the rank-and-file Italians.

Shortly after the meeting with Meade, I went with Dan Wolf and his daughter Margaret, and with Wally Popolizio, to Arthur Avenue in the Bronx; it was the worst, the most vicious event imaginable. Mario Biaggi and Bess Myerson also were there. Arthur Avenue was a center of enormous strength for Cuomo. They had a headquarters nearby and the area is all Italian. Mario Biaggi, the local Democratic Congressman, had been supporting Cuomo throughout the primary but then, like a good Democrat, when I won the primary he came over and supported me in the general election. So Biaggi is there, too. And we have this flatbed truck and Biaggi gets up to speak to this crowd of several hundred Italians and they shout him down and they won't let him speak—they booed him off the stage, in effect. So he comes over to me and he says, "Let's get out of here—it's not possible to speak."

I say, "No. Nothing doing." So I take the microphone and I say, "Whether you like it or not, I am here and I am going to say hello and I am going to win."

They are yelling, "Fag, queer, Jew, kike." They were the most vicious, vile people imaginable. So then I jumped down into the crowd and walked through it saying, "Let's shake even if you don't like me." Well, some of them shook hands and others didn't, but the remarks were terrible as we walked through the crowd. At one point while Bess was in a campaign car a carload of locals drove by screaming, "Faggot." Bess leaned out of the car's window, gave them the finger and yelled out "Fuck you!" That's a real supporter.

They have this rather large indoor public market there, which we went into—sort of to take cover. I got on the microphone and talked to people. A few people would come over to me, and some whispered, "*Shalom*," indicating they were Jewish and they were scared

146

shitless. I'll tell you one more thing: I could tell that those people out in the street were shocked, really shocked, when instead of just driving off in the truck we jumped down onto the street and reached out to talk to them.

Almost a year later, on Saturday, September 23, 1978, I went to a festival on Arthur Avenue in the Bronx. It was a love fest. When I entered the market, the North Bronx Retail Market, at 2344 Arthur Avenue, the butcher took the microphone and repeated again and again, "Ladies and Gentlemen, the Mayor of New York City, Ed Koch, is here in the market. . . . You're the best. . . . you're doing great, Mr. Mayor. . . . Ladies and Gentlemen . . ." After a walk around the corner onto 187th Street, the festival committee asked me to draw the winning raffle ticket. Before making the drawing, however, I took the opportunity to address the community. When the applause died down, I said, "Listen, whether you are for me or against me, I am for you, because I look at these houses and I see houses that are old. The same kinds of houses exist five and six blocks away from here and they are burned out and deserted. Here you have a thriving shopping street. It is not the housing, or the stores. It's the people. And I am going to be supporting you because we need people like you in this city." They cheered as if I'd grown up down the street. Then I drew the raffle ticket and kissed the winner and then I made my way to my car. A woman appeared with a plate of cannolis and cream puffs. She insisted that I take the whole plate and she told me I was the best mayor New York ever had and to come back anytime for more pastries.*

As I have said, one quality that is particularly wonderful about the Italians is that they are forgiving—in this instance, I forgave them.

---

*Two years after my election, in January 1980, some 81 percent of the Italians in New York City thought I was doing a good job. That was better than I was doing with the Jews at the time. There, only 73 percent approved of my performance on the job.

7

A Liberal with Sanity

IN 1956 I WAS A STREET SPEAKER for Adlai Stevenson. They gave you an American flag, which was required by law in those days, and I had my chair to stand on, and I would go out and make speeches in support of Stevenson.

One of the best places to draw a crowd was at the corner of Broad and Wall Streets in lower Manhattan in front of the Sub-Treasury Building by the statue of George Washington. I could get a crowd of twenty-five or thirty at lunchtime. It was a favorite place for all kinds of street speakers.

So I go there one lunch hour with my chair and my flag. My law office was just up the block. And I start to speak and a big burly cop comes along and says,

"Where's your permit? You can't speak without a permit."

I say, "Oh no, Officer, that is not the law. The law does not require a permit if you are not using an amplification device."

He says, "Listen, you can't speak without a permit. Let me see your permit or I'll have to arrest you."

I said, "I don't have a permit because there is no permit required for this kind of street speaking. Just my flag and I have that."

He says, "Okay, I'm going to arrest you if you don't move on."

At that point, I see an evangelist across the street who is talking to a crowd of about seventy and who I knew was generally at that corner every day of the week and speaking to similarly sized crowds. I say to the cop, "What are you going to do about him? You never asked him for a permit, and he's here every day!"

The cop looks at me and says, "He's different. He's a fanatic."

I picked up my chair and I left.

●　　　　●　　　　●

When I was running for Congress for the first time, in 1968, the key to running and winning was getting the Liberal Party endorsement. I was actually sure of getting that because Alex Rose—the legendary longtime vice-chairman of the Liberal Party, and the recognized real head of the party—was for me. That came out of my friendship with Henry Stern and also, very key, my support of Lindsay and the Liberal Party when Lindsay had run for mayor in 1965.

In 1968 I appeared before the county executive committee for the Liberal Party. One of the questions I was asked was, "Where do you stand on the Condon-Wadlin Law?" (That law prohibited strikes by municipal employees. It was subsequently changed and became known as the Taylor Law.)

I said, "I am for the Condon-Wadlin Law because I do not believe that civil servants have the right to strike." Nothing much else was said.

However, the next day at my law office I got a call from Victor Gotbaum of District Council 37, the municipal employees' union, whom I didn't know; I had probably met him but really didn't know him. It was followed by a call from Al Shanker of the United Federation of Teachers. Both of them used almost exactly the same phrases.

Victor said, "Ed, I just heard and I can't believe what I heard and I am sure it is not true and that is why I am calling you."

I said, "What, Victor?"

He said, "I just heard that you are against strikes by municipal employees and that you support the Condon-Wadlin Law."

I said, "I do, Victor. I don't believe that municipal employees have a right to strike."

He said, "I can't believe that you take that position, and if you do, then we will have to seek to do what we can to deprive you of the Liberal Party's endorsement.''

I said, "I would hope, Victor, that you would look at my whole record as a member of the City Council and what I stood for, and you should know, Victor, that I picketed in support of the right of hospital workers to organize and stood in front of Montefiore Hospital with the pickets to get them the right to organize."

He said, "That doesn't make any difference. If you are against our right to strike we are against you."

I said, "Well, if that is the only issue that concerns you, then, of course, I will understand your being against me."

Then I had exactly the same discussion with Al Shanker five minutes later, so they had to have synchronized it. Then they sought to organize against me and to elect Peter Berle—an Assemblyman representing an East Side district—who was seeking the Silk Stocking congressional nomination from the Liberal and Democratic parties. The district was a Republican one, and so the only way a Democrat could win was if that person ran also with the endorsement of the Liberal Party. Shanker and Gotbaum then cooperated in support of Berle, who came out against the Condon-Wadlin Law saying he was for the right to strike by municipal employees.

I was very worried and I called Henry Stern. Henry said, "Don't worry about it. You have to understand, Alex Rose and all of the other leaders of the Liberal Party are not fanatical on this issue. They don't think that municipal employees should have the right to strike, either. No matter what they might say publicly, they are with you on this issue.''

And, in fact, they were. They gave me their support. The county executive committee had already done it and then I went before the full county committee and they gave me the Liberal Party nomination, which, by the way, was essential for any Democrat who wanted to win.

In fact the Liberal Party gave me 14,000 votes on their line in the general election and I won against Seymour by what I recall was a margin of 2,500. So obviously the Liberal Party's endorsement was key.

●   ●   ●

Now let me tell you about my feelings about reformers and regulars in New York City. I like regulars as human beings better than I do reformers. I like conservatives as human beings better than I do liberals. Philosophically I agree with the reformers more than I do with the regulars, and I agree with the liberals more than I do with the conservatives. But as human beings, reformers and liberals care comparatively little about human beings except in the abstract. They love them in the abstract; they just don't like them in the particular.

What do I mean by that? I mean they don't care about the impact of their actions on the individual. What they care about is some general axiom, some philosophy, and not how it impacts on somebody immediately. It's like Stanley Geller saying to me when the Lindsay administration was trying to force low-income housing into Forest Hills, Queens, "The Jews in Forest Hills have to pay their dues," in support of some philosophical concept that he had. He didn't care about that poor guy who spends his whole life getting his family to Forest Hills in order to get out of a section of Brooklyn which was falling apart or a slum in the Bronx. He doesn't care that that guy has worked his whole life to give his kids a better life. He doesn't care about that—Stanley Geller. No. What he cares about is some utopia down the road. That's what the reformers and the liberals are talking about. They don't care what's happening to individuals at the moment in a whole host of substantive areas.*

Anyway, the regulars and the conservatives are more understanding of human frailty and human error. They'll accept disagreement. They'll say, "Oh, sure, he's wrong on this, but he's right on that. Ah, I understand why he did this—he had all those pressures. Next time he'll be better." Reformers and liberals never do that. They never excuse human frailty. They have absolutes that everybody has to meet, an absolute test. But the test changes from day to day. That's the point. It's not "What have you done?" No. It's "What are you doing today?" You may have been with them on a hundred issues, and then on a single issue you will not be. Everything gets wiped out. They don't care about what you did. Absolute allegiance is expected of you. I don't

*Several years later we laughed about our earlier differences and our friendship was restored.

really like many of them. It is unrealistic to think that someone will be with you on every issue.

With regulars and conservatives, on the other hand, loyalty is important. There is little loyalty with reformers and liberals. That's an overstatement, but it is more correct than incorrect.

Another example of the sort of grand design that transfixes liberals was the liberal response to the plight of integrationist whites in the South in the sixties. My trip to Mississippi, in 1964, was fascinating and scary. I had a number of civil-rights cases to defend, and I was there for about eight days. I have already recounted much of what happened there in an earlier chapter.

The last day I was there, there was a picnic—I was not at it—of blacks and whites. They were called COFO workers—they were college students recruited from around the nation to help register blacks to vote in the South. So these workers on a day off were attacked at this picnic by some Mississippi white rednecks with chains, and some of the workers were beaten up, and the rednecks beat up the whites, the white college students, most of all. When I heard of it I was horrified. And at that very moment the Democratic national convention was going on in Atlantic City, and the major fight was the seating of the Mississippi delegation and Fannie Lou Hamer, a very courageous black woman who was a major civil-rights and equal-rights advocate. Others were testifying before the Credentials Committee, and Joe Rauh of the Americans for Democratic Action was the attorney of the black delegates challenging the regulars. It was very exciting watching it on television, and I thought, My God, I must get to Atlantic City and tell them about this latest obscenity.

So I fly to New York and when I land, instead of going home, I take another flight direct to Atlantic City. I get to the convention hall and I go in where you announce your presence, and I say, "I've got to see Mr. Rauh. I must see Mr. Rauh. I have important news from Mississippi." I felt like I was carrying the message from García—that sort of thing. And I sent up my card, my attorney's card, with a little note saying: "Mr. Rauh"—I'd never met him—"I have important news from Mississippi. I must talk to you."

Some guy came down and said, "You can go upstairs," and I go up to see Rauh. "Mr. Rauh," I say, "I've just come back from Mississippi and I want to tell you something that happened down there. There was a riot where civil-rights workers were unmercifully beaten with chains. It was just awful." And he said, "What color were the people who were beaten?" I said, "They were white."

He said, "Can't use it." The only thing that would have been dramatic so far as he was concerned, as it appeared to me at that convention, was if blacks were beaten up, not if whites were beaten up. To me that is a double standard. He now denies that the incident occurred that way, but that is my recollection, and it had a profound impact upon me.

To return to the story about Forest Hills: I felt that the people in Forest Hills were being pushed around in an unfair way by the Lindsay administration. They were being made the goat. A low-income housing project was being placed in their midst: three buildings twenty-four stories tall and about three thousand residents. A substantial number of those three thousand were going to be welfare recipients.

The city administration was lying when it said that 40 percent of the project would be devoted to the elderly. The fact was they weren't going to have 40 percent of the buildings occupied by the elderly. They might have elderly persons in 40 percent of the apartments. But elderly people generally live either alone or in pairs. They don't have kids with them. And so the vast majority of the population of that project was likely to be welfare families, not the elderly.

When I first heard of it in 1971, I thought it was wrong to do. I didn't really say anything at that time—it wasn't in my district. I did mention it, however, to Ben Rosenthal, who was the Congressman in the district. I said, "Ben, I think it's terrible what they're doing to those people, and if you ever want me to join with you, I'll join with you." I was then on the Banking and Currency Committee, and that committee had jurisdiction over housing matters.

He wasn't keen on getting involved. And the reason was that, although he knew that what was happening was wrong, the issue of stopping the project had been seized by the fanatic right. Jerry Birbach was one of those people, and nobody on the left likes to be identified with the fanatic right. That's true on a whole host

157

of issues where you'd like to get involved and you stay out of it simply because you don't want to be identified with the right. Fluoridation was another one of those issues.

One Sunday morning—this must have been in early 1972—a friend of mine, George Bady, said, "Would you like to have breakfast?"

I said, "Sure."

So we start to go looking for a place to eat breakfast, and he says, "You know, I'd like to go out and see this Forest Hills project," which was then a hole in the ground. "Have you ever seen it?"

I said, "No."

So we drive out to Queens. I didn't know there was going to be a demonstration going on at the time, but we drive out there, and there may be two thousand people circling this hole in the ground with signs and yelling and screaming. We get out of the car, and some of them see me and they recognize me and come running over saying, "Congressman, we're so glad you're here. We'd like you to say a few words."

Well, all you have to do is give a politician a microphone and he's off. I said, "Sure," because I have never feared speaking to any group, whether they were for me or against me. I love the combat of the street in politics. So I say, "Keep up the fight—you can turn City Hall around. They can't impose this on you. It's wrong." And I made all the statements that I believed were true then and are certainly true now and they've become true in the sense that others have recognized the validity of them.*

Well, there were radio people out there, and this was all carried on the radio. And when I got back to my apartment the calls began to come in from all of my friends: "Ed, we heard you on the radio and you sound like a racist and what did you say?"

I told them what I'd said.

"Well, it doesn't come over that way. After all, it's Birbach who's out there."

I say, "I can't help it if Birbach is on the same side of the issue as I am, or I'm on the same side of the issue as he is. I'm interested in the issue." Well, it didn't satisfy anyone, particularly the VID and the liberals on the East Side. They were very upset.

I go back to Washington and I get a call from Stanley Geller. I remember the conversation so well. He says, "Ed, I understand that you're against public housing."

I say, "No, Stanley, I'm not against public housing. I'm against the Forest Hills project because it's too big. It's got to be scaled down."

---

*On May 17, 1972, Mario Cuomo, then a law professor at St. John's University, was appointed by Mayor Lindsay to look into the Forest Hills project situation as an "independent fact-finder." In the two months that elapsed between Cuomo's appointment and the day he rendered his report to Lindsay (July 25, 1972) Cuomo interviewed all the partisans, engineers, planners and others then familiar with the dispute. I was one of those interviewed; and when the report was issued its conclusions were nearly chapter and verse my conclusions.

He says, "You can't be against public housing, no matter what the size."

I say, "No, no, no, Stanley. That project, if it's built that way, will destroy that neighborhood and the Jews will move out. It's got to be scaled down."

He says, "I don't care if it destroys the neighborhood and the Jews move out." And then that line: "The Jews in Forest Hills have to pay their dues." That's the literal quote, because it never went out of my head.

I said, "Stanley, you're such a nice guy, and we've known each other for such a long time, and you're a rich man and you've used your money for good causes. In fact, you've helped me. For that I'm very appreciative." He had always supported me financially as well as with his feet in the streets. "And you have this brownstone in the Village, and I wish I had one like it. And you have this marvelous home in the Hamptons with this near-Olympic-size pool, and you've invited me there, and I wish I owned one like that. On the day your kids were born you registered them in private schools. And you're telling me that the Jews of Forest Hills have to pay their dues. I am telling you they are willing to pay theirs; they are just not willing to pay *yours*."

On the same subject, I had lunch with Alex Rose. He by then was obsessed with crime; and he was also very down on my stand on the Forest Hills housing project. It was 1972 and I was seeking the Liberal Party's endorsement in my reelection campaign, but our relationship was strained.

I go to the Toy Center at 200 Fifth Avenue, where there was a seedy European-style restaurant. Alex Rose had a permanent table there. God knows why; the food wasn't very good.

I come in; he is already seated at his table; I sit down.

He says, "Ed, you know it is very upsetting to us, the position you have taken on Forest Hills."

I say, "Alex, let me explain my position to you. That project, as it is now planned, will destroy Forest Hills. If you allow this to be done to the middle-class neighborhoods, you are going to witness the destruction of this city. The city will be destroyed."

He says with great intensity, "The city is destroyed already. I can't walk out on the streets at night. It isn't safe. It's over!"

Ultimately I received their endorsement—for Congress. Not for mayor. I blame the latter on the fact that Alex died before the mayoralty election in '77.

What all of this indicates is the large gulf between fantasy and reality with these so-called liberals. In their minds the world should be changed—just as long as the changes don't impact on *their* day-to-day lives. What they often propose is fantasy, and that is why they are in reality ideologues. Believe me. No one knows them better than I do.

My tough stand on Forest Hills ultimately was a major source of strength, but it also accounted for some of my major weaknesses as a candidate for the mayoralty in 1973.

As a result of my opposition to the Forest Hills project, I was censured by the Lexington Democratic Club—a wealthy reform club that had been a power in East Side politics since reform came to the Democratic Party. It was a grueling moment for me and not just because of Stanley Geller. I responded publicly to the Lexington Club censure. My retort was, "The East Side reformers are for low-income housing projects, just so long as they're built in Forest Hills."

Forest Hills was, for me, a rubicon. It meant creating problems for me in my heretofore safe limousine-liberal constituency on the East Side of Manhattan. The immediate effect, and the one that was devastating to my 1973 candidacy for mayor, was visible when I tried to raise campaign funds. The "exotics"* wouldn't give me anything, because they said I was against housing for poor people. And the middle-class people, of whom I was one, in the city at large didn't know me well enough yet to send their $10, $25, $100 contributions. So my campaign went broke in forty-five days, and I had to pack it in and withdraw my candidacy. I learned a lot about liberals in that Forest Hills fight. And since then I have continued to take my own positions—which I describe as "liberal with sanity"—without regard for where the "liberals" are on the issue.

●　　　　　●　　　　　●

*It was Congressman Charles Wilson, from Texas, my friend, who first used the word "exotics" to describe the archliberals living in my district.

In the mid-sixties the State of New York changed its policy in a major way regarding the keeping and housing of mentally incompetent people. As a result of that policy change the streets of New York City, and undoubtedly those of other communities, became not only less attractive but also more dangerous. This development caused concern among New Yorkers. In the late winter and early spring of 1981 I went on several early-morning (5 A.M.) inspection tours of places like Pennsylvania Station where shopping-bag ladies were known to sleep. My intention at that time was to interview these women, describe to them the ways in which the city was prepared to help them, and in general to enhance my understanding of the ways in which homeless people think and survive in New York City.

Following one of these tours I mentioned to a reporter my thought that obviously mentally disturbed people ought to be picked up and taken to centers like the newly opened Antonio Olivieri Center on Manhattan's West Side for a seventy-two-hour program of washing, delousing, feeding and medical care. When the experts read of this suggestion they informed me that such a program was violative of the Fourth Amendment of the U.S. Constitution, the amendment that forbids "unreasonable searches and seizures."

I responded, "Well, then the Constitution is dumb."

For that I was roundly attacked in the liberal press. Beth Fallon, in the *Daily News,* for example, ran a column entitled "Ed vs. 'Dumb' Constitution: You

Lose, Smartie!'' in which she described her quarrel with me as being based upon my statement's ''repugnant and demonstrable untruth and with the bloated arrogance that could make so offensive a remark.'' In that March 30 column Fallon concluded by bemoaning my ''monumental insolence to call the Constitution of our country dumb.''

If I had said the Constitution was dumb at the time women could not vote because of the Constitution, no one would have gotten upset. If I had said the Constitution was dumb when it said that a slave was only three fifths of a person, no one would have gotten upset. I tried out a different way of dealing with this by saying to some people, ''If I had said the Constitution on this issue is archaic, would you be upset?'' They said, ''No.'' I said, ''But who would have understood that? Many people wouldn't have gotten my meaning.''

Still, I wanted to help. So I met with Jack Krauskopf of the Human Resources Administration, Nat Leventhal, my deputy mayor for operations, and Hadley Gold from the Corporation Counsel's Office. I told them that I wanted a new program immediately that would allow us to hand out literature that would tell these shopping-bag people where they could go for food, showers, medical treatment, overnight accommodations, etc. The immediate response from Krauskopf was, ''We don't have room for them.''

I said, ''Not acceptable. Here I am saying that I want to help what some have estimated to be thirty-six thousand* homeless who are out there, and I am being attacked by the press as a monster for (a) not helping and (b) offering to help the way I did. I want to help; all the homeless people in this town won't come in; but at least let's tell them the services are available. In a city with a fourteen-billion-dollar budget, I am not going to take the position that we can't deal with this problem.''

At 4:15 A.M. one day next week I was back out at Penn Station handing out the new pamphlet and talking to shopping-bag ladies again. I had moved up my arrival time at the station because I had found in my earlier expeditions that the Port Authority police would begin moving the shopping-bag ladies out at about five o'clock so that the passengers on the commuter trains could use the ladies' rooms.

That was a week in which I again incurred the wrath of the liberal press. On April 6 the *Times* ran an editorial entitled ''Judicial Discretion, Mayoral Indiscretion'' in which the editors criticized me for criticizing individual judges publicly. This was the old dispute, reminiscent of my attack on Judge Bruce Wright in 1979 during which I called Wright's policy of little or no bail ''bizarre.'' This time I openly criticized Justices Hortense Gabel and Irving Lang for being too lenient with two Brinks guards who had turned out to be thieves. According to the city's Department of Investigation the two had stolen an estimated $1.2 million in

*The totally overstated figure often used by the advocates for the homeless.

quarters from the City of New York. They had been responsible for guarding the quarters that the Department of Traffic personnel took out of the city's parking meters. Instead the thieves had developed a scheme with which they routinely skimmed several hundred pounds of quarters off the parking-meter take each day. The justices had fined the two $2,400 and $2,500 respectively and ordered that they each spend sixteen weekends in jail. I expected the defendants to pay their fines in quarters! Those sentences, I said, "encourage people to steal from the city." It was to these comments the *Times* editors took exception.

Hardly had the editors taken a hopeful breath before I was on the attack again. This time the defendant was a young white male who, upon being apprehended for a minor crime, ordered his German-shepherd dog to attack a black police officer who was then in the process of taking the man into custody. I was outraged at the young man's defiance of the police officer's dignity and duty. I hoped for harsh punishment.

On April 8 Judge Stanley Gartenstein found the defendant guilty and sentenced him to pay a small fine, make an apology to the police officer, and write a five-thousand-word essay entitled "The Untenability of Disobedience to the Authority of the Sovereign: The Views of Hobbes, Locke, Rousseau, Mill, Bentham, Thoreau and Holmes Compared." No jail. I hit the roof! In Judge Gartenstein's decision he explained in this way his failure to send the young man to jail:

He [the defendant] would be immediately subject to homosexual rape and sodomy and to
brutalities from fellow prisoners such as make
the imagination recoil in horror. In short, while
incarceration is merited, rape, torture and brutality are not. We take judicial notice of defendant's slight build; his mannerisms; dress; col-
or and ethnic background and are cognizant of
the unfortunate realities that he would not last
for 10 minutes on Riker's Island.

I was aghast at the discriminatory statements of
Judge Gartenstein. First, the city's Department of Cor-
rection segregates from the rest of the jail population
those inmates whose appearance might make them the
subject of a sexual attack. All homosexuals, for example, who request it are segregated from the rest of the
jail population. Of course it would be foolish not to
acknowledge the possibility of violence in a jail system
that nightly houses nine thousand inmates. But what did
Judge Gartenstein actually say in that decision? To me
he said that only black and Hispanic persons should be
subject to the possibility of these brutalities. He advo-
cated the very kind of two-tiered justice which was
what the civil-rights struggle was conducted to abolish.
His is a notion that is repugnant to me and to civilized
society. The jail door must be color blind; and those
who belong in jail must be sent there, regardless of
race. Instead, what was that sentence? It was worthy of

a prep-school teacher, not of a judge presiding over a criminal trial.

Of course I was not attacked by the liberals for my stance on this one. It was, after all, a white-against-black case.

Meanwhile, still following up on the parking-meter cases, Beth Fallon had decided to go to court to watch Justice Lang for a day.

In her April 10, 1981, column Fallon detailed her day in court. She had watched as the bailiff brought a "chronic undifferentiated schizophrenic" before Acting Justice Lang. He was charged with attempted armed robbery with a knife, and he pleaded guilty. The state's policy on accepting these individuals into its mental institutions is clear: proof must be made that the defendant was insane when he committed the crime. It is easier for a court-appointed attorney to clear him off the docket with a guilty plea. "One to three years," said Lang.

"The law is an ass, the state is an ass," wrote Beth Fallon in her next-day column.

"Dear Beth," I wrote on April 10. "Why did you call the law an ass? Don't you know that the law can never be an ass and that the Constitution can never be dumb? All the best. Love, Ed."

•   •   •

The next one, which is a favorite of mine, was beginning in 1981 as the other was wrapping up. I have always believed that graffiti has an adverse impact on everything that we have going on in the subways. It adds to the oppression. If you look at the Port Authority Trans-Hudson (PATH) subways that come across from New Jersey in the Hudson–Manhattan tube, you'll see no graffiti. And those subway cars are stored in Newark, which is no rose garden. And so I made an inquiry: How come? And the answer was very simple: The Port Authority protects those cars in areas that are guarded, fenced in. The Metropolitan Transportation Authority (MTA) was not protecting its cars in the same ways. So several years back I took the matter up with Jay Goldin and City Council President Carol Bellamy and Council Majority Leader Tom Cuite at one of our regular Wednesday meetings, and I suggested that we jointly urge MTA Board Chairman Dick Ravitch to fence in the yards and thereby protect the rolling stock. They agreed. So we sent out joint correspondence to the effect, Why don't you do this, to wit, enclose the yards? And Ravitch's responses, and now I am referring to a number of responses, were, "No, we can't do it. I have given it to our people and they don't think it will work."

I said, "But the proposal is that you would have a fence and a dog in the yard."

His response was, "No, if you put a dog in there the dog would step on the third rail and get killed."

I said, "Listen, I don't believe dogs step on third rails. How come the vandals don't step on the third rails? And if you do find a dog that has stepped on the third rail, then replace him."

Well, this went on for a little while.

Then I said, "But, in any event, if that is what is bothering you, then build two fences around the yard. And have the dog run between the two fences. Then he can't step on the third rail."

The response to that was, "Well, somebody might climb over the fence and if they did they would fall between the two fences and then the dog would bite them."

To that I said, "But I thought that is what the dogs were supposed to do! However," said I, "if you are afraid that the dog will bite somebody, then what you should do is put a wolf between the two fences." Because—and here I drew on my prodigious memory—I had read once that no wolf had ever bitten a human being, except if it was a rabid wolf; wolves had a bad rap against them. I said, "You should put a wolf there because wolves don't bite people." And I announced this to the world at a press conference.

The next day Clyde Haberman of the *Times* came in and said he had wanted to check out whether my information was correct, so he had gone to the zoological library, and: "The facts are different from what you suggest, Mayor. You are half right and you are half wrong. It is true that no wolf in the wild has ever bitten a human being in any recorded case. But there are a number of cases where wolves in captivity have bitten human beings."

So I say at that point, staring at him, "But of course. I know that. I would never use a tame wolf. I only would use wild wolves. And when the wild wolf

1

Adlai Stevenson and Estes Kefauver (top) receiving the Democratic nomination for President and Vice President in 1956, cheered on by former President Harry Truman and New York Governor Averell Harriman. Stevenson's speeches seemed all-encompassing in their breadth. Those speeches got me to speak in the streets for him in 1952 and '56. Harry Truman, with his candor, honesty and common sense, is still an inspiration long after Stevenson has faded.

3

Fiorello La Guardia will always be remembered as the Mayor who set the standard for all mayors to come. Some of the legend is fact and some is myth.

2

In 1961 Jim Lanigan and Carol Greitzer were elected Greenwich Village district leaders. I served in their campaign, and two years later in my first successful run for office I succeeded Lanigan. I won that one by the skin of my teeth.

4

Saints and sinners, depending on the election in each year: (left to right) Senator Herbert H. Lehman, Mayor Robert F. Wagner, Secretary of State Carmine De Sapio. Wagner and Lehman did me in in 1962 when I lost the Assembly nomination to William F. Passannante (below); then they helped elect me district leader in 1963 as a way of stopping De Sapio's comeback. Defeating De Sapio in 1963, '64 and '65 gave me my start in politics, so that I can now say jocularly I owe him a lot.

5

Assemblyman William Passannante held on to his seat in 1962 by defeating me in the primary. He's still in Albany and I'm here. We're both happy.

6

Carmine De Sapio, shown here in the early '60s, explaining to the Greenwich Village planning board all that he had done to help prevent a roadway from running through Washington Square Park. Carmine could be charming, sophisticated, gentle, generous, venal and tough. He could be all things to all people. I defeated him for district leader and I said during our debates, "Carmine, you turned your back on the people of Greenwich Village when you moved uptown." He had moved from the primarily Italian South Village to the Brevoort on lower Fifth Avenue, where the richies and the upper middle class live.

In 1965, talking with Italians living in the South Village and trying to convince them to vote for Carol Greitzer (standing) and me and to reject Carmine De Sapio's comeback.

7

8
John Lindsay. His campaign theme was "He is fresh and everyone else is tired." He looked the part but fell apart.

9
Henry Stern: brilliant, idiosyncratic, friend. He convinced me to cross party lines and endorse Lindsay for mayor in 1965. He even wrote my endorsement statement. Today he is the New York City Parks Commissioner.

The *Village Voice* when it was a great newspaper, under the brilliant editorship of Dan Wolf (right, with pipe), here shown with publisher Edwin Fancher, a friend (left), and Jerry Tallmer (center), the writer.
10

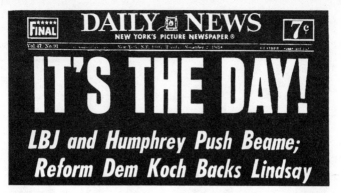

FINAL ★★★★★

DAILY ⬧ NEWS

NEW YORK'S PICTURE NEWSPAPER ®

7¢

Vol. 47, No. 91   New York, N.Y., Tuesday, November 2, 1965   WEATHER

IT'S THE DAY!

LBJ and Humphrey Push Beame;
Reform Dem Koch Backs Lindsay

11

My first banner headline. Some say it may have made the difference between Lindsay's winning and losing.

My first campaign for Congress in 1968. I was the underdog, running as a Democrat in a district that had been Republican for 31 years. That year I ran against the posh and successful lawyer and then State Senator Whitney North Seymour, Jr. Who would have thought a guy with two names could beat a guy with four names in the Silk Stocking District?

12

In Washington in the congressional studio, sitting for the picture that nearly every congressman sends home to his district.

13

14
Bob Morgenthau, a superb public servant, former U.S. Attorney and now Manhattan District Attorney. Bob is shy and reserved, and early on in his career he was shocked to find he had to talk to voters to get elected. He learned how.

15
Representative Ron Dellums. There are very few people in Congress of whom it can be said that when they take the well of the House the House falls silent and listens. Ron Dellums is one of those few. A gentleman and a friend.

16
One of the many Israeli Day parades and demonstrations that I have attended and that I now, as mayor, lead. I love the parades and I march in all of them from the Korean to the Ukrainian and a dozen in between.

17

When I ran for reelection to Congress in 1972 I had a new constituency added to my district. It was Hispanic and it was the Lower East Side of Manhattan (known in the community as LOISADA). So I had the Fortune 500 crowd in the north of my district and LOISADA in the south. I loved it.

18

In Iowa beef country. At the invitation of then Congressman John Culver, Congressman Ben Rosenthal (behind me in cowboy hat) and I visited small cattle-fattening feedlots and participated in a 4H contest. I asked where the nearest subway was.

19

During the 1968 school strike some of the public school students helped in my campaign. They were the best campaign workers I ever had. You gave them a mission, they would die to get it done.

20
Participating with Coretta Scott King in a civil-rights demonstration evoking the memory of Dr. Martin Luther King, Jr.

Forest Hills was for me the Rubicon. Lindsay called it "scatter-site housing." Forest Hills was not in my congressional district, but the housing project, as proposed, was funded by my congressional committee. I decided to protest the imposition of about 3000 people, most of them on welfare, on a middle-class Jewish neighborhood. The residents of Forest Hills believed the project would severely and adversely impact on their neighborhood. As a result of the efforts of a lot of people, myself included, the project as shown below was ultimately reduced in size by half. This finally became the first low-income co-op of its kind in the nation.

21

22   23   24

BARRY GOLDWATER, JR. We worked together on a privacy bill. He had only one original idea to contribute. I had about 37 that he had to accept. We agreed, and became known as the Gold Dust Twins on this issue. As a result of this unusual alliance between two members, one perceived as an archliberal and the other as an archconservative, we prevailed in the Congress. • WAYNE HAYS. A petty tyrant, but fair, as chairman of the House Administration Committee. • DAVID ROCKEFELLER. He's now been to both Egypt and Israel.

I opposed the Vietnam War when I first ran for City Council in 1966 and consistently thereafter until the American troops were finally withdrawn. My position was that both North and South Vietnam were oppressive governments and that they deserved each other. In retrospect I think North Vietnam was by far the more oppressive. Nevertheless Americans should never have been sent to die there.

25

26

My most poignant and memorable congressional moment—when U.S. citizens reading on the steps of the U.S. Capitol from *The Congressional Record* the names of the American war dead in Vietnam were arrested for that simple, peaceful protest. A federal court subsequently directed Congress to allow the public to peacefully petition Congress in this way, thereby prohibiting all such arrests in the future. I was a witness at the trial. Three members of Congress had joined and read with the protesters: Charles Diggs of Michigan, George Brown of California and myself.

27

The 1977 Mayoral Zoo. Top row, left to right: Roy Goodman, Joel Harnett, myself, Percy Sutton. Bottom row: Bella Abzug, Herman Badillo, Mario Cuomo and Barry Farber.

28

My father, Louis Koch, his second wife, Rose, both now deceased, standing with Bess Myerson (one of my most important supporters in that race), help me claim victory in 1977.

29

The inauguration of my first administration on January 1, 1978, which included the swearing in of Jay Goldin (top left) as second-term City Comptroller and Carol Bellamy (top right) as first-term City Council President. At bottom right is Governor Hugh L. Carey, a great governor and a friend.

At campaign headquarters, swearing in the first appointments to my new administration: (from left) my political adviser, John LoCicero, and Deputy Mayors Ronay Menschel, Herman Badillo, Basil Paterson and David Brown. I appointed seven deputy mayors at first and then two years later reduced the number to a more manageable three. I have found that number to be the best.

30

31   **32**

The first fence with razor-sharp barbed wire protecting some of the subway cars from graffiti vandals. This fence was backed up by one pregnant German shepherd and one toothless German shepherd, both useless for the purpose of guard--dogging.

33

Denny Farrell, the New York County Democratic leader who ran against me in the 1985 Democratic mayoral primary.

Meade Esposito, retired Brooklyn County Democratic leader. He helped me win in 1977 by not endorsing me but having his organization work on my behalf. He's been a supporter and a friend ever since.

Prince Charles and First Lady Nancy Reagan on the pier about to board Malcolm Forbes's boat, the *Highlander*. It was there I detected and reported on the Prince's emerging bald spot.

34   **35**

36
Without its ethnic parades New York would be a city without diversity.

Mother Teresa (center) with a sister from her order, the Missionary Sisters of Charity. In my opinion Mother Teresa is one of the few living saints.
37

38

His Eminence Archbishop Iakovos, Primate of the Greek Orthodox Church of North and South America. We are pictured here at a rally in opposition to the occupation by the Turkish Army of 40 percent of the island of Cyprus, which regrettably continues today. There are few people who radiate saintliness; Archbishop Iakovos is one such person.

"Only in New York can a cardinal and a mayor sue each other and still be friends."

39

40
Bernhard Goetz: the subway gun-man. Victim or villain?

41
Reverend Jesse Jackson: charis-matic, occasionally demagogic, and moving toward the center. Religion never got in the way of his political pragmatism.

September 10, 1985—primary night. Winning with 64 percent of the vote after nine long months of campaigning. On the platform with me were (left rear) my nephew Jared Thaler, (on right) my friend and a great congressman, Robert Garcia, and (right rear) my brother-in-law, Alvin Thaler. In the general election two months later, I won with a record-breaking 76 percent of the vote.
42

becomes tame and begins to bite people you replace him.''

I have told this story I don't know how many times by now. I have told it at the most sophisticated luncheons, I have told it to the largest of audiences and the smallest of audiences, and it always gets an enormous response. And it embarrassed the MTA so that they finally in May of 1981 said that they would build the fence as a pilot project in the Corona yards.

I put Ronay Menschel* on it to follow it through. She came in one day and said, ''Well, they are building the fence. It is going to cost $1,039,165.'' Why a fence should cost over $1 million is beyond me, but nevertheless I was not going to complain. She brought in a model of the fence. She said, ''However, it is 3800 feet in circumference, this yard, and they are only going to build the dog run for 710 feet.''

I said, ''What kind of fence is that? How can they not build a fence around the whole yard?''

She said, ''Well, Ravitch doesn't want to put the dog run next to a tennis court, because some of the tennis players might put their fingers into the fence and the dog might bite their fingers.''

I thought to myself, This is absolutely crazy. So then I said, ''Well, tell him they should put a blanket up which would shield this part of the fence from the tennis players so they wouldn't put their fingers in the fence.''

*She was then the executive administrator of the Office of the Mayor as well as a member of the MTA's board, a position she still holds.

Then she came back and said, "Okay, they decided that they will manage that."

But then she said, "They decided that they don't want to build a part of the fence that runs for about five hundred yards because it is within observation of people who walk in and out of the yard and they don't think it is necessary."

I said, "This is ridiculous. These people don't work. These people don't watch. These people don't care. You are going to have to have a fence all the way around there." They finally agreed and they finally built the whole fence.

When I went out there in September 1981 to open the fence, so to speak, there were these two dogs. These dogs didn't bark much. But nevertheless there were these two dogs. The next day an enterprising reporter goes out and finds out that one of these dogs doesn't have any teeth and the other is pregnant; it gives birth five days later.

Nevertheless the fence has led to a reduction in vandalism and graffiti. How do I know? Because before this each month the MTA had to clean out of the Corona yards alone something in excess of five thousand spray paint cans. The month after they put the fence and the dogs in, only five cans were found.

Now, there is one thing to be learned from that story. And that is, when you do not appoint someone, when you do not have the power to hire and fire, as I as mayor do not with the MTA, then there is only one way to get anything done, only one weapon you have. And that is to go out and publicly criticize and embarrass and castigate those people until they do what they should be doing. Eventually you can shame even liberals and bureaucrats into doing what common sense dictates.

8

No Punching Bag

In 1973, as I said, I ran for mayor for forty-five days and then I withdrew from the race because we couldn't raise the money necessary to continue. But it wasn't because I didn't try.

Joan Davidson was one of my finance committee people. In the '73 race for mayor she told me she wanted to help. Good! But when I called her for the money she had pledged, which was $500, she kept putting me off. And we were in desperate straits.

It's so demeaning to have to ask people for money. I find it awful. But if you have to pay campaign salaries, as I did, you have to make those calls.

So I called her. And she began to avoid my calls. Then one day she told me she had to meet with

Congressman Herman Badillo and Assemblyman Albert Blumenthal, who were my opponents.

I said, "What do you mean you have to meet with Badillo and Blumenthal? You're supporting me for mayor."

She said, "Well, I have to meet with them in all fairness." So immediately I knew she was a screwball. If she's already told me she's for me, and she's made a $500 commitment, what does she mean, meet with Badillo and Blumenthal? That's not exactly sensible.

Then she gave a party for me, to her credit, at her home, to meet people. Not a fund-raising party—oh no, she wasn't going to do that—it was to have me meet people.

I go to her house. She had a fancy apartment. There are maybe twenty people. And I make my presentation. She gets up and says, "Oh, Ed, where is the charisma? We need charisma." I wanted to hit her. I really wanted to hit her.

"Well," I said, "I'm not exactly charismatic. I can only tell you the things that I am familiar with."

The people she had there were like her: richies. I don't do too well with richies. I do well with people who are rich and made the money themselves, but not with the sons and daughters of wealthy people.

In any event, her father, Jack Kaplan, gets up at that point and says, "I have never heard a more honest person. I want you to know that I will do anything to elect you, and I will give you twenty-five thousand dollars."

I said to myself, My God, I feel like kissing his fingers. But I controlled myself.

So that changes the discussion in the room. Nobody makes any pledges, because we weren't asking for money, except her father who did it voluntarily.

So then in the next couple of days I start calling him, writing to him. He doesn't take my calls. He doesn't answer my letter, I can't get through to him. And I am furious—we need the money desperately. Well, ultimately he doesn't give anything.

Joan Davidson called David Brown, who was running my campaign, and said to him, "If Ed gets out of the race, I'll send him the money." What a despicable thing to say.

Anyway, then comes her turn. The next election: '74. And she is running against Roy Goodman for State Senate. She calls me up. She wants advice. Should she run? Shouldn't she run?

I always tell people, "If you want to run, you should run. It's not a question that anybody else should answer for you. You have the bug, you should run." I never tell people not to run.

"Do I have to move?" she says. "I don't live in the district."

I said, "Definitely. The law requires you to be a resident of the district."

"Well, I could get this apartment, so I could have the two residences." She didn't want to give up this really nice place she had.

I said, "Listen, I'm going to give you my advice,

then you do whatever you want to do. If you do not really move, and if the residence that you're taking is in effect a phony residence, a technical residence, then you're going to get your ass thrown off the ballot, because Goodman will go after you."

She says, "That's what my lawyer told me."

I say, "Well, listen to your lawyer."

She didn't ask me whether I would support her. I see her a couple of weeks later at a party and she says to me, "Ed, I've decided to run. I hope you'll support me."

I say to her, "Who are the other candidates? I'll have to have lunch with them. And then we can discuss it."

She subsequently arranges to come in and see me, because she has been told by someone, as she says to me, "Yours is the single most important endorsement in this race. And I know that you're angry with me, but I want you to know that I want your support."

So I say to her, "Joan, I'm an up-front guy, and I'll tell you exactly what I think. I never volunteer it, but you ask me, I'll tell you. In your race I'll do for you what you did for me. I'll decide is it good for me to endorse you? At the moment the answer is, it's not good, so I'll decide at a later time." I think I also told her about what her father did, a little bit of that.

She wrote me a letter, very upset with herself, apologizing: "I don't want your endorsement now. Hope you will at a later time. Certainly understand your feelings." Well, actually I did endorse her, because the guy she was running against in the primary was just bizarre.* But that's the way I handle it: right up front. You punch me, I punch back. I do not believe it is good for one's self-respect to be a punching bag.

●   ●   ●

Eight years later, during my 1981 mayoral reelection campaign, I went out to Brooklyn to make the announcement that I was endorsing Norman Rosen† for Brooklyn district attorney. At the end of that press conference I went outside his storefront headquarters because the press wanted to ask me questions on other subjects. When I was outside there was a noisy heckler who was very obnoxious and kept trying to interrupt the press conference. I ignored him. After I finished with their questions I went over to my car and got in. And this guy kept haranguing me: "You broke all your campaign promises! There hasn't been a sanitation truck on my block in months. . . . " He went on and on. So, as we were driving away, I indicated my contempt for him with the use of my hand.

Then he began to scream, "Look what he did. He gave me the finger! Isn't that a terrible thing? Mayors shouldn't do that!"

When I got back to City Hall, Maureen Connelly, my former press secretary, who at this time was managing

---

*After I became Mayor Joan Davidson and I became good friends. I named her as the chairman of the Gracie Mansion Conservancy and she did a superb job.

†Norman Rosen had been an assistant district attorney under Eugene Gold when Gold stepped down. He was Gold's man as well as Meade Esposito's. Rosen's campaign slogan was "Good as Gold."

my reelection campaign from David Garth's office, called and said that she had heard on the radio that "the Mayor engaged in an obscene gesture towards a heckler."

Then all the City Hall reporters came into my office. They asked, "Did you give him the finger?"

I said, "Did anyone take a picture?" They laughed and said, "No." We all recalled the famous photograph of Nelson Rockefeller using his middle finger toward a heckler. I said to the press, "No pictures, no finger." Then I went on to explain: "What I did was the three-finger Boy Scout salute." And then I demonstrated it. I said, "Now, it may look like a single finger, depending upon your angle of view, but if you look carefully you will see that it is really three fingers stuck together."

They said, "Why use three fingers, why not one?"

I said, "Because they expect one finger and I give them three. But they know what I have in mind."

On the streets over the weekend people kept calling out at me, saying, "Give 'em the Boy Scout salute, Mayor." They knew what happened and it was a lot of fun.

When someone upsets you in politics sometimes you can react immediately, as in that case, and sometimes you have to wait a little. But the wheel always turns eventually.

●   ●   ●

I'll give you another example: Arthur Levitt's campaign literature in 1974.

In that race Levitt was running for reelection as state comptroller and we decided that for the East Side of Manhattan (where I was running for reelection to Congress) we would put together a single piece of literature. Instead of having ten different pieces of literature for the Assemblyman, the State Senator, the Congressman, the Comptroller—I mean there were so many candidates running and people just throw away that literature in the subways because there's so much of it. So we decided we would print something like a million pieces of literature, assess the costs to everybody depending on the area that they covered (it wasn't very much, like $300 would be Arthur Levitt's share, for an assemblyman maybe $150), and then one person can hand out one piece of literature for ten people. We called up the campaign managers and said, "Do you want to do it?" and they said, "Oh, yes—delighted." So we told them what their share was.

F body sent in their money with the exception of Ar evitt. He didn't send in his $300. We printed the literature, but he never sent in his money, and we were furious. I mean, here's the Comptroller of the State of New York not sending in his $300 for the literature. Who does he think he is?

Well, we have a second chance at this, because while we don't get paid for the literature, on election day we have a palm card, which is something you give to voters on the day of the election, telling where candidates are on the machine. And we call his office up again, and we say, "We're printing the palm card, and the three hundred dollars includes both the literature and the palm card.'' Then I have one of my campaigners call up saying, ''Congressman Koch wants you to know that unless we get the three hundred dollars, Comptroller Levitt's name will not appear on the palm card.'' And the guy handling the Levitt campaign gets furious, as campaign managers do.

A few minutes later the phone rings and it's the campaign manager, and he wants to speak to Congressman Koch. He gets on and says, ''Congressman, I just got a call—I know it's not someone speaking for you—that unless we provide three hundred dollars you're not going to put Arthur's name on the palm card.''

I say, ''No, that's exactly what I told him to say, and unless we get it either in cash or by certified check today, you're not going on.''

Well, he is astounded. He says, ''We are going to hold a press conference and denounce you. What is this, a holdup?''

I say, ''Please let me know when you're having the press conference—I'll be there. But if we don't get the check, I'll tell you what we're going to do on the palm card. When we get to the office of comptroller, we'll put this line in: 'Guess who?' and then we're putting in every other name.'' Oh, he was yelling, he was screaming. That afternoon the check was delivered.

•   •   •

Early on in my 1985 campaign for reelection as mayor, we scheduled a fund-raiser in Washington, D.C.

The thought was that we would invite the lobbyists representing different sectors of society who knew and supported me when I was a congressman. We hoped that just as they had contributed to my congressional campaign, they would, for old times' sake, contribute to my reelection campaign for mayor. In fund-raisers of this kind it is preferable to attract the sponsoring of major public officials, like senators, former administration officials and congressmen.

I called a number of members of Congress. First the Speaker, Tip O'Neill, and then the Majority Leader, Jim Wright. And then other members from both the New York delegation and the Massachusetts delegation, all of whom were my friends and with whom I had served in Congress before I was elected mayor in 1977. Everyone I called agreed to be listed as a sponsor. While they were not all sure they could attend the event, they said they were happy to support my reelection.

I then called the senior Senator from New York, Pat Moynihan. My conversation with him went something like this: I said, "Pat, I am going to have a fund-raiser in Washington, D.C., and I would like to list your name as one of the sponsors of my reelection campaign. If you can't attend the event, that is okay, but I do hope that you will be able to come."

There was a pause on the telephone.

Then he said, "Well, okay, but don't tell my staff."

I assume that telling his staff meant it might get him into trouble. They might not want him to be a sponsor.

I said nothing, but I thought it was peculiar that he should worry about what his staff thought regarding his political endorsement of me.

Then he said something that was not only strange but not worthy of him. He said, "Ed, you won't be upset if Denny Farrell calls me and asks that I allow him to use my name for his fund-raisers, and I do, will you?"

I thought to myself, This is bizarre. Herman (Denny) Farrell was running against me at that time. How could Moynihan possibly believe that I wouldn't be upset that he wanted to endorse both me and my opponent? And how could he believe for a moment that I would want to use his name under those conditions? Bizarre.

I simply replied, "Sure, Senator," and then I hung up the phone.

I decided at that moment that we wouldn't use his name, and we didn't. And that I wouldn't forget it. Over the course of the campaign, he never again raised the question of his endorsement or suggested we participate in a joint appearance for that purpose. And, of course, upon reflection I did not want it, nor do I think it would have carried any weight with any significant number of people. There was no endorsement by Moynihan during the primary.

On October 11, a month after the primary results were known and less than a month before the general election, I went to WABC, Channel 7, to appear on what had by that time become a weekly news event where I was interviewed. As I waited to go on the air, I saw that Pat Moynihan was in the studio being interviewed.

He was talking about the recent PLO hijacking of the ship the *Achille Lauro* by Palestine Liberation Organization terrorists and the death of the American Jew, Leon Klinghoffer, at the hands of the terrorists. The U.S. Navy in a brilliant maneuver had located the Egyptian airliner that was taking the murderers to Tunisia and freedom, to Egypt's shame, and forced the airliner at President Reagan's instructions to land in Sicily, where the Italian government arrested the four terrorists. On board was another PLO high official, Mohammed Abbas, who our government believed was the mastermind of the original piracy and murder. I watched Moynihan on the monitor, talking with great authority about Mohammed Abbas and the need to hold him and try him for his terroristic activities over the years. As I waited in the holding room, suddenly Pat Moynihan, who had finished his segment of the show, walked in.

He said, "Ed, I have been trying to arrange a time when I could endorse you. I have called David Garth, and I told him I would like to come up and endorse you."

I had already told Garth in advance of his receiving the call that Pat Moynihan had called John LoCicero of my staff for that purpose. When John asked me what he should do, I told him to refer the Senator to David Garth. I then called David and said, "Tell him that I don't want his endorsement."

Garth said, "Well, I won't be that direct, but I will say we simply don't have a time slot within which to schedule it."

However, in my conversation with Pat Moynihan at the television studio I thought to myself, Why not tell him what I really felt about his not having endorsed me in the primary when it might have been important? I certainly didn't want or need his endorsement in the general election, where such an endorsement would be almost worthless.

So I said to him, "Pat, the election is over."

There was a moment of silence. He is a very smart man and he understood exactly what I was conveying, that in my judgment he had been playing it too safe too long.

His response was, "Oh. So, from now on you are simply going to do your governmental work and not campaign."

I said, "You got it."

•　　　　•　　　　•

If you are going to be rough on people and if you are going to have a long memory about slights, then you must also have a long memory for when people are decent to you and for those who do the right thing when they don't have to.

On January 16, 1975, the Democratic Caucus of the House of Representatives met to decide the fate of Wayne Hays, the crotchety Ohio Democrat who was then chairman of the House Administration Committee. Hays had been weakened by news that he had put on his congressional office's payroll a young woman who couldn't type but who might be doing other things for him. The preliminary meetings had been going on for weeks. Legions of Hays's antagonists had finally spoken up after years of silent anger, and on the morning of the sixteenth things looked pretty grim for Hays. It was just my kind of fight: the opposition was nasty, the air was filled with invective, and the terrain was clearly uphill.

Hays was a peculiar man. He was a very gifted man, but he was also a very petty man. He was undoubtedly anti-Semitic. And yet he could be very fair.

I was on his committee, and he ran the committee very fairly, although when he dealt with staff people, either on his own staff or with other staff members in the Congress, he was a miserable petty tyrant. But in terms of conducting the committee and what it stood for, he was okay.

Indeed, with respect to voter reform legislation, he took all the heat in opposition to certain provisions—for example, public funding of candidacies, which most people are not for. It is the do-gooders who are for it. And I am using that term both pejoratively and not pejoratively. The elitists like to schlepp us around by the nose. This week it is fashionable to change this, next week they may have a new fashionable thought and move to something else.

Now, John Brademas, the Indiana Democrat,* was in the lead in terms of getting the voter registration changes that Common Cause wanted, and I was supporting him.

*Now the president of New York University.

The conservatives on the committee, both Democratic and Republican, did not want changes, because the changes would affect them adversely. It is relatively easy to raise money if you are an incumbent, so if you make monies available to all candidates you are helping your challengers and adding to your own problems. The public doesn't want it, either. They don't want monies taken out of the treasury for congressional campaigns. Ultimately the compromise was to make monies available for presidential and vice-presidential candidates but not for congressional races.

There wouldn't have been anything of any substantial worth coming out of committee if it had not been for Wayne Hays. He got a majority on the committee to vote for it. The majority on the committee was not liberal; and he got people to change their minds and vote for what would be termed a liberal position. I appreciated that. Now he was under attack. He had alienated the leadership. I'm speaking now of the Speaker, who was Tip O'Neill.

Wayne Hays came to me and asked me if I would speak for him before the Democratic Caucus, which consisted of perhaps 250 people. It was the same morning that his removal was to take place. He was testing me and he also needed me. I thought to myself, As the chairman he is doing a good job. The reason that he is going to be removed is not because of the way he chairs the committee but because of his personality. His colleagues don't like him. And I can understand that, since he once denounced me on the floor of the Con-

187

gress. He called me an "emissary from Hanoi," because I was opposed to our involvement in Vietnam. At that time I sent out his statement in my congressional newsletter asking, "Whom do you agree with, me or Wayne Hays?" He called me up one day and said, "Stop it already, I'm getting all these letters saying they agree with you." It was really interesting.

I also had lunch with him in the members' dining room nearly every day. About a year after he had called me an "emissary from Hanoi" he said to me, "You know, Ed, if I had known you then as I know you now, I never would have called you a Commie."

All those things went through my head. I also happen to like the underdog. That's another aspect of it. I happen to think it is very American. It may also be pure rot. But I like the underdog.

So the leadership was going to try to take this chairmanship away from him that morning, and Wayne Hays says to me, "Will you speak for me?" He's going to fight it. He put Jim Stanton of Ohio in charge of the fifteen minutes that were allocated to him to defend himself, and they asked me, "Would you speak for two minutes?"

I said sure. I didn't know what I was going to say, but Wayne Hays wanted some liberal getting up and speaking for him. And I made what some consider to be my best short speech and one that members of Congress to this very day will refer to and remember and talk about with a great sense of humor. They loved it when I said what I did, and I know exactly what I said, because it was a two-minute speech. I hadn't planned it. I got up when they called on me, walked to the well of the House in the Democratic Caucus and said, "A lot of you are wondering what's a nice guy like Ed Koch doing down here in the well speaking for a guy like Wayne Hays?" The place roared. "I'll tell you why I'm doing it. Not that he's such a nice guy. In fact, he's a bully. But he is a superb chairman, and I have worked on his committee and I know whereof I speak. And I'll tell you something else. He's not been so nice to me. Once he referred to me as an 'emissary from Hanoi.' Oh yes," I said, "he apologized—a year later." I continued, "My feeling is that if you can't stand the heat of the debate, you don't debate. I don't believe we should remove chairmen because of how they debate or because of philosophical differences, as long as they are in the mainstream of the party. Hays is in the mainstream of the party, and he is an excellent chairman. He is fair to the Democratic majority and to the Republican minority."

After I finished, Tip O'Neill comes over to me and says, "If he wins, you did it." The place was in pandemonium. It was a marvelous compliment. And Hays did win. And he came over to me—they stood in line to shake my hand. People like Bolling from Missouri, who had spoken against Hays and wanted him deposed, came over to me and said, "If I ever need a lawyer, I'll hire you."

•   •   •

189

Now another one, just to demonstrate that even a political hairshirt from Greenwich Village can become infected by congressional collegiality. Frank Brasco and Bert Podell were both congressmen from Brooklyn; they were both Democrats; and they were both indicted for crimes, independently of each other, in 1975. I served with Brasco on the Banking and Currency Committee; we sat next to each other and we got to know each other.

He did something rather odd on the Banking and Currency Committee which was the subject of newspaper articles. It was in October of 1972, when Watergate was just coming to the public attention but there wasn't an opportunity to subpoena any material that would open up the matter. We had not yet reached the impeachment stage. But the late Wright Patman of Texas, the committee chairman, who was a wily old man, a little senile, but wily, dreamt up that we on Banking and Currency could get into Watergate because there had been some laundering of money by American banks in Mexico. Under our rules, in order to subpoena, the chairman had to get the approval of the full committee. And there was a hearing on whether or not there should be a subpoena of various banks, and the Republicans were absolutely against it. This was in October of 1972, one month before the election.

There was a vote, and six Democrats voted with the Republicans against our subpoenaing the records.

There was a story—I think it was in the *Washington Monthly* and some other papers, magazines—that the six Democrats all had problems with the Administration. One maybe wanted some help with a bank that he was a director of—various problems. And Brasco, it was alleged, had the problem that he was the subject of an FBI investigation for having conspired with his uncle to sell a contract with the Postal Service. Brasco was also on the Post Office Committee. The thought expressed in the papers was that he had gone along with the Administration, because Attorney General John Mitchell said on some Watergate tape that he had called all of the New Yorkers on the Banking and Currency Committee. It's not true; he never called me. Maybe he called all those he could do business with, and Brasco would be one of them, and Brasco did vote his way. It didn't save Brasco, because ultimately he was indicted, and ultimately he went to trial. And he asked me whether I would be a character witness.

Now, a character witness has only one function at a trial. A character witness does not get into the charges against the defendant. The character witness basically responds to the questions "Do you know the defendant? What is his reputation for truth and veracity?" That's really the single question. And then if the court is lenient, they'll permit you to get into "How long have you known his family?" and things of that kind. But basically it's "What's his reputation?"

So Frank asked me to be a character witness, and of course obviously they want the very best people from their point of view that the jury will respond to. So they decided, since the trial is in Manhattan in the federal district court, the Southern District of New York, the best people would be: Ed Koch, Bella Abzug, Charles Rangel. There you've got a liberal Jew—that's me, a reformer; you've got a radical like Bella Abzug, a woman; and you've got a black, Charlie Rangel.

Now, I said, "Sure, I'll be happy to do it." And I go and testify, and the defense counsel asks me the question that I've just indicated he's allowed to ask: "What is his reputation in the community for truth and veracity?"

My response: "Excellent." And it was, in the political community, with the people that I knew. He was liked, which has nothing to do with whether or not he committed the crime. And I had no knowledge of that.

Well, I was criticized in the papers for doing that, and liberal friends—really not so liberal when you think about it—said, "How could you go down and testify for Brasco?" But my former law partner Allen Schwartz, who had been in Manhattan District Attorney Frank Hogan's office as assistant district attorney and had known Brasco when Brasco was an assistant district attorney in the Brooklyn DA's office, said to me, "Brasco's reputation was good." He liked him. He thought he was an honest guy. And Allen thought I was rather brave to do it, knowing the political repercussions.

You can't win. My response to people would be, "Don't you think more highly of Dean Acheson that he gave character testimony for Alger Hiss and said he wouldn't turn his back on him and testified for him, as did a number of people? As did Justice Frankfurter. Aren't you obliged to provide testimony in the most unpleasant of cases, where all you're required to do is tell what you know?" But liberals have a sense of morality that's a very personal one. If it suits their morality, it's okay. There are no eternal truths for many liberals.

In any event, he's convicted. And I'm telling you there were a couple of newspaper reports that were not very good from my point of view—associating me, so to speak, with Frank Brasco who's convicted.

Well, then Bert Podell was under indictment. He was under indictment for having represented a client for a fee before a federal agency, which is a violation of the law if you're a congressman. He was a lawyer. But he was a congressman and he did receive money. His defense was that it was a campaign contribution. But the way it looked was just peculiar. As I recall it Podell made out the checks. He really could only be described as after the buck.

In any event, he's tried. Now, I know Bert Podell— an interesting guy—and he asks me to be a character witness. Well, what are you going to say? Especially when he calls me up at home either on Rosh Hashanah or on Yom Kippur. And he says, "Ed, my case is coming to trial, and we need you as a character witness. Will you come?" What am I going to say? No? I don't know whether he's committed a crime or taken money. Again, it's not the substance of the case that's involved. His reputation is good in the circles that he moves in.

Well, I say, "Okay, Bert." But I say, "Bert, I don't think you should call me." It's the same courthouse here in New York County where Brasco was tried and found guilty, and Podell asked for the same people as witnesses plus Tip O'Neill and a couple of others. I said to him, "I believe, Bert, that if I testify for you they'll ask me did I not testify for Frank Brasco, who's been, as you know, convicted. That can't help you."

"Oh, they can't ask you that question."

I said, "I think they can. Ask your lawyer whether or not, in view of what I just raised with you, you wouldn't be better off not having me come there. But if you ultimately decide you want me to come, I will come."

He said, "We will suit your convenience."

I said, "It would be helpful to me to have it on a Friday, so I don't have to come up specially and lose any time from legislative work."

"Of course," he said.

Well, he calls me back maybe a day or two later, and he says, "I spoke to my lawyer. My lawyer said absolutely they can't ask you that question, and we want you to come and we can put you on the stand this Friday. The prosecution is on its case, now, but we'll get them to consent to my calling you out of turn so that you can come in now instead of waiting."

"Okay, Bert, I'll be there."

I go to court—it's the same courthouse. It's the same prosecutor. They call me. The defense counsel asks the same question: "What is his reputation?"

"Excellent."

The federal prosecutor, a guy by the name of Michael

194

Shaw, had not asked me a single question with Brasco, which is the sensible thing to do in a normal case. You don't try to cross-examine character witnesses. You can get very little information from them other than to reinforce a positive aspect for the defendant. You just get them off the stand very quickly. Not this time. This time Mr. Shaw says, "Congressman, meaning no disrespect, but weren't you a character witness in this very courtroom for Congressman Brasco?"

"Objection," says the defense counsel.

I wait for the judge to rule. And the judge says, "Objection overruled."

My response, "Yes."

"And did you not say in response to a question concerning the reputation for truth and veracity of Congressman Brasco, that his reputation was excellent?"

"Objection," says the defense counsel.

I wait for the judge to rule. And the judge says, "Objection overruled."

My response, "Yes."

"And wasn't he convicted?"

My response, "Yes."

"No other questions." I felt like a schmuck.

Well, then Podell puts in his case a couple of days later. In the middle of the trial he withdraws his plea of not guilty and pleads guilty. That really bothered me, he calls me as a character witness and then he pleads guilty.

What do you do? Now, obviously you should never tell an untruth. But you can't run away from your responsibilities as a citizen—in this situation, of being a character witness. I would never have said anything about Frank Brasco or Bert Podell that was not true. The testimony I gave was accurate. And it wasn't helpful to me as a politician to give it. But you can't win.

Now, I happened to be in the cloakroom right off the House Chamber and Tip O'Neill was there the very day that Podell changed his plea to guilty. And Tip O'Neill is recounting the following: "What do you think of that son-of-a-bitch?" says he about Podell. "He calls me as a character witness and he pleads guilty. You know what happened to me? Bert asks me to be a character witness. I go up and I'm a character witness. 'What is his reputation?' 'His reputation is excellent.'" This is Tip O'Neill speaking.

"Then the prosecutor says, 'Meaning no disrespect, Congressman, have you ever been a character witness for anyone else associated with Congress?'"

"'Objection.'"

"'Objection overruled,' says the judge."

Tip O'Neill says with a heavy heart, "Yes."

Says the prosecutor, "Who?"

Says Tip O'Neill, "Voloshen."

That's the guy who was convicted of using Speaker McCormack's office to commit gross fraud.

9

Sharing

DURING MY NINE YEARS IN CONGRESS, I introduced more legislation and certainly co-sponsored more legislation than most of my colleagues. And I put more statements into *The Congressional Record* than most people in Congress. I used *The Congressional Record* almost every day and I did it for the purpose of educating—educating the public and educating the members of Congress—and also to identify myself with certain issues.

I would deliberately pick issues. Health care was one. Privacy was another. Transportation was another. If you put statements into the *Record* week after week, while the individual members of Congress don't necessarily read them, their staffs do; then you suddenly become the recognized expert.

I started that with privacy, for example, in 1969 and I became the expert. I mean I became overwhelmingly the expert on the subject. Barry Goldwater, Jr., took one small aspect of it, one that related to protecting the Social Security number, preventing it from becoming the universal identifying number. Of course, that is a lot of bull. You need such a number. And you need it for a whole host of reasons.

Goldwater's proposal caught the eye of Nat Hentoff, a writer for *The Village Voice*. Nat Hentoff and I have had a stormy association for about twenty years. Hentoff, I believe, generally likes what I do, but he is always attacking me. And if there is anyone else who does anything in the same area, he will favor the other guy. In this case, I had done all this work on privacy, and Barry Goldwater comes up with this one idea, preventing the abuse of the Social Security number. Nat Hentoff goes ape over Barry Goldwater. He also had a column in which he asked why Barry Goldwater and I didn't get together.

I said to myself, That's not a bad idea. So I went to Goldwater and I did get the two of us together. I said, Let's join forces; and we did. He had only one idea that I had to accept. I had about thirty-seven ideas he had to accept; and he did. So we became the Gold Dust Twins on this issue.

The best illustration of the impact of that combination was that we got our legislation through. We got the

Study Commission through and we were named by the Speaker two of the members of the Privacy Commission. It was really unusual. And our recommendations were quite good. Then what we had was a debate on the floor of the House. That debate is called a special order. A special order occurs when after the business of the day is over you stay and only the people who are in accord with you stay and you get up and speak in support of whatever it is you are seeking to give public attention to. On rare occasions opponents participate in such a debate. And we had this special order on privacy. Maybe sixty members either came or inserted their statements into the *Record*. The best statement of all, indicating great support for what we were doing, was made by right-wing Republican Jack Kemp of upstate New York.

He gets up and says, "I am pleased to be supporting this legislation which is supported by a liberal like my friend Ed Koch from New York and a conservative like my friend Barry Goldwater from California and a moderate like me." He was serious. I raised the issue of privacy in a nonideological way and I think it left a mark.

• • •

An equally odd collaboration accounted for the decriminalization of marijuana. I am primarily responsible for the decriminalization of marijuana. There is no question about it. I started the campaign in 1969 when I got the legislation made the subject of hearings. I brought down to Washington Bill Buckley, whom I had met and who had written a column supporting the analysis. He didn't say he was for it, although obviously he was. When he came down to the hearing, he was terrific. Every member of the committee on both the right and the left came over to shake his hand.

He made a superb statement saying that he thought there should be an examination of this issue. He said, "I once took a trip three miles outside the continental limits of the United States and I lit up and I didn't blow up." It was classic. We got the bill passed—that is, a bill to establish a commission, which became known as the Shafer Commission, after its chairman, Raymond P. Shafer.

Eleven years later, on November 12, 1980, I went up to Radio Station WPLJ-FM, one of New York's rock-and-roll stations. There, with my earphones on, I played records and fielded listeners' queries in much the same way I have on a number of other radio stations in town. One question was, "Mr. Mayor, have you ever smoked pot?"

I had made it a matter of public record in 1969 that I had previous to that smoked pot once. Everybody wanted to know at that time, and I told them: "Once, several years ago. It made me dizzy. I wouldn't recommend it." But by 1980 I guess if anybody ever knew what I had said in 1969 they had forgotten it, because it seemed to come as a surprise to people that the Mayor had smoked pot. It got quite a bit of coverage.

But what was interesting was that then the reporters

POLITICS

went out and asked Jay Goldin if he had ever smoked marijuana. And Jay's response was, "No, I prefer sex." Well, while that is somewhat witty it is also flip, because sensuality is not something that people would normally associate with Jay. But the really interesting one was Carol Bellamy. She was described that night in the *Post* as having used marijuana a number of times. But apparently she didn't like the looks of that, because the next day she was quoted as having said, "Once, while I was in college—just like the Mayor."

The Shafer Commission's report led ultimately to decriminalization statutes in at least nine states.*

I was pressing for a federal decriminalization statute and I appeared before a committee on my legislation to decriminalize. I remember a very conservative Republican on the committee saying, "Well, who are these people who are smoking marijuana?" I had given him the statistics, which were something like eight million smoked it regularly (regularly meaning several times a week) and thirty-five million had smoked it sometime during their lives.

I said, "You can't put all of these people in jail. If you put them all in jail it will cost about seventy-nine billion dollars a year."

And he said, "Well, who are all these people?"

I replied, "Based on the statistics available to us,

*I did not favor legalization; and I believe that the sale of cocaine and heroin is the scourge of America. I now have doubts that the decriminalization of marijuana was wise; indeed, it may have led to the extension of hard drug usage.

eighteen percent are Republicans." That was the proportion of registered Republicans in the country at that time.

• • •

Another issue that attracted strange partners was aid to families with children in parochial schools. I was against parochial aid for a long time before I went to Congress in 1969, and then I decided after looking at the issue, What is the sense of this thing? Why shouldn't people, basically middle-class people or lower-middle-class, who want their kids to go to parochial schools be able to get some assistance? I don't see any problem in terms of a constitutional issue—no problem of church against state—because I don't happen to think the use of parochial schools by people is destroying this country. I think it—the diversity of schooling—benefits the country by our having three competitive systems.

Regrettably the public schools have become lousy in many places. I think what we're doing is simply compelling the middle class, and the lower middle class particularly, and the Catholics and the Orthodox Jews to keep their kids in public schools so as to keep the whites from leaving. But the richies, as I like to refer to them—they take their kids out and send them to private schools or to the posh parochial schools and they complain about the working poor and middle-income whites sending their kids to the local parochial schools.

I'm very sympathetic to the whites in Boston. I've come to the conclusion that the busing and the underly-

POLITICS

ing thing, which is imposed racial balance—that every school shall have, wherever possible, a fixed percentage of minorities in it even if that means taking kids out of their local school settings and shipping them by bus to a school that's much farther away simply for the purpose of establishing racial balance—doesn't work. I think it's destructive, and I'm not for it, even though I have voted for busing because it's such an emotional issue, and you really have to have a lot of facts before you take a position that reverses what you've said and voted for in the past. But I ultimately came to oppose busing because I have an obligation to lead people and speak for what I believe to be rational.

It was nice to see William T. Coleman, who as an attorney was one of those responsible for the original Supreme Court decision, ultimately say that simply having racial balance in schools hasn't helped black kids and it hasn't helped white kids in any substantial degree in terms of their skills, but it has destroyed many of the schools because the white kids have been taken out. I know in my own congressional district the figure showed that when I was in Congress about 50 percent of all the kids went to private or parochial schools. So, in my judgment, if the Supreme Court—and I don't want to blame the Court—had put the same emphasis on equality of opportunity for jobs that it did on racial balance in the schools, we would have been much further ahead. And I believe an ever growing number of blacks agree with me.

Quality education does not come from racial balance

or sending black kids into white schools or white kids into black schools unless, as was the case at one time, doing so will make the school better because (this was the theory and probably the fact) black schools did not have enough parents who were interested in the schools or their kids or didn't have political clout and therefore didn't make the demands that white parents made on the boards of education. They weren't militant and therefore didn't get what they wanted; and, secondly, in many states less money was appropriated for the black schools than for the white schools. I do not believe that to be true anymore, certainly not in New York City. It may have been true in the sixties and prior thereto, but it's not true anymore. Black parents today are often more militant than white parents, and black schools get more money than white schools in the City of New York. Title I money, which is federal, goes to schools with children of poor families, overwhelmingly black and Hispanic. They should—I'm not quarreling with that—but the two reasons that I once believed were legitimate reasons for moving kids around have been disposed of, or at least in New York City.

Now, there are others who in a philosophical way say, ''Well, listen, you know, education is improved by black kids and white kids being mixed according to the racial balance of the population, because they'll get to like one another better.'' It's just not true. Black kids and white kids when they are not living in the same neighborhood generally don't mix. That's my understanding. And I happen to remember what the story was when I went to elementary school in Newark, New Jersey. The public schools that I went to were integrated and more than 50 percent black, and white kids and black kids did not mix. You sat at separate tables, not because the school authorities required it, but because you had your own friends. It continues so today to a great degree when the kids are bused in.

Also I recall and have often applauded the fact that Dr. Kenneth B. Clark, the City College psychologist and New York State regent who was responsible for decentralization in New York, said in May 1972 that he had been wrong. He said that decentralization had been a failure and had embroiled the school system in unnecessary politics. So he left Nat Hentoff out on a limb. Hentoff was the big decentralization advocate, who, if it had been somebody other than Ken Clark, if it had been Ed Koch, would have been denouncing me as a fascist. But Hentoff to Ken Clark is saying, "Oh, how can you leave us?" and urging Ken Clark to come back to the reservation. On the other hand, Hentoff is a guy who sent his kids to Dalton, which is a posh private school, but simultaneously urged everybody else to send their kids to the integrated public schools—so what's new?

In my congressional district, as I've said, and here again because we had this limousine-liberal philosophy, we had just about 50 percent of all the children in private and parochial schools. Those were mostly white children. But you had the odd situation in the borough of Manhattan that the Catholic parochial schools were more integrated than the public schools, because the

Catholic Church gives black children and Hispanic children the opportunity to come at low or no cost. They subsidize them and make a very special effort. So the attacks made on the parochial-school system are just an outrage, in my judgment. I happen to be very supportive of providing reasonable funding for parochial schools to the limits of the Constitution. That's not a position that is acceptable to liberals, but years ago I took that position, and it was contrary to my original position. Why shouldn't children who go to parochial schools receive governmental assistance? The rich who can afford it send their children to them, don't they?

I once had five women come to see me in Washington from a national Jewish women's group—very nice ladies—and they said, "We want to know your position," and they went through the usual litany of causes. Abortion? "Oh, yes, don't worry about it. I'm for abortion." I can't even remember all the others. Then they came to "And of course you're opposed to aid for parochial schools?"

"Oh, no, I'm not. I believe in aid for parochial schools."

Shocked, one said, "How can you say that, Congressman?"

I said, "Listen, every one of you has a husband who's making fifty thousand minimum, and tell me where your kids are. You—where's your kid?"

At some private school—every one of them except one, whose son was an adult already. Two of the five had their kids in Protestant schools. One was with the

Quakers. The other was in an Espiscopalian school—
that's very big with some Jewish parents.

.I said, "You should be ashamed of yourselves telling
me we shouldn't permit public funds for the poor—the
Irish poor, the Catholic poor—to send their kids to
these parochial schools, some modest assistance. I'm
not saying that it shouldn't cost them anything. You
have your own money. You can do it yourselves. Why
don't you send your kids to public school if you're
going to take this position?"

One woman said, "Congressman, I'm ashamed,"
which I thought was nice. If I can get that kind of
reaction occasionally, it makes it all worthwhile.

What I want to make clear about racial integration is
this: I believe that we should have the severest penalties
for people who would stop blacks or anyone else from
moving into areas where they can afford to move.
There's no question that government today cannot,
without violating the federal Constitution, prevent you
from moving where you can afford to. Government
today has the role, and quite correctly, of enforcing
laws which prohibit racial discrimination in areas of
employment, housing and places of public accommoda-
tion, and although they aren't always enforced, the laws
are there and should be enforced. And when I read
about somebody on Staten Island or maybe in Queens
planting a cross or throwing garbage on somebody's
lawn or perpetrating some other racially motivated in-
dignity, I'd like to put that person in jail—not just give
him a fine but put him in jail.

The bottom line here is that people who have the same lifestyle, and I'm talking about economics—low income, middle income, the wealthy—have a right, an absolute right, to live where they can afford to. But there's something wrong, in my judgment, about government's saying that people of different economic strata shall be picked up and put into the high-income areas with government money. The idea that low-income people, who are living at poverty levels and on welfare in many cases, should be picked up and put into middle-class areas on the grounds that somehow or other the middle-class values will rub off on the economically deprived is just wrong. It does not often happen, in my judgment. What happens is that the middle class, rightly or wrongly, and I think rightly, believes that the low-income people, particularly those on welfare and particularly children in those families, have a different style of life, different values and a great deal of anger, and will ultimately adversely impact on their neighborhood, and that will too often lead to physical attacks on their kids, the elderly and so forth. So they move out—the middle-class whites and blacks move out—and ultimately the neighborhood becomes a slum.

I think the problem of lifestyle is a class problem and not a racial problem, but that's an abstract analysis, because in the City of New York poverty happens to be overwhelmingly minority. So it makes my position easier to postulate by saying, "Well, it's not racial— it's class." And I really believe that. The fact is that in the City of New York class and race happen to work out very often in the same way. But that can change over time. And in the meantime we ought not to become locked into futile programs.

What should always be remembered is that the black and Hispanic middle class, the black and Hispanic property owner, feel exactly the same way as their counterparts in the white middle class. They don't appreciate any more than the whites appreciate low-income housing projects filled with welfare families in their middle-class neighborhoods. Those who are obsessed with race, on the right and the left, ignore class as a determinant of social attitudes. They are wrong, and they do an injustice to whites, blacks and Hispanics.

10

Ethnic Politics

IN MY CONGRESSIONAL DISTRICT there were about 65,000 Hispanics. I always liked to say to people, "I come from a district that is extraordinary. In the north I have David Rockefeller, in the south I have sixty-five thousand Hispanics—in effect the richest man in the country in the north and the poorest people in the country in the south. And he thinks his one vote cancels out theirs, but with me it doesn't." Not a bad line, and I used it a good deal. It happened to be true.

I liked the Puerto Rican constituency. It was located between Houston and Fourteenth Streets and from Second Avenue to the East River. As a congressman I made a couple of friends there, and I'll tell you how I made a couple of friends there. I worked very hard. I worked with a guy named Arturo Santiago, whom I met when I first got that neighborhood attached to my district, which I think was in 1972, when they had redistricting. I got that neighborhood on the Lower East Side in exchange for Central Park West running from Fifty-ninth to Seventy-fourth, which was a very good area for me because it's mostly Jewish and Jews are very good Democrats, too.

So one day I got a call from two guys saying they'd like to come up and see me. Arturo Santiago was one of them. I can't remember the other guy's name. They came to see me and they said, "You're now our congressman; we'd like to take you on a tour of the Lower East Side," so I went with them. It was interesting. I learned a little, saw the incredible housing, everything torn apart. And that's how our relationship started.

Now, when I ran for mayor in '73, Arturo Santiago and a couple of other guys from that neighborhood said they wanted to help me. Santiago had put together a group of Puerto Ricans, militant ones. They're almost all militant there. Throughout my congressional career I never met a politically involved nonmilitant Puerto Rican in that neighborhood. And again they're almost all very revolutionary about ending Puerto Rico's involvement with the United States. They wanted independence for Puerto Rico, and my position on that was very good.

I would say, "Whatever the Puerto Ricans want they can have. I'm not for holding them here against their will.'' The fact is, many Americans would love it if Puerto Rico became independent; they consider it a financial drain because Puerto Rico's citizens and businesses do not pay federal income taxes but do receive federally paid-for programs. There's no question about that. It's not a put-down of Puerto Ricans; it's just a fact of life. I don't, however, include myself in that group. As I said, I like Puerto Ricans, and New York is richer because they make up 20 percent of our city and add to our diversity and traditions, and if Puerto Rico wants to stay in the U.S. as a commonwealth or become the fifty-first state it's more than okay with me, and indeed I hope they decide to do that. My view is that those who put Puerto Ricans down are just changing their victims from Jews to blacks to Puerto Ricans. And sooner or later it will be another group taking their place; those who know history will recall that they once said in Boston and elsewhere—the bigots—''No Irish need apply.''

Santiago reiterated that he'd like to help me in my race for mayor. I was never sure, not that I had any personal reason to disbelieve Arturo, but, with Herman Badillo running, almost every Puerto Rican was going to vote for Badillo. And they didn't like him. They think he's arrogant, that he left them when he moved from the Barrio to Riverdale, that he married two Jewish women, that he's no more Puerto Rican than I am. Except that he is Puerto Rican by blood, by name, and by culture originally. So it appeared to me they'd vote for him in the end no matter how much they attacked him.

I knew that before they told me they were going to vote for me. So I never counted on it. And I didn't find any problem with that. There's nothing wrong with ethnic politics. A lot of people like to talk about the melting pot. It's all bullshit. There is ethnic politics in this country and in this city in particular, and it's okay. More Jews will vote for me than for an ordinary non-Jewish candidate.

But I want to make a distinction here. Jews are peculiar in politics in a whole host of ways. One is, they love to vote for someone whom they consider to be an FDR, a WASP with power and money who they think loves them. And they'll vote for an FDR in preference to a Jew, because they much prefer to get someone they can think of as more classy, see. They loved Lindsay for a while. I don't think they do anymore, but they did for a while. And that was one of the reasons why my own success was unique in a way, because this syndrome that I'm talking about was accentuated on the Upper East Side of Manhattan, where you had upwardly mobile Jews. These were not the economically deprived, these were not the religious orthodox, and voting for me as they did overwhelmingly was really unique.

All people have ethnic aspirations. A black would love to see a first-rate black mayor. It's ridiculous to think that if Charlie Rangel or some other well-qualified black ran he wouldn't get the overwhelming majority of black votes. To be sure, some people shrink from ethnic politics. They would say, "If a white man were opposing him, how awful it would be if whites voted overwhelmingly for the white." Well, I guess it might be in the best of all possible worlds, where everybody trusts everybody and you don't have any special affinities racially and culturally. But that's not real life.

The bad part is the double standard. If blacks vote in a bloc, that's good. It's called community empowerment. If whites vote in a bloc, that's racist. This is the language that's employed by the media as well as by liberals in general. I deplore that kind of characterization. Free choice is the requisite element. Ethnic politics is not racist, in my judgment, not at all. It doesn't mean that blacks don't get elected—they do. The whites in Charlie Rangel's district could easily put up a white against him and beat him. But they won't. They have a high regard for him and they will support him. The difference between racial politics and ethnic voting is this: in racial politics no distinction is made and you vote simply on the basis of race. In ethnic politics, if the candidates are roughly equal, as perceived, an ethnic group will quite naturally vote for someone they identify with. So in Harlem, the Assemblyman is black, in Riverdale Jewish, in Bensonhurst Italian, in the South Bronx Puerto Rican. But if there is perceived to be a major difference in the candidates, ethnicity will not apply. Jews voted for Hugh Carey over Howard Samuels for governor in 1974, and blacks voted for Joe

Addabbo over Simeon Golar, who is black, for congressman in Queens in 1984.

Okay, getting back to the Puerto Ricans, we had a couple of meetings at my house. I remember one that was really an eye-opener. Arturo invited maybe ten or fifteen people to come to my house, and they came one at a time on a Saturday morning, and the first one to come—I'd never met him—the bell rings, there's this young, about twenty-four years old, Puerto Rican guy. He introduces himself. He's still at the threshold of the door when suddenly there's a loud noise, and a knife has fallen from his belt and it's on the floor. And he's very embarrassed, very embarrassed. I said to him, "Don't worry about it. I have only one rule. All knives get checked at the door."

I thought about it. I was not affronted. Obviously he hadn't brought the knife because he was afraid of me. If I'd lived in the environment that he was living in, with the crime in his neighborhood—it was not safe to walk around—I'd have carried a knife, too, and I'd understand carrying a gun although I would disapprove of it. So I'm not upset by that.

Now, I had one meeting in 1973 when Arturo had put together some of his Puerto Rican political constituency for me for mayor, and it was near the end of the period when I'd already decided I'm not able to stay in the race because I can't raise the money. I had raised $100,000, and there was no hope of my raising any more, and it had all been used up, and I wasn't going to go into debt. I will not ever get into a race where I have

215

to carry the financial burden and worry about paying back people years later. I just don't want it. I'm a person of very modest financial resources, and I'm not going to carry debt on my back—I won't do it.

Okay, so, knowing all this, we go to this meeting on the Lower East Side in some apartment, and one of the more radical guys—he's really a revolutionary—says, "You know, we can put together this group for you and we'll open a store for you and we'll really organize for you, and we have figured out our budget, and our budget comes," says he, "to twenty-five thousand dollars." I've never given a group anything for its support. There are some expenses you have to pay for. If you open a storefront, that's okay—you pay the rent; that's part of a campaign operation. But this operation was obviously a ripoff. I mean I'd give them $25,000, and $24,000 would go into the pockets of the people in that room. So I said, "Well, we'll think about that." But it was clear that I was not going to do it, and suddenly the guy says, "This cat doesn't have any money." And we didn't and he knew it. And that changed the atmosphere.

•   •   •

Somewhat later the Puerto Ricans in that area were involved in a dispute over the public schools. Luis Fuentes, a Puerto Rican, was superintendent of School District 1. The question was: was Fuentes engaging in anti-Semitic practices against teachers and removing Jewish schoolteachers? The Puerto Ricans wanted to move the Jewish teachers out, not through attrition, not through working their way up through the civil service, but just remove them and bring in Puerto Rican and black teachers. Now, Jews don't like to be removed any more than anybody else does. So they fought back, and the big fight was basically that of the union, the UFT, against Fuentes. On that issue I sided with the UFT.

I tried nevertheless to make peace between the UFT and the Puerto Rican community by meeting with Dora Colazzo Levy, a Puerto Rican who was a Democratic district leader on the Lower East Side. (Her husband is Jewish.) She came to my house with some other Puerto Ricans at my invitation. I had already had a meeting with the UFT and had proposed to them that I try to mediate the dispute, and they had said, "Sure."

So I said to this group of Puerto Ricans, "Listen, I could try somehow or other to mediate this, to work out something, but it will never happen so long as Fuentes is the person it's all revolving around. I don't think that the UFT would oppose a Puerto Rican majority on the school board [which was elected in local elections anyway], but they're never going to give up if it's Fuentes you're fighting for."

So Dora said, "Listen, we wish we could get rid of him. He's not the battle. We know he causes us damage."

I said, "Well, why don't you just dump him? Get rid of him. Then we could put this thing together."

And she said, "No, we can't. We're stuck with him. He's a symbol, and we just couldn't do that."

So they were stuck with their symbol. The others

217

were stuck with theirs, and so the whole thing fell apart and I was never able to do anything there.

Later Santiago became a district leader. As such, he was involved in a demonstration over cuts in community programs, and he was in charge of a community program. I believe he was honest and decent, and I liked him. And when the last budget reduction cut off his telephones, he said, "How are we supposed to run a community program providing services if we are told by the city that we can't have telephones? How can you do that?" Obviously it was a stupidity on the city's part.

So they had a demonstration. The demonstration closed off the East River Drive. He and a number of others just went and lay down on the highway to call attention to the problem. They were arrested. He told me he was charged with resisting arrest because he lay down and wouldn't cooperate in getting up and walking into the patrol wagon. They had to carry him in. That's called resisting arrest, and that's a very serious charge.

He said to me, "You know, I wouldn't mind being prosecuted if everybody was prosecuted. But the cops did exactly what I did. When they were laid off, they blocked the Brooklyn Bridge. They weren't arrested."

I said, "You're absolutely right. That's really wrong. And the first thing I want to tell you, Arturo, is that when your trial comes up, if you need a character witness, I'll be happy to come. Just let me know. And, secondly, I'm going to see if I can do something to help."

So I wrote a letter to District Attorney Bob Morgenthau, and I said in effect, "I believe we have to have justice, and justice means equal application of the law. Arturo Santiago was arrested on two charges, and cops who did the same thing weren't arrested, because they're cops. I just think it's wrong."

Well, shortly thereafter, Arturo's case comes up. I didn't even know it, but a few days later I met his lawyer, one of the poverty lawyers, and he said, "You'll be pleased to know that they dismissed the charges, withdrew them." (Actually—it was technical—in contemplation of dismissal, they adjourned it. If you're a good guy for six months afterward, then they drop the charge.) And he said, "You know, your letter was there. The assistant DA had it and they were waving this letter around, and that did it."

Now, Arturo thanked me later. It was very moving in a way. He said, "I want you to know, if you run for mayor again [i.e., in 1977], I want to help you. I really want to help you. But I also have to tell you that publicly I have to be for Badillo."

I said to myself, I understand that. I mean he had his cross to bear, which was Herman. He couldn't get away from it. That's ethnic politics.

●   ●   ●

My cross to bear was some of the Jewish organizations. Before I went to Congress I had never been a Jewish activist. I'm very proud of being Jewish, but I had never been a Jewish activist. But I *am* an activist,

219

and in Congress I was getting involved in every civil-liberties issue for the blacks and the Puerto Ricans and the women and every oppressed group in the country except the Jews. Well, I quickly changed that, and made the Jews one of my priorities. A lot of people, by the way, in my district at that time did not know I was Jewish. My name is not particularly Jewish. K-o-c-h for many people is not Jewish—more German, although it is both a Jewish and a German name. So I came up with the idea—William Stern of the Workmen's Circle had suggested it to me—that I introduce legislation that would allow and encourage Soviet Jews to come to the United States.

At that point the Jackson-Vanik amendment, which provided that no U.S. credit would be available to the Soviet Union unless it allowed Jews to emigrate, was being discussed in Congress, and if it became law it would be very helpful in getting Jews out of the Soviet Union. The problem there was: if they got *out* of the Soviet Union, there was no automatic way they could come *into* the United States, because in order to come into the United States they had to fit into what we no longer call a quota system but what in fact was a quota system. So I said, "We ought to allocate special additional visas to emigrés from the Soviet Union if they can get out and we should provide them with refugee status here." I was successful in getting the Justice Department to permit Jewish and all other emigrés who wish to come to the United States from the Soviet Union to enter. I was heavily involved in those kinds of issues.

But I don't believe life should be a one-way street, so a few years later I made a complaint about the refusal of the major Jewish organizations to give any kind of credit to the Jewish congressmen here in New York who were seeking to help Jews. The whole thing came to a head in the gubernatorial race in 1974 when there was a rally at Dag Hammarskjold Plaza. This Jewish group had invited Senator Jacob Javits and Ramsey Clark, his Democratic opponent, to speak and said that nobody else could be on the platform. There may have been 100,000 people in the plaza. Nobody else could be on the platform. All the other congressmen and dignitaries are sitting right below the platform but are not allowed up there. And Dick Cohen, who is the assistant director of the American Jewish Congress, is guarding the staircase up to the platform. Nobody can go up.

Then along comes Hugh Carey, who was then a congressman (he was running for governor at the time), and he's bringing Senator Scoop Jackson along to the rally. He escorts Jackson up. Dick Cohen says, "Jackson can come. Carey cannot." And he turns Carey away.

I see this, and I go over to Cohen, and I say, "Do you know what the hell you're doing? You're turning away the next Governor of the State of New York. Are you a nut?"

He says, "I don't care what he is. So far as I'm concerned, he's just another congressman," which puts down congressmen too, right?

So I then engage in my correspondence. I write to everybody, every Jewish organization. I also write to

Rabbi Israel Miller, chairman of the Conference Presidents of Major Jewish Organizations, and I send copies to all the presidents of the major Jewish organizations. It's an umbrella group of which Rabbi Miller is the chairman, and every major Jewish organization in the city belongs to it. And I outline this whole business. I go into a long diatribe about how miserable they are to congressmen. I'm not only talking about Jewish congressmen. They make no effort to even invite congressmen to come to the parade that precedes the rally. I said, "I got invited to help lead the Saint Patrick's Day parade. And I never even got an invitation to the Israel Day parade. Are you people nutty?" That was the thrust of it.

That started a furor in the whole Jewish community. I got letters from everybody saying, "You're right, you're right." And it changed their whole operation, so that later the Jewish congressmen said, "What did you start? Now we have to turn down invitations." That's really very funny, and the correspondence is very funny on this whole business. Meanwhile Dick Cohen tries very hard to be friendly to me. I'm very difficult to be friendly with once you've insulted me, but I do sometimes try.

•   •   •

On the subject of insults, sometime in June of '75 there was a vote in the House on a cutback in our military forces, and I had supported that proposal at least once and maybe twice in prior years. It was called

the O'Neill-Mansfield proposal. It would cut back something like 100,000 or 125,000 personnel. But the wisest
opinion at that point was that to do that, immediately
after our withdrawal from Vietnam, would be a signal
to all our allies that we're giving up on them in Europe
and elsewhere. Senate Majority Leader Mike Mansfield
and House Speaker Tip O'Neill and many others had
withdrawn their support of that proposal, and I had,
too. So I vote against it. And it goes down. It got maybe
100 votes. (The year before, it had gotten maybe 175.)
And the fight in support of the bill was led by Democrat
Ron Dellums of California. Ron Dellums is black and
radical; he looks about six foot six maybe; at that time
he had a huge Afro. He is a very dapper dresser. He's
very articulate, yet he also uses a lot of street language.

So I'm sitting in the front row of the House the day
after the vote, and Dellums comes over. He has a rather
soft voice except when he gets excited, and he says,
"How did you Eastern liberals vote on my amendment
yesterday?"

I said, "I don't know how the Eastern liberals voted
on the amendment; I don't speak for them, but I voted
against it."

He says, "You white racist motherfucker."

So I say, "Why do you think you can talk to me that
way, and how do you think that helps your cause?"
He's towering over me and I'm sitting down. Congressman Stephen Solarz of Brooklyn was next to me. Then
I say, "You know, Ron, you're a smart guy, and I'm at
least as smart as you are."

"Oh," he says, "that's right—you're one of the chosen people."

I say, "What are you trying to convey to me when you say I'm one of the chosen people? Spit it out. What are you trying to tell me?"

He says, "You call me anti-Semitic and I'll knock you down."

I say, "I haven't called you anti-Semitic. I haven't even told you I'm Jewish." Then he walks away.

Solarz says to me in amazement, "Did you say to him, 'I'm at least as smart as you are'?"

A few minutes later Dellums comes back and says, "I'm sorry," and he holds out his hand.

I say, "No, no, no, no. We're not going to shake on this thing. You'll do it again." So he walks away.

In June I went on a trip to Europe, the NATO trip to visit European countries. It was a two-week trip. Congress was back in session when I returned. And I'm very correct in the way I handle Dellums. I see him, he nods to me, I nod to him, but it's obvious I'm very cold toward him. So he comes over one day shortly thereafter in the corridor outside the chamber and he says, "Ed, I'm very upset. I know you're mad, but you shouldn't be mad. You know, when I called you a motherfucker, that's not intended to be anything other than street language. It doesn't mean anything."

I said, "Oh, no, no, no. I know what the word means. And that's not all you called me. You called me a white racist motherfucker, and that doesn't make us friends."

He says, "This Congress is chickenshit."

A week later he is sitting in the chamber and I pass by and he says, "Ed, come on over here. I want you to know it's really bothering me what's happened, and if we can't be friends, let's at least have a détente."

I say, "Listen, Ron, you did several things that are unforgivable. You called me a white racist motherfucker, and you called me a member of the chosen people, intending it to be a pejorative, and you threatened to knock me down, and nobody can intimidate me. Having said that, I'm willing to forget about it." It's hard to forget those things, but at least you can have a working relationship.

Now, just to show how in politics the wheel eventually turns, in July of 1985, right after I declared my intention to seek reelection as mayor, I am given by a reporter a copy of a book about me, a poorly written biography, that is intended to be a hatchet job. The only problem is there's no hatchet. There's nothing in the book that's damaging, it's only boring. So I read the book and there's one part that says in 1975 I referred to Ron Dellums at a private dinner as "a Zulu warrior" and as a "Watusi prince." It is clear to me that these terms are included in this biography in an effort to cast an adverse light on me. The intimation is that I used these terms in a pejorative way. And I also know that the key guy here is Dellums. And Dellums will be asked what is his reaction? So I call him up. And I explain to him what has happened.

He's very friendly and says, "Ed, there are too many

substantive issues for us to work together on. There's too much work to be done. I know that these guys will try to come between us. But we won't let them.'' And that was it and he said that to the press.

So then I am asked what I meant. I know I am walking in a minefield here. I said, after recounting my conversation with Dellums, ''It happens you can't compliment someone more than if you referred to them as a Zulu warrior. Zulus were the major tribe of extraordinary bravery in Africa. They defeated the Boers and the English in combat. The Zulus, with their spears, beat the Boers and the English using guns. They didn't win the war, I'm sorry to say. I'm sort of an aficionado on this subject. King Shaka is renowned as one of the great Zulu kings. A very brave man. A man of extraordinary courage. Now, I think lots of people know that. I think Ron Dellums knows that. I also think that lots of people may not know very much about the Watusi, but I do. The Watusi were kings in their own lands, the two countries of Burundi and Rwanda. And they're very extraordinary people—very tall, very handsome. There's no question but that Ron Dellums is the most imposing figure that you'll ever meet—when he comes into any room he dominates the room.... But more than that, he was very much involved in debate on the floor of the House. And I was very much involved in debate on the floor. His positions would be more radical than mine, so we did indeed differ substantively. But you should know this: there are very few people in Congress who, when they took the well of the House, the House would fall silent and listen, whether they agreed or disagreed. And Ron Dellums was one of those few people."

After that incident, and his standing up for me, I forgave him for calling me a white racist motherfucker. I do now consider us to be friends. If he had wanted to he could have been insulted, condemned me and created problems for me in my pending reelection campaign. He didn't, although he probably was asked to, and I'm grateful to him. I owe him one.

One other story about Dellums. After the Yom Kippur War of 1973 or maybe even during it, the $2.2 billion to provide arms to replenish Israel was on the floor. And prior to that, because of the deteriorating relations between blacks and Jews, Ben Rosenthal, Dellums, Rangel and I had had a dinner meeting at Duke Ziebert's, a restaurant in Washington. It was a very candid discussion, rather loud for a dinner meeting, where we got a lot of steam off. It was a good meeting, though, talking about blacks and whites and from my point of view how the black leadership had screwed both the Jews and the blacks by presuming that almost every white is anti-black; and they in turn countering that the Jews and other whites had screwed the blacks.

In any event, as a result of that conversation, and just the night prior to the vote on the $2.2 billion, I'm home sleeping in Washington and there is a telephone call about one-thirty in the morning. It's Ron Dellums. He says, "Ed, I knew you wouldn't be sleeping. I know you're a cat like me," whatever that means. And then he proceeds for an hour and a half to tell me how he's going to ruin his career because he can't vote for the $2.2 billion. He can't vote for it because he doesn't believe in arms, and then he says, "If my son were being held up on the street and a guy had a gun on him, and I had a gun, I wouldn't give it to my son."

I said, "Ron, you're full of shit. You are not a pacifist, and if your son were being held up by a gun and you could stop the guy and kill him with a gun, you would and you know it and I know your son's life is very precious to you—and here Israel's life is at stake."

So he says at the end of this conversation, "I'm glad I called you, because I'm going to vote for it." This is the end of an hour-and-a-half conversation. Of course the next day he doesn't vote for it. I can't remember whether he abstained or voted against it.

•   •   •

There's one other little incident that occurred at that time, with Congressman Parren Mitchell of Maryland. I happened to be standing next to Parren Mitchell when he voted. We had an electronic-machine operation and you put your plastic card into the machine. He's the brother of Clarence Mitchell of the National Association for the Advancement of Colored People. Well, Parren puts the card in and pushes the "no" button, and it flashes up on the wall "no"—against the $2.2 billion. Then I think he probably has second thoughts. He has a 20 percent Jewish constituency maybe and other things, so he decides maybe that's not the right thing to do, and so he goes over to the controller of the electronic system and he says to him, "Can I get off the machine altogether?" What he wants to do is not vote. And the guy says, "No, once you're on the machine, you can't get off. You can change your vote from 'no' to 'present' or 'yes' or any combination of that, but you can't get off the machine once you're on." So then Mitchell moves his vote to "present," which I thought was very interesting. He's not good on the issue of Israel.

Before that, very soon after I got to Congress, I was sitting behind three Democratic members who were in the front row and were unaware that I was sitting immediately to their rear. It was during a debate on appropriations for Israel, and there would be a vote shortly on an amendment. My recollection is it was an amendment to increase or decrease the appropriation for Israel in the foreign-relations appropriation bill. The question would always be, Who was going to vote how? And these three members were talking about it. And how they were going to vote. I couldn't help but hear what they were saying. I don't regret that I heard it, but there's no question that I felt like an eavesdropper at the time because of how revolting their conversation was.

One of the three, Clarence Long of Maryland—who was not yet the chairman of the Appropriations Committee's Foreign Operations Subcommittee, which he subsequently became—said that he really did not want to vote for this amendment which would give money to Israel.* He said he was much more sympathetic to the Arabs, and his reference to the Arabs in this particular case was to the Egyptians. But he did have, said he, a sufficient number of Jews in his district and no Arabs or Egyptians and therefore he was going to vote in support of Israel.

The second, Otto Passman of Louisiana, who was then the chairman of the subcommittee, said that he personally couldn't care less except that as a rule the Jews were always seeking more than they should have. Still, he said, he was going to vote for the bill, too, because he didn't need trouble in his district. And oddly, there's no question that while he was chairman of the subcommittee he was extremely supportive of Jewish and Israeli requests for help, but the tenor of his conversation was such as to show it was not moral or philosophical support, it was simply grudging and pragmatic political support that came probably as the result of campaign contributions from Jewish organizations.

The third one was Julia Hansen of Washington State, and I don't really know how she ultimately voted. But her comment stuck in my head. She said, "You know, I was once cheated by a Jew. He was a storekeeper, and what he did was to sell me inferior merchandise." And the thrust thereafter of her conversation was, from that

---

*To his credit, when he became chairman and I served on his committee, he became a great friend of Israel, and we also became great personal friends. People sometimes have a change of heart.

time on she didn't like Jews. I thought to myself, And this is the way the United States Congress works?

•   •   •

I had been in Congress only a brief time before I heard about the prayer breakfasts in the members' private dining room. I had never been invited and had not sought an invitation. But one day on the floor of the House of Representatives I had the following conversation with Congressman Sonny Montgomery from Mississippi. He came over and in his Mississippi accent said, "Ed, have you ever heard of the prayer breakfast?"

I said, "Yes, Sonny."

He said, "We would like you to come and be our next speaker and to talk to us about Judaism." And then he paused and he said, "You are Jewish, aren't you, Ed?"

I said, "Yes, Sonny, I am Jewish and I'd be delighted to come." I was thinking at the time, I know next to nothing on the subject. But in two weeks any good lawyer can become an expert on anything by just going to the library, and that's what I did. And so over the next two weeks I read a couple of books and discussed the matter with a rabbi whom I knew. And I came loaded for bear and very erudite on the subject and I would certainly know more than all of these congressmen, none of whom was Jewish.

I spoke for about fifteen minutes on the three branches of Judaism: Orthodox, Conservative and Reform. I told them about the various dietary laws and I dredged up as much exotica as I could, and then I took questions. And they asked me a lot of questions. But it was clear to me that the question that they really wanted to ask they were too embarrassed to ask, and so I said to them, "You know, you've asked me a lot of questions, but there is one question that you want to ask me that you haven't asked and so I'm going to pose it for you. The question that you really want to ask me is, Do Jews have dual loyalty?" And their eyes lit up, because that was the question that they wanted to ask and they were fearful of offending me, so they hadn't asked it. I then proceeded, "You never ask that question of an Italian as to whether or not he might have dual loyalty, or of a Frenchman or an Englishman or an Irishman. That question is asked only of a Jew."

Then I paused, and then I said, raising my right hand at the time that I made the statement, "I want to assure you and to solemnly swear that if Israel ever invades the United States I shall stand with the United States."

And they roared with laughter and goodwill.

•　　　•　　　•

As a congressman I went to Israel on two occasions. One was in November 1973, immediately after the October war, and the other was in 1975, when I went as a member of the Appropriations Subcommittee on Foreign Operations. The second time I went with two fellow Democrats, Congressmen Joe Early of Massachusetts and Dave Obey of Wisconsin (who later be-

came chairman of the Subcommittee), and we went first
to Portugal, then to Egypt, Syria, Jordan, Israel. It was
a fascinating trip.

We were traveling as an official group, accompanied
by a State Department person. I went, frankly, because
Dave Obey was very bad on Israel. He's a charming
guy, very highly regarded and a hard worker and a very
dangerous adversary. So he approached me one time
and asked if I would like to go with him to Israel—the
Mideast, I really think he said. And of course I would
want to go—one, to see Israel, but also to bird-dog
him. I knew that whatever he would do would be
anti-Israel, and if he sees something, I want to be there
to see the same thing so I can give the other point of
view if there is another point of view, because his
would never be pro-Israel.

Now, you might ask whether there were any problems. Only in Syria. When we got to Syria, I had
already made up my mind that I was going to go to the
Damascus Jewish quarter. When we got off the plane
we were told by the American ambassador, Richard W.
Murphy, that President Assad of Syria was entertaining
the President of North Yemen and therefore would not
see us. He was the only leader of any of the countries
we visited who did not see us, and it had been my
intention to ask Assad if I could visit the Jewish quarter
and the synagogues. When the ambassador told me
that, I said, "Well, then, I would like to go to the
synagogue tomorrow," as though it were a religious
matter.

Very upset, he said, "Well, we'll see if we can arrange it."

I said, "Why can't you arrange it?"

He said, "Well, we'll let you know shortly."

Then he told Obey that he was very upset that I had not alerted them in advance about having this desire, and Obey said to him, "It was Congressman Koch's intention to take the matter up with Assad, and since Assad is not going to see us, he's taking it up with you; and I think you ought to provide the means to do that." Obey, by the way, as a result of the application of seniority, was the chairman of the three of us, he being the oldest subcommittee member in seniority on the trip.

About an hour or two later Murphy sends word: Yes, we can go to the synagogues tomorrow morning, but the trip has to be undertaken very early in the morning; we have to leave the hotel at five-fifteen in the morning— as though that were going to deter me.

I say, "Fine." And then Joe Early (and for this alone I will always have the highest regard for him) said to me, "I'll go with you, Ed, if you'd like." The reason I think he offered was that we all were under tension in Syria; it was not a comfortable place. And the thought of my getting up and going to a Syrian Jewish synagogue at five-fifteen in the morning—I wasn't exactly comfortable with it. So I really appreciated that offer and I said, after first saying it wasn't necessary, "Fine, Joe, that's very nice of you."

The next morning Early and I meet downstairs about

five o'clock, and the car is to pick us up about five-fifteen, and we're joking. It's very dark in Syria in August, very dark, at five-fifteen in the morning. And I say to Joe, who's Roman Catholic from Worcester, Massachusetts, "Joe, I can see the headlines tomorrow. The headline will read: 'Two American Congressmen Found in Jewish Quarter of Damascus with Their Passports Stuffed in Their Mouths, Dead.'" So he laughs and says, "No, that's not the headline. The headline is: 'One American Congressman Found with His Passport in His Mouth Dead—The Other Returned Safely to His Hotel.'"

At that point the Syrian Foreign Ministry people arrive—one the driver, whom I didn't see, and the other someone who had met us at the airport the day before. He said he was going to take us to the Jewish quarter. Well, we get in the car. You go for miles and then you get into the old part of the city, which is very much like the old part of Jerusalem, very narrow alleys. It's clear after a while, and our guide says it: "We're lost. I've never been down here before, and we just can't find the way." And as we go down one alley after another, we finally get to an alley where the car can't go any farther, and I'm thinking, Oh, shit, what's going to happen now?

So we get out of the car, and it's very dark, and we walk; and we come to a rather large plaza, an open area, and there we see at the other end of the plaza a guy, an elderly man, wearing a yarmulka, and he's walking. I say, "He'll know where." And we rush across the plaza to get ahold of this guy. I'm thinking to myself, He must think, "My God, it's a pogrom!" So we rush across and we get him, and the Syrian asks him where the synagogue is, and he takes us there. We never would have found it without him.

So we get into the synagogue, and it's a very small building, and there are about twelve or so people—two or three adolescents, the others middle-aged. And they're praying, and as we come to the door I say to the Syrian Foreign Ministry guy, "Just tell them that I'm Jewish; we're two American Congressmen and Mr. Early is Roman Catholic, and I'm here to pray. Early here is my friend."

So we go inside and they didn't take much note of us. The synagogue is Eastern—Sephardic. Among other things, it means that there are no chairs; you sit along the wall on a sort of wooden plank that's covered with pillows and rugs, very Oriental. Even some of them are sitting cross-legged on this platform against the wall. One of the members of the congregation brings over tefillin, which are the phylacteries you put on your left hand and over your heart—they contain prayers in two little boxes, an ancient tradition mentioned in the Bible. Actually, you don't put one on your heart; you put it on your arm, and your arm touches your heart. The other one you put on top of your forehead over your brow. I hadn't done this since my bar mitzvah, and I didn't know how to do it—there's a special technique. So I said, "I don't know how to do it," and I didn't take them. Then I pointed to a tallith, which is a prayer shawl, and they brought one over to me, and I put it on around my shoulders.

Then at that moment the guy sitting next to me says in English, "Well, what do you think?" I was shocked.

I said to him, "Is it okay for us to talk?" I was thinking to myself, There are two Syrians in this synagogue. Isn't he going to get into trouble? I had already made my decision that I was not going to engage in any political discussion with the Jews, because I didn't want to endanger their lives.

He said, "Sure," So then I thought to myself, because he's sitting there with a hat on his head, I'll ask one more question. I said, "Are you Jewish?" He said, "No, I'm your driver"—whose face I had not seen. "I'm a refugee from Jerusalem."

From there we went to another synagogue. In the second synagogue there were no people, just the caretaker—in Hebrew it would be the *shammes*—who takes care of the synagogue when nobody is there. Our Syrian Foreign Ministry guy says, "We understand that the services here will start in about twenty minutes. Would you like to wait?" So I said, "Sure."

At that point three guys come in, in their early thirties, maybe late twenties, obviously Arab, very threatening-looking. They have the Arab worry beads, which they're manipulating in their hands. Aside from the fact that they didn't look Jewish, with these worry beads in their hands and their threatening manner, I thought, as Joe thought, We're in a lot of trouble.

These three guys came over, and one of them, the

leader, says in Arabic, "What are you doing here?"
And the Foreign Ministry guy translates it. I said, "Tell
him that we're American congressmen and we're here
to visit the Jewish quarter." And they stand there rather
threateningly. I said, "Ask him who they are." He asks,
and the reply is, "I am the teacher in the quarter, and
we are Arab refugees from Jerusalem." Everybody
comes from Jerusalem. It's considered to be prestigious. No matter where you come from, if you ever
were in Palestine, you say Jerusalem.

So the atmosphere is tense, and I'm saying to myself,
My God, supposing I was here alone. I'd really be
worried. At least I've got the Foreign Ministry guy
from the Syrian government and nothing's going to
happen.

So the Syrian ministry guy says to me, "There's a
third synagogue, where they're actually now praying.
Would you like to go there?" I say, "Yes," thinking, I
want to get out of this empty room. And I'm so furious,
because I feel this is an attempt to intimidate me.

As I leave the synagogue, there is a mezuzah, a little
religious box, on the door. I want to make a statement,
so to speak, so I go over to the mezuzah on the door,
and I kiss it so that this Arab can see me do that. I want
to say, I am Jewish, you can fuck off. That's the kind of
feeling I wanted to convey.

So we go outside and go to the third synagogue, and
those three Arabs accompany us. In the third synagogue
they're praying, and there are about thirty-five to forty

people there. And they continue to pray, and then when the prayer ends, they sort of come around and ask us what we are doing. Again, I didn't want to ask them any political questions. After all, I've got these two Syrians and now the three Arab refugees in tow, I wasn't going to create any problems for the Jews. So the conversation was sort of inane. One fellow said, "Have they found the cure for cancer yet in America?" I'm sure that wasn't on their minds, and it wasn't on my mind. Then they asked whether we would like to have tea, and they made the tea. It was just a very emotional, moving experience for Joe and me.

As we leave, I'm walking with the three Arabs, and the leader of the Arabs says, "Can I ask the Congressman a question?"

That's translated to me. I said, "Sure."

He says, "What do American Jews think of Israel?"

I say "American Jews support Israel."

He says, "I am the teacher in this quarter, and this boy is one of my students," and he points to an Arab child.

I say, "Do you teach the Jewish children too?"

He says, "Yes, and this boy"—one of the adolescents who had been in the first synagogue and who had walked with us—"is my student, too."

I had been walking around with this kid, this Jewish kid, from the first synagogue, and I placed my hand on his shoulder; I sort of wanted to convey a bond.

The teacher said, "Yes, he's my student, too."

Then in a very melodramatic way—it wasn't intended that way, but that's the way I see it on reflection—I say, "Take care of all the children."

The reason I tell this story is that the morning before we went to the Jewish quarter I had spoken with the highest Syrian official who saw us, whose name is Dr. Immadi, who was the Finance and Economics Minister, and he spoke English. And when we were introduced to him, he was very friendly and he said that he had gone to New York University and I said, "Oh, then we're brothers. I went to New York University, and I live four blocks away, and we're brothers." It was sort of silly, but I wanted to convey a little warmth so that we could talk. I raised the question of the plight of Syrian Jews with him, and he just denied that there was any problem; he said they had the same rights as others. And he wouldn't know where the Jews lived, and it's just an outrage that Syria is being unfairly criticized.

So I said, "Well, why don't you let them go?"

"Let them go?" he said. "They don't want to go."

I said, "Well, offer to let them go. Those who want to go will go. Those who don't want to go won't go. But in the meanwhile, whether or not you are persecuting them—and I'm not suggesting you are—let them go. You've got a very bad reputation, and you can end that bad reputation by letting them out if they want to go. Those who don't want to won't go."

So he got a little upset. I said, "You know, it is said that you put on the internal passbooks the word which in Arabic means Son of Moses, so that these people have problems; and they are not allowed to emigrate when others are allowed to.''

He denied it all. He said, ''They have the exact same rights. If a Syrian who isn't Jewish can emigrate, they can emigrate.''

Then he said he was going to be in Washington the following week, when we are returning—the week after Labor Day—as a delegate to the International Monetary Fund. And I happened to be a delegate to the International Monetary Fund. My technical title was adviser, I believe. William Simon, Secretary of the Treasury, had put me on that. So I just stored that in my head, and the following week when we returned I go down to Washington. The Congress was not in session, and I go right to the International Monetary Fund. I had no intention of going there, because those things are generally very boring. There's a big room, I think it's in the Sheraton Park Hotel—maybe a thousand people sitting at tables representing different countries. I get a map and I find out where the Syrian table is and go right over to the Syrian table, and there's Dr. Immadi, sitting by himself. So I go over and I say, ''Hi, Doctor, remember me? We met in Damascus last week.''

So he gets up, very friendly, you know, and he says, ''Oh, yes, of course.''

I sit down and then I said, ''Why don't you let them go?'' Then I proceeded to tell him about my incident in the Damascus synagogue. He's writing it all down. I said, ''You know, when we were together you told me that you wanted American Jews to come. You said,

'Senator Javits should come and other American Jews should come and see that we're not torturing the Jewish community.' " I said, "I went, and I'm not suggesting that you're torturing them, but I must say to you, I felt intimidated, and supposing I was a simple citizen, not a Congressman, not accompanied by a member of the Foreign Ministry. How would you like to walk into a synagogue and suddenly be confronted with three militant Arabs who are not Jewish?"

He's writing it down. He said, "I'm writing it down. I will see that it doesn't happen again." Very lethal. I worried for those three Arab militants.

Then he said, "I must tell you that we are very desirous of encouraging Americans to come. We had an economic fair last year, and there were some bombings of American exhibits, and not very long ago—several weeks ago—we executed the five people who were found to have engaged in those bombings. So we are very tough on that." Then he said, "Supposing one of them had been Jewish. What would you have said?"

I said, "Good point. Okay." I said, "Let's keep in touch." And then I went back to my office.

The next week there is a letter denouncing me by the Syrian ambassador in this country, Dr. Kabbani. I had written an article on the trip for the travel section of the *Times*. The letter of Dr. Kabbani said, "What an outrage that any American Congressman should convey that there is any danger in Syria," and he made some reference to my having used that description of two American congressmen found with their passports in their mouths—I'd worked that into my little article. And the *Times*, as they always do, gave me an opportunity to respond to his letter, so they had a little paragraph from me responding to that. And I thought to myself, I've got to do something about this. I'll call him up. So I called up Kabbani and I get through to him and I said, "Listen, Doctor, we should not be corresponding through *The New York Times*."

He said, "I didn't start it." Which I thought was a very good line.

I said, "Let's have lunch."

So he said, "Okay."

I arranged for lunch with him, and then I invited Joe Early, and the three of us had lunch the following week. The ambassador is a very sharp fellow who had been in the States some time, spoke English fluently. The repartee was rather nice. At one point, Dr. Kabbani says, "I hope this food is kosher—" he laughs—"because I don't eat pork." I say, "I do. I'm not as strong as you on this. I happen to love pork. I know I shouldn't eat it, but..." So it was very nice.

At one point I said to him, "Listen, you've got such a bad public image on this Jewish thing. Why don't you let them out? The Iraqis let them out." And that's true. The Iraqis are just as bad as the Syrians, but the French were able to get out a few hundred Jews who were left there, except for some who in fact probably didn't want to go.

Finally I said, "Will you do anything to reunite families?"

He said, "On a case-by-case basis."

I said, "If I then give you lists of names of people who are here in the United States who have families there, would you look into the possibility of allowing them to come out and join their families here?"

He said, "Yes. "

So then I got in touch with HIAS, the Hebrew Immigrant Aid Society, and I got in touch with the American Jewish Congress—which, as it happened, was going to do a big article on Syria using my earlier article as a takeoff and some other things I have gotten involved in. For example, I had correspondence with Henry Kissinger's office—he was then the Secretary of State—where they admitted that there was a problem in Syria for Jews and they were trying to help but in a very soft-sell way, and how any Jew who was allowed out of Syria and got to any other country would automatically be given refugee status to come to the United States. The American Jewish Congress was going to do a big article on that. I called up Phil Baum, who was the director in charge of this operation, and I said, "Don't run the article; don't do it, because I might still be able to get some Jewish families out." I told him what had happened, and I said, "Send me a list of some Jewish families, and I'll put them all together," and he did. In the meanwhile, I had sent to Dr. Kabbani a list of thirteen Jewish families, and I prepared the letter to be signed by Joe Early and myself, very soft-sell, saying, "In the interests of compassion, of reuniting families, here is a list of names." It was a first step.

•   •   •

In early 1982, after I had been reelected as mayor, I got into another contretemps on a related issue, once again in defense of Israel, this time in opposition to those in the United Nations who were seeking to drive Israel out of the UN. In early February of that year the UN General Assembly passed a resolution that denounced Israel as not being a peace-loving country. It urged its member nations to withdraw their member diplomats from Jerusalem. Further, the resolution was a tacit threat to Israel of imminent expulsion from the UN.

Shortly after the resolution I received a call from Yehuda Blum, the chief Israeli delegate to the United Nations. The call concerned the inscription on the "Isaiah Wall" on First Avenue opposite the United Nations. The inscription read: "They shall beat their swords into plowshares, and their spears into pruning hooks; nation shall not lift up sword against nation. Neither shall they learn war anymore."

He said, "Who owns the Isaiah Wall?"

I said, "Why?"

He said, "Well, I would like to send a telegram to whoever owns it asking that the inscription on the wall be removed because of the hypocrisy of the UN. It is an embarrassment to Isaiah that it be there directly across the street from the UN."

I said, "The wall and the inscription are owned by the city and I don't think I would remove it. I might simply add an inscription from the Bible which would denounce with moral indignation and outrage the hypocrisy of the UN."

Blum then said, "Well, you do your thing and I'll do mine."

I said, "Good. Send me a copy of the telegram."

I then spoke with my speechwriter, Clark Whelton, and with Dan Wolf and asked them to try to find an appropriate quote from the Bible, preferably another one from Isaiah but, if not, then from anywhere else.

The *Times* ran a piece on my search for another Biblical passage, and the whole little story started heating up nicely. A deputy secretary at the UN told a TV reporter that the UN might move out. I called the UN "a den of iniquity" for their monolithic insistence on bowing to the economic blackmail of the Arab nations and the Soviet Union. A reporter asked me what kind of quote we were looking for. I said, "One that would refer to hypocrisy, immorality and cowardice."

Then I went to a meeting of the Foreign Press Association, and they asked me about it. So I gave them my thoughts. I said, "You know, it is interesting that the United Nations hasn't taken similar measures against anyone but Israel. Here you have Iran and Iraq killing each other. And silence from the UN. Here you have the Soviet Union, which, in my judgment, has killed more people than Nazi Germany. I would say it is conservative to estimate that fifty million people have been killed by the Soviet Union since it was established in 1917. Whole ethnic groups have had their cultures destroyed. If the Soviet Union is a peace-loving country, then we have changed the meaning of the English language. What you have here is economic blackmail and countries that march in lockstep to it. You call Poland a peace-loving country after what they have done to their own people? Why doesn't the United Nations focus on that?''

Okay, so everybody wanted to know the quote. And everybody wanted into the act. They made suggestions. They denounced me. There were editorials. The *Daily News* said I was "off the wall—the Isaiah Wall—for inviting the UN to get out of town."*

Finally, I decided that the best thing to do would be to announce my quote and then not put it up. Al Thaler, my brother-in-law, suggested it to me—Isaiah 10:1, "Woe unto them that decree unrighteous decrees." I think I made my point. You focus attention. That's what you want to get out of these things. And you have a little fun.

I closed the incident by saying I would put no quote up but would leave everyone with the freedom to think of what should be invisibly inscribed there so as to shame the United Nations. I knew that if I actually inscribed a quote, it would be covered with graffiti from

Daily News editorial, Feb. 12, 1982, p. 29.

day one unless I put a cop on permanent duty to protect it. And that made no sense.

•   •   •

In 1980 I went to China with an official City Hall delegation. In Peking we met with Vice-Premier Wan Li. I asked him, "Mr. Vice-Premier, why is it that on almost every street corner in Peking there is a picture of Joseph Stalin?"

He said, in translation, "Because he was a very good Marxist dialectician."

I said, "Yes, but a brutal, wicked man. It is hard for me to understand how you can be so distressed with the current Soviet leadership and still be supportive of Stalin."

Wan said, "Stalin did not invade Hungary, Czechoslovakia or Afghanistan."

I said, "No, he didn't do that. He invaded Poland, Lithuania, Latvia, Estonia, Finland and Outer Mongolia."

His adviser said something to him in Chinese. I was told by my interpreter that the advice to Vice-Premier Wan was, "Don't answer him [me], it won't help."

I have made numerous statements on behalf of dissidents and against Communist governments. I was instrumental in bringing pressure against the Soviets to release the Ukrainian dissenter Valentine Muros. I led the fight in Congress to end most-favored-nation status for Rumania. This criticism of the Rumanian government had the effect of making me a sort of local hero to the Hungarians from Transylvania—now a part of

Rumania—living in New York. Every year I attend their annual celebration; and every year they call on me to tell the story of the Waldorf-Astoria Debate. This is what I tell them:

It was on a Sunday night in 1978, very soon after I had become the Mayor. I was staying in my apartment on Washington Place and I got a call at about midnight from my friend Matthew Nimetz at the State Department in Washington, where he was then counselor. He said there was a problem with President Ceausescu of Rumania, who was at that time supposed to be staying at the Waldorf-Astoria Hotel. The problem was that there were several thousand demonstrators outside the hotel and he couldn't get to his room. There were all these Hungarians outside the hotel yelling and screaming at him. Matt gave me the number of the Rumanian Consul General.

First I called Police Commissioner Bob McGuire to tell him what was happening. I held him on one phone and then I called the Consul General on the other phone. He said that Ceausescu had gone to visit the Rumanian Mission to the UN, and that when he had tried to return to the hotel he couldn't get in because of all these demonstrators. Now, the Consul General said, Ceausescu is back at the Rumanian Mission and he is threatening to cut his visit short, and that would cause an international incident.

I said, "Police Commissioner McGuire will call you right away and he will arrange to get the President back into his hotel. If there is anything else I can do, please let me know. And if you think it is helpful I will be happy to come up and express my regret to President Ceausescu in the morning.'' I told all this to McGuire; and he went up there and got the President through the picket line.

Next morning there is a call from an envoy at the Rumanian Mission. He says, ''The President would like to see you.'' This is about 8 A.M. and I am at City Hall. ''Could you come up at nine?''

Well, that's pretty short notice, but I thought to myself I had better do it, so I say I'll be there at nine with the Police Commissioner.

The envoy says, ''That's good, because there were thousands of people yelling and screaming beneath the President's window all night and he couldn't sleep.''

I say, ''What floor is he on?''

He says, ''The twenty-ninth.''

I say, ''You call twenty-nine floors down 'beneath his window'?''

So McGuire and I go up there, and while we are in the car he tells me what occurred the night before. He describes how there was an egg thrown at the President's car, and he tells me of the President's upset. We get to the hotel and there are State Department people and the city's commissioner to the United Nations, Gillian Sorensen, and others, and we all go upstairs together to meet Ceausescu.

The President says, ''This was an outrage. You should not permit this picketing of me.''

I say, ''Mr. President, firstly, you should feel

250

complimented. They only picket very important people. They demonstrate against me all the time. I don't mind. I walk right through the picket lines. They demonstrate against President Carter when he comes. All it means is that you are important." Well, he was a little mollified, but the State Department people are pacing back and forth.

He says, "Well, if President Carter came to Rumania I would not permit any picketing of him."

I say, "Well, you have to understand we have a different kind of society here."

He says, "Well, if in the future you can't control your people let me send in my troops."

I say, "No. Thank you for your offer, Mr. President. But that won't be necessary."

•   •   •

From time to time when I speak out about foreign affairs someone will say, "You are a mayor. This is not your business."

To them I always say, "Did I lose my First Amendment rights when I became Mayor? I don't think so."

In the third week of June 1981 three international events occurred that stirred me up. That was the week the government of South Africa broke up a memorial service being attended by blacks in Soweto Township. The government's troops were reported to have teargassed the church. I was appalled and angered by the raid. I called, once again, on the South African government "to provide for the full and equal participation of all South African citizens in the life of their country." My comments on Soweto were not carried in the press.

The second week in June was also the week the United Nations condemned Israel for its air attack on an Iraqi nuclear installation. The United States had joined the Soviets, the French and others in that condemnation resolution. I called the vote a "joke" and the diplomats "hypocrites" and a "pack of fools." I also characterized Iraqi President Saddam Hussein as "a certified madman bent on the destruction of the world." All those comments were carried in the press.

The big story of that week was, however, the visit to New York of Prince Charles, Lady Di's affianced and the heir to the British throne. The Prince's visit, I had been told, would require a two-thousand-police-officer presence costing the City of New York approximately $300,000 in police overtime. Would the State Department reimburse the city? The State Department reply: No, his visit is not official. We have our rules. I said publicly, "Well, maybe I should just send one cop."

But when the Prince arrived on June 18 everyone got their money's worth.

Malcolm Forbes had arranged that Prince Charles have lunch on Forbes's boat, the *Highlander*. Mrs. Reagan, the First Lady, and some fifty other people, myself included, also went on the lunchtime cruise around Manhattan.

At lunch Prince Charles said that he was sorry he couldn't come to City Hall, but that it was a matter of security. I said that we would have loved to have him and that the people at City Hall, particularly the young women, were very disappointed. But, I said, "I told them all that I would note down what you had said and that I would report back to them. I will be your Boswell."

Then Mrs. Reagan arrived and I went over to greet her. I said, "I saw you on Barbara Walters' show and you were terrific, particularly at the very poignant moment when you spoke of the assassination attempt against the President."

She said, "Oh, well, thank you very much."

Then someone said, "You know, Mrs. Reagan, Ed Koch here has just been endorsed in his reelection bid by the Republicans."

She said, "Well, he certainly deserves it."

During the boat ride the Prince said that he is very sympathetic to the plight of the Irish Catholics. He said, "You know, there is a lot of bigotry up there amongst the Protestants and it is directed towards the Irish Catholics."

Someone asked him why Britain stays in Ireland.

He said, "Well, it is certainly unfair to refer to the British presence in Ireland as 'colonization' while a majority of those who live there wish to continue their tie with Britain. That is the democratic principle."

I asked him if he had any upsetting incidents as a result of this trouble in Ireland.

He said, "Yes, but not too many. There have been a lot of obscenities hurled at me, and it is especially hurting when you recall that my great-grand-uncle,

Louis Mountbatten, was killed." Then he said, "Mr. Mayor, I want to compliment you on having brought fiscal stability back to your city. It was a messy problem. How did you solve it?"

I said, "Very simple. We don't spend money we don't have."

When I got back to City Hall, Tom Goldstein, the former *New York Times* reporter, who was then my press secretary, told me that he had heard from people at the dock that the Prince had actually been requested by Prime Minister Margaret Thatcher to cancel the visit to City Hall, and that she said she would be personally offended if he came there, because of my remarks over the last ten days—that England should get out of Ireland.

When I met with the press back at City Hall, I mentioned to them that the Prince was going bald. And that seemed to get a lot of attention. I said, "Well, he is a nice guy, 'a nice chap,' as we say in England, but you know he's going to be bald. It has started on the back of his head at the top. You can't see it really, unless you are very observant like me. I'm an expert on this and I can tell you he's not going to end up looking like a billiard ball, but he will be balding soon."

"How was the food, Mayor?"

"Fit for a prince, and a mayor."

"Did he say anything about Northern Ireland?"

"Well," I responded, "yes. I thought he was rather responsible in his comments. He mentioned that he was very sympathetic to the plight of the Irish Catholics in

Northern Ireland. At the same time he said it was unfair to refer to the British presence there as 'colonization,' because a majority of those living there favor the tie. Now, what I have continually said is that I do not believe that it is fair to associate the monarchy, and particularly Prince Charles, with the position of the Thatcher government. Therefore I have no hesitation in meeting with the Prince and I think he's a first-rate chap. At the same time I reserve my right to be critical of the Thatcher government."

"Mr. Mayor, were you able to impress upon him your views?"

"I did not at all seek to persuade him to any point of view. This was not a political setting. I was welcoming a representative of the British monarchy to the City of New York; I wanted him to have a good time. But I did say to others who asked me, 'I believe the British should get out of Ireland.'"

"There has been a great deal of criticism of the role of some Irish-Americans in New York in supplying money to what some believe may be the IRA. What's your view of that?"

"Well, I'm absolutely opposed to the activities of the IRA provisionals. They are a terrorist organization. And I deplore terrorism whether it's committed in Ireland by the IRA provos or by the PLO in Israel, or by the Black Liberation Army or the Puerto Rican FALN, or the Jewish Defense League in New York City. Terrorism around the world has to be deplored and punished. But that doesn't mean that the cause of the

Irish people for the reunification of the thirty-two counties in Ireland cannot be supported. And indeed I do support that reunification.''

That afternoon at about five o'clock Tom Goldstein got a call from Patrick Nixon of the British Information Services, based in New York. Nixon said, "Mr. Goldstein, is the Mayor unaware that all royal conversations are privileged?''

Tom said, ''Yes, I believe he is unaware of that.''

Nixon said, ''Well, that is the case. Now, if you would call the media and put a halt to their reporting of Mayor Koch's conversations with the Prince . . .''

Tom quite rightly said, ''That will be well-nigh impossible. You see, the press conference was by general invitation and it has been over for an hour at least. The stories are on the wires.''

At that point Nixon gasped and said, ''We thought it was just one interview. We didn't realize he'd told everybody!''

Tom came into my office to tell me about the call. I said, ''They're trying to censor me,'' which they of course weren't. They would have liked to, but they knew that was impossible. What they wanted was to have their royal privilege upheld.

The following morning all the reporters wanted to talk about ''royal privileges'' at the morning briefing.

''Mr. Mayor,'' they said, ''the British are upset that you have violated this royal privilege.''

I said, ''I welcomed Prince Charles. I think he is not to be held responsible for the abominations of the

British government. I believe England should get out of Ireland. Am I supposed to change my views because Bonnie Prince Charles comes to New York City? Am I supposed to change my position because the English don't like it? The British press prefers hypocrites to people who tell the truth. Is that my fault?''

"But, Mr. Mayor, the royal privilege?"

"Well, nobody told me about it. I don't hang around with princes much.''

●　　　●　　　●

Now one more. It relates to the Greeks.

The rabbi I most relate to happens to be the rabbi of the synagogue I'm a member of, the Park East Synagogue. It's on Sixty-seventh Street, right across from the Soviet Mission to the United Nations. The rabbi's name is Arthur Schneier, and he's a very good friend of mine.

To be more precise, I go twice a year. He invites me to come and I go; and after the High Holiday services he'd ask me to come over for dinner, and I often went.

I recall one dinner in particular, when I was still in Congress. He had said to me on earlier occasions—he'd been very interested in my mayoralty race—"You know, you really ought to get to see Archbishop Iakovos. He's a good man. He works with me.''

For whatever reason, I didn't do it. And then the Greek-Turkish crisis arose, and then I happened to have a conversation with Arthur Schneier in New York. And he said, "Have you spoken to Iakovos?''

I said, "Arthur, I haven't. I'm delinquent. I'll call him right now and I'll arrange to see him." Archbishop Iakovos is the Greek Orthodox Archbishop of North and South America. He's the highest primate of the Greek Orthodox Church in the Western Hemisphere. I said to my secretary, "Call up the Archbishop's office and tell him I'd like, at the Archbishop's convenience, to come up and meet him." So she calls up, and a few minutes later she says, "The Archbishop is on the phone: he wants to talk to you." So I got on and I knew the correct form of address, which is "Your Eminence." I said, "Your Eminence, I'm really calling to arrange to come up to see you at your convenience. Rabbi Schneier suggests that I do that, and I would like very much to do it."

He said, "How about about this afternoon?"

So I said, "Of course, Your Eminence."

I go up there, and this man is a saint. There are some people who exude saintliness, and he's one of them. I hadn't met anybody else like him, not even my rabbi. I really was quite impressed. He said to me (and he's a man who was born in Turkey), "Mr. Kahtz"—he called me "Kahtz," as though it was spelled that way; I think that's the Greek pronunciation for Koch—"I'm so pleased that you came. I feel ashamed that I am an American, and I *am* an American, and I represent two million Greek-Americans and others in North and South America, and I have tried to get an appointment with President Nixon and with Henry Kissinger, and they refuse to see me. My heart is heavy." Then he said,

"What is it that your people and my people have done that they must suffer so through the centuries?" A very moving statement. I was really very taken with him.

And at that moment there's a call. The secretary says, "Senator Kennedy is on the phone, Your Eminence." All I can hear, of course, is the conversation at this end. "Yes, Ted. Yes, I thank you. Yes, I'm going to Greece tonight and I will tell the Prime Minister your thoughts. Yes." And I had the feeling that I was sitting in Martin Luther King's cell when Jack Kennedy called, as you may remember, during the election of 1960.

Then there's another call. This time the secretary says it's John Brademas. And the conversation goes, "Yes, John, yes. Your colleague is here, Congressman Kahtz." So he finishes.

And then I say, "Your Eminence, I don't know if I can help, but I'd like to try. Let me try to call somebody in the State Department—I know some people there—and see if I can't do something to be of assistance."

He says to me as I start making my calls, "You are an unusual man, Mr. Kahtz. You do things. You don't just talk." Because I started making calls right in front of him. And I called Phil Trimble, who was then a lawyer in the State Department. He had just joined State that year and was running an economic-law section. This is the same Phil Trimble who had worked in my councilmanic office. He had worked on several of my campaigns. He's a Democrat. It amazed him he was able to get a job with the Nixon Administration. Anyway, I said, "Phil, I'm sitting in the office of the

Archbishop of the Greek Orthodox Church. He's just gotten two calls, one from Ted Kennedy, one from John Brademas. He says he's been trying to get in touch with the Secretary of State for a number of weeks, nobody takes his calls, nobody answers his letters; he's not given an opportunity to meet with the President or the Secretary. He is furious. I think you're all crazy down there. Why don't you at least talk to him, even if you can't do anything?''

Trimble says, "Let me see what I can do and I'll call you back." He calls back a few minutes later and he says, "What they say is, 'Will it be okay if Joe Sisco calls him?' and he'll do it right away."

I say, "Of course it will be okay."

He says, "The Secretary just can't call, but Sisco will." Joseph Sisco was a very important guy in the State Department who became the number-one guy on the Middle East, a very able guy.

I say, "Your Eminence, I've spoken to my friend, and my friend says that Undersecretary Sisco is going to call you in a few minutes if it's okay."

He said, "Yes."

A few minutes later, his secretary says, "Your Eminence, Undersecretary Joseph Sisco is on the phone."

The Archbishop takes the phone, and I can hear his side of the conversation, which goes basically, ". . . Yes, I shall convey that to the Prime Minister." Iakovos was going that very night to Greece, and Sisco is filling him in on the U.S. government's position. The Archbishop hangs up and says to me, "You are a wonderful man."

I say, "Your Eminence, I must tell you, I'm really so overwhelmed with your pain, and I want you to know that whatever I can do, you just have to let me know. And if it's within my power, I'm going to do it. I'm going to help you."

Well, of course, I became involved in the fight to cut off aid to Turkey. The leaders of that fight were Ben Rosenthal, who was on the Foreign Affairs Committee—the cutoff measure became known as the Rosenthal Amendment—and two Greeks. There were five Greeks in the House at the time, but only two took major roles. One was John Brademas and the other was Paul Sarbanes of Maryland, who is now a senator. They're two very smart guys. And I took a role, too, speaking, supporting.

Subsequently the Archbishop had a dinner, his annual dinner where they raise money for charity, at the Waldorf-Astoria, and they invited as special guests Rosenthal, Brademas, Sarbanes and me to sit on the dais.

Well, the star was Rosenthal. When he came in, the place erupted. You had a thousand Greeks in there. It would be like a thousand Jews on something involving Israel of momentous importance to them. The Rosenthal Amendment had carried at that point, and I've never seen such a response for the size of the group. It was wonderful. And Rosenthal made one of the best speeches I've ever heard. It was a very short one.

He said, "I was wondering what I would say here tonight, and I thought I'd tell you a story. You're probably not going to appreciate it in the way that it's meant, but I'm going to tell you anyway." He said, "I had lunch with my mother, who lives in New York, today; and she asked me what I was doing tonight, so I said, 'I'm going to a dinner, Mama, that will honor two of my friends in Congress, John Brademas and Paul Sarbanes. And, you know, Mama, they're probably the two smartest men in Congress.' My mother said, 'Are they Jewish?' and I said, 'No, Mama, they're not Jewish—they're Greek.' My mother said, 'Are you sure they're not Jewish?' I thought a moment and then I said to my mother, 'Mama, I think they're half Jewish.' " And then he said to this crowd, holding out his hands, "Tonight I'm half Greek." And the place erupted. I think it's the best story I've ever heard for an audience of that kind. It was wonderful, just wonderful.

I've always felt that if you are honest in your emotions, expressing them, telling people what you think, of course on occasion you're going to get people upset and angry, but more times than not they are going to respond in a positive way.

11

Zealots

I AM SOMEONE WHO HAS ALWAYS BEEN SUPPORTIVE of minorities. That comes naturally simply because I'm a Jew. So I take pride in having been very active in support of the blacks in their struggle for voting rights. I support the gays in their fight for equal rights. And I support the women and the Ukrainians and the Armenians, the Irish and every group that has been the subject of or is currently subject to discrimination or oppression. That's my nature. And with respect to women my support has two facets. One is I believe in equality of opportunity; the other is that support of women's rights is politically a plus. It is getting less so, just as support of equal rights for blacks or bringing them to the point where they have equal rights in a whole host of areas is less salable because some people now believe that blacks have achieved equality and that what blacks want now is preferential treatment. Being for equality is to me still the right thing to do. And I will support efforts to secure equality for blacks and women until the goal has been achieved. And that goes equally for gays.

When I was district leader, beginning in 1963, and in particular in 1965, we were having a severe problem in the Sixth Avenue/Eighth Street/Christopher Street area with male prostitutes. It was vile. You couldn't walk along these streets without being solicited. Now, I happen to believe, as Pierre Trudeau summed it up, that ''the government has no business in the bedrooms of the nation.'' On the other hand, I also believe that public solicitation, whether it's male or female prostitution, is something that people do not have to be subjected to. I'm not offended by the concept of prostitution, and I believe that in private consenting adults should be able to engage in any sexual behavior that they want to. Still, there are rights for those who don't want to get involved and who are offended—and they don't have to be subjected to harassment. So, for example, on prostitution my position is that we should adopt the English approach, which is that prostitution is illegal only if it includes public solicitation or pimps. But I believe that someone who engages in prostitution in the privacy of his or her home is not engaging in an illegal act. I believe that that is a very sensible approach. I don't believe in a red-light district. I don't think the government should cordon areas off. I just don't think it's the business of government to get into licensing prostitution or harassing prostitution, subject to these limitations that I've just described. And when I make this point in front of audiences, as I have done on occasion, they say, "Well, how will they find one another?"

I say, "Love will find a way."

Now, of course, in England what happened is that they use the media. They put up cards. They use newspapers. They're very blatant. Everybody knows what they are. And that's okay. People reading it know what they're reading. I'm not for censorship.

All right, now getting back to the gays, in '65, when we're running again for the district leadership, Carol Greitzer and I, one of the issues was: What the hell's going on on Sixth Avenue? You can't walk down the street without being accosted. And so we undertook to get the cops to stop it. And this was considered to be a vile, antihomosexual drive and we were denounced by the Mattachine Society. In fact, I think Carol and I were in a book they put out. Very denunciatory. And I remember getting letters from some of the leaders of that group. I felt very bad about that, because it's easy to victimize gays, even though in the Greenwich Village area you would certainly lose votes—there are areas on the Upper East Side where you might not. But I would consider that to be heinous, to use them as whipping boys. And, besides, the gay men and lesbian women are deserving of support on the basis of justice, notwithstanding the occasional zealot who makes your life miserable with unfair attacks for giving such sup-

265

port. On an issue such as this you will be attacked on one side by the Mattachine Society, which is seeking to protect every conceivable right that in their estimation gays have, and on the other side by some of the militant block associations and community groups. One will say you are doing too much, the other will say you aren't doing enough. And I will say, "I must be doing something right if I am being attacked by both extremes."

• • •

When I was a congressman I had a constituent hour every week. For years we met on Friday mornings from nine to ten in churches, synagogues, community houses, the YMCA, wherever we could get a room at no cost to us. My staff mailed and handed out about ten thousand cards a week notifying people where we would be that week. I did that immediately after the 8 to 9 A.M. hour, when I handed out literature in the subway. In 1975 I started doing it on Saturdays because Congress started meeting on Fridays.

In any event, one day we met at the YMCA. I say a meeting, but what I mean is that people came in and lined up. Sometimes it was two people, sometimes it was thirty-five people, with personal problems. That's what the card they get in their mailbox says, "If you have a problem," and I list the kinds of problems I can be helpful with, "then come and I'll try to be of help." And I was able to help in many cases.

So this particular meeting hour in 1974 or '75 was filled with people. I was expecting some disruption at this meeting, because the U.S. Labor Party people had called the day before saying they wanted to see me and where would be my next public appearance? And my staff—we never hide these things—said, ''Tomorrow he will be at the YMCA on Twenty-third Street near Seventh Avenue.'' And so I knew that they would come.

Well, there are fifteen, twenty people in the room sitting on chairs around a table waiting for me to get to them separately, and in walk these two guys. You can tell them right away, because one of their techniques is to take pictures. One of them is always a photographer. God knows whether he has any film in the camera or not. It's to intimidate you: taking pictures all the time.

As soon as they walk in, I know who they are and I say, ''Stop taking those pictures, you cannot take pictures of my constituents. You can take pictures of me, but not of my constituents. Take that goddamn camera off your neck and put it on the table or get the hell out.'' This always takes them a bit by surprise, the direct confrontation.

So, okay, he takes the camera off his neck and puts it down on the table, and they both sit down like the other people waiting.

Finally comes their turn, and one of them takes out a petition that was rolled up like a Chinese scroll, puts it on the table, and says, ''Sign.''

I say, ''Can I read it?''

So I started to read it, and it's filled with idiocies: we've got to pay $60 billion reparations to this group and $40 billion reparations to that group. It's the silliest kind of program. They are philosophically to the left of Chairman Mao.

As I am reading this, I say, "I'll take this home, I'll read it, I'll study it."

"No, you're going to sign it now." And they begin to yell.

I say, "Okay, get the cops somebody. I want a cop."

And at that point, one of the constituents who's waiting, who must have been about seven foot tall—he looked like Frankenstein's monster, I mean he was Boris Karloff incarnate—gets up, he's got the plodding type of movements, and walks over and puts a hand the size of a plate on the shoulder of one of these guys and says, "Congressman, I'll take care of him."

So I say, "No, no, no, put him down. The cops are coming. Not you. Sit down. I appreciate it, but don't get involved." Sort of like treating some huge giant who has half a brain. "Sit down!" And he sits down.

Then the security officer from the Y comes in and ushers these two U.S. Labor Party people out of the room.

Comes the turn of Boris Karloff, he says to me, "Congressman, I need your help. I've been wrongly accused of assault." Well, really?

The U.S. Labor Party is a group of basically young men and women in their late twenties, early thirties; the ones I have met are mostly Jewish but not all; and they are all nuts. They are also, the ones that I know, the sons and daughters of very wealthy people. One of them happened to be the son of a good friend of mine, which is interesting. The sins of the fathers are visited upon the children. He was a radical, and then the son was even more radical and the father was suffering.* The daughter of another friend is in the same category. There are a number of very wealthy people who have children who give them great pain. I don't know what the psychological reason is. An obvious possibility would be resenting the money they have available to them and they would like in some way to expiate their sins, so they go out and commit nutty acts in support of people they consider to be the downtrodden. But they are very strange cases. Now let me just give you a couple of my experiences.

First of all, they engage in violence. I have never been the subject of their violence. I have been the subject of their vilification. Let me also point out the nuttiness. They have said that Bella Abzug is a CIA agent. Now, I happen to dislike Bella Abzug intensely, immensely. I can't think of words I could use that would be broad enough. But to call her a CIA agent makes them nutty. Okay?

Of my experiences with the U.S. Labor Party, the most hilarious was when I took Bob Morgenthau on a walk down the East Side of Manhattan. Morgenthau was running for Manhattan district attorney. I was very instrumental in getting him the nomination in the prima-

---

*The son later broke with the group and is now middle class once again.

ry and also in getting him elected, although getting elected is easy once you're the Democratic candidate here in Manhattan. In any event, he asked me to take him down the East Side of Manhattan and to introduce him. He wasn't a very good candidate in the sense of being able to handle crowds or people. He was an unusual candidate in that respect. He just didn't know how to do it.

As we walk down Lexington beginning at Eighty-sixth Street on a Saturday morning in the summer of '74, as we walk down from Eighty-sixth Street to Fifty-ninth shaking hands and talking to people, I am introducing Morgenthau. I say to people, "This is Bob Morgenthau. You know Morgenthau. You know the name!" And they look at me sort of wide-eyed. And I say, "That's him!" Morgenthau doesn't know what to do. If he could, he'd creep under a manhole cover, he's so embarrassed by it.

In any event, as we get to Fifty-ninth Street and are approaching Bloomingdale's, there are crowds, you know, hundreds of people on the street; and there are three guys, young guys with megaphones, and they see us, they probably knew we were coming. Suddenly they are shouting into the megaphone, "Here they come, the two war criminals, Morgenthau and Koch—there! War criminals, yes sir, here they come—the two war criminals."

It was incredible. Me it doesn't bother. Morgenthau, if he could, would have jumped into a cab and gone across town—anything to avoid the embarrassment. In fact, he said to me, "Let's go over to the West Side."

I said, "No, you can't let them drive you off the block."

But, in any event, as we get right under the Bloomingdale's canopy overhang, one of these guys sticks the megaphone next to my ear and he yells, "War criminal! War criminal!"

I say to him, "Fuck off!" And he really is very upset and very shocked at this.

He says to me, "Can I repeat that?"

I say, "Sure."

And he yells into his megaphone, "Congressman Koch just told me to fuck off." And hundreds of people started to applaud and cheer.

●   ●   ●

The U.S. Labor Party activists are as sheep compared to the militant Irish-American irredentists. I was quite active in supporting the Irish-Americans in their quest for rights for the Catholics in Northern Ireland. I'm avoiding saying that I supported the Irish Republican Army provos, because I never intended to support the IRA provos, although probably my efforts may have been doing that. But that was not my intention. They're bad people, these terrorists—there's no question about it. They've killed and maimed innocent people.

In any case, it was the thing to be for several years. Lester Wolff was elected in his new congressional district—I guess it was 1972—based on the Irish vote against a conservative Irishman, because Wolff had taken the lead on behalf of the Fort Worth Five, Irish-Americans who had been picked up for gunrunning across Mexico's border. The five wouldn't say anything before the grand jury, and they were being held in Texas. And the big campaign was: how unfair it was that they should be held for contempt of court in Texas and away from their families.

I got on that issue with a lot of other people. Our position wasn't really wrong, because unfair methods had been used by the U.S. government, and ultimately the prisoners were released. I think one could probably have argued both sides of that one, but I was quite active on the prisoners' behalf and I have no regrets about that. I was honored with about seven or eight other members of Congress. Bella was one of them; Liz Holtzman (who is now Brooklyn district attorney) was another; and Ben Rosenthal. What we did was to create a mood nationwide, and Paul O'Dwyer was at its head.

Subsequently—I think it would be early 1973—I get a letter from a guy who was sort of the head of the Irish group in this country. The letter says, We would like you to denounce the British government for keeping the Price sisters in Britain and force-feeding them and treating them horribly; we want you to urge that they be taken to Northern Ireland. You know, one of those letters.

By that point I had already decided that this group is probably more militant than I really want to be involved with, and I don't really know what the situation is with the Price sisters. So I write a letter, as I did almost customarily in such situations, to the federal agency that might have some facts. In this case I wrote to the State Department, and I say, I've received a request concerning the Price sisters to protest their maltreatment and urge their removal to Northern Ireland jails instead of being kept in England. Can you tell me what the situation is?

They write back: The Price sisters were responsible for explosions in England that killed five people and injured a hundred others in restaurants and other public areas. They are incarcerated in an English prison because the crime took place in England. They have protested their treatment, but two left-wing members of Congress (and they gave their names) have examined the situation and have found they're receiving excellent treatment. They are being force-fed because they've gone on a hunger strike and the prison officials want to make certain that the Price sisters don't die.

Well, based on that letter, I write back to the guy who had written me, and I say:

This is the situation, it appears to me, since the crimes had been committed in England, I cannot in good conscience urge that the prisoners be transported to jails in Northern Ireland. Nor do I consider the forcefeeding cruel. My own feeling is: If somebody wants to die, they should be allowed to die; so I wouldn't force-feed anybody. But it's not an inhumane thing to do. That's a philosophical concept which you can take either side of. But I don't really see how I can get involved here. The treatment apparently is reasonable.

And then I put in a line that went something like this: "And, as I hope you know, I am opposed to terrorism, as I hope you are."

So a few days later I get a letter not from this guy, but from Paul O'Dwyer, the local spokesman for the group, who also happened to be the President of the New York City Council, and the thrust of the letter, the feel of it—I could see the page burning up—went something like this: Who the hell asked your opinion on terrorism?

It was a thoroughly denunciatory letter. I was fit to be tied. And I was going to send a real zinger back to him, but it's just a few days before the St. Patrick's Day parade, and I know I'm going to be marching in that parade with him, and who needs confrontation? And so on advice of my counsel—David Brown—I decided not to respond by letter.

Ultimately, I cannot say he apologized, but he said that he wanted me to know he wasn't angry. This was months later. And I didn't see the benefit of getting into a donnybrook with him.

•   •   •

In the area of zealotry there are few individuals who bring more passion to their cause than the animal protectors. Sometimes they are justified in their zeal—and after all it is the zealots who get things done—but sometimes they go too far.

I had received a lot of mail from constituents who were concerned about experiments taking place at the Museum of Natural History. Allegedly the experiments included the torturing and blinding of cats. And it was being done, said those who were opposed to it, with federal monies. They were taking lots of ads at the time, and the ads had pictures showing cats being tortured with electrodes in their brains.

My personal belief is that vivisection is a necessary evil, if you will. It is a tool required for advancing science, to help human beings and animals on occasion, but certainly there are benefits for human beings. It's abused, but nevertheless if we obey the desires of the antivivisectionists, we wouldn't have today a polio vaccine, which came as a result of experimentation with monkeys. And there are many other such cases. However, in this case the deluge of mail was so extraordinary that I decided to go and look at the experiments. So I called up and asked whether I might visit and I was told that I could.

I appeared one morning with Ronay Menschel. The director of the facility said to me he was sorry that the doctor in charge of the experiment was not in.

I asked, "Where is he?"

He said, "He was stung by bees and is now in the hospital."

I thought to myself, Probably deserved.

I said, "Does he have an assistant?"

The director said, "Yes," and he introduced me to a young woman who was with him.

I said, "Can't she take me through?"

He said, "If you'd like."

So we went upstairs to the area in which the experimentation was taking place, and I was taken into a room that was loaded with cats in cages. I personally prefer dogs to cats. I am uncomfortable with cats. I always have the feeling that they are going to spring in an unexpected way. And cats seem to understand that I have that feeling, because they seem always to spring at me in an unexpected way. Ostensibly they will be seeking to sit in my lap or on my shoulder. It makes me very uncomfortable. Cats are much smarter than dogs. I am convinced they know exactly what they are doing.

In any event, I say to the young woman, "What is it that you do? What are you seeking to find out?"

She says, "Our experiments are directed to ascertaining what additional knowledge we can get on hypersexual activity and hyposexual activity," which means lesser activity than normal.

I say, "Well, what do you do?"

She says, "What we do is the following. We take a male cat and we put lesions in its brain."

I say, seeking to keep the record straight, "What does it mean to put lesions in its brain?"

She says, "When you put lesions in a cat's brain you are destroying brain tissue and areas that motivate certain functions."

I say, "Well, after you've done that, what do you do?"

She says, "Well, then we take this male cat and we put it into a room with a female cat and a female rabbit."

I ask, "Then what happens?"

She says, "We watch what the male cat with lesions does after it enters the room."

I ask, "What does the cat do?"

She says, "The cat mounts the rabbit."

I say, "Well, now, look. After you put lesions into a cat's brain and you take this brain-damaged cat and you throw it into a room with a female cat and a female rabbit, and this brain-damaged cat mounts the rabbit, what have you got?"

There was silence. No response.

I say, "By the way, how does the rabbit feel about all of this?"

There was no response.

I say, "How long have you been doing this?"

She says, "About twenty years."

I ask, "How much has this cost the federal government?"

She says, "About four hundred thirty-five thousand dollars."

I went back to Congress and told the story on the floor of the House of Representatives. It had great impact.

●　　　●　　　●

Now I'll just tell you one other little story, because it happens to come to mind. It involves a woman named

Alice Herrington. And by way of background you should know that in my congressional district in the 1970s, in terms of issue interest on the basis of number of letters, it was "Save the whales," "Save the porpoises," "Save the Jews"—and in that order.

Alice Herrington calls me up right after I was first elected to Congress. She's the leader of some friends-of-animals group. She's the one who was the moving force every year in running those ads showing some cat in a torture chamber and baby seals being clubbed to death—really gory stuff. She writes and asks me to support legislation that would outlaw kosher slaughtering. Specifically, she demanded that the animal has to be stunned—struck on the head and rendered unconscious—before its throat is slit. This would violate the law of kashruth, which states that the throat has to be slit while the animal is conscious. It happens that death is instantaneous when that particular artery is cut, but she wanted me to take up this legislation, which she had been propounding for years, to ban kosher slaughtering. I said, "No."

Then she calls up and wants to come in and see me.

I say, "I'll see anybody."

She comes in with a movie projector, a self-contained little movie projector. In the meantime, I had been studying up on this thing so that I'd be able to respond to her. She shows me this movie of a slaughterhouse. It's very gory. All these cows are being slaughtered and there's blood—it was very gory. But that's what a slaughterhouse is: very gory.

At the end she says, "I hope now that you will help outlaw kosher slaughtering."

"Oh," I said, "no, I couldn't do that. That's a matter of First Amendment rights. In addition, it happens that kosher slaughtering is not painful. The fact is, it's probably the least painful. What is painful results from the civil law that requires that the cow be shackled and hoisted." They hoist the animal up, shackling one of its legs, in order to make sure that when its throat is cut it doesn't fall into its own offal. I said, "It happens that there is something called the Weinberg pen that prevents the need for hoisting and shackling." What the Jews had done was to get the ASPCA to develop a pen that keeps the animal together and doesn't permit it to fall. I said, "I have no objection to requiring states to use the Weinberg pen. They use it in Israel, and they use it in Pennsylvania."

"Oh, no, we're not interested in the Weinberg pen," she says. "We want kosher slaughtering stopped." Very tough.

I say, "No, not me. You've got the wrong guy."

She says, "You're going to hear from your constituents."

I'm always going to hear from them. That's always the threat. I say, "That's fine. Get the letters moving."

Then I say, "By the way, if you have a little extra time, can I tell you something that is on my mind that bothers me about the way animals are handled? I cannot get over or accept the fact that there are people who take living lobsters and scald them to death before they eat them! Is that any way to treat a lobster? And there are other people who eat animals alive—clams and oysters, alive! Isn't that terrible? If you have a little extra time, Miss Herrington, get those outrages stopped.''

So she looks at me like I'm crazy, as I was in a way, and she leaves.

I didn't hear from Alice Herrington again until I introduced a piece of legislation that was called ''The Commission to Provide Humane Treatment for Animals.'' This issue came to me because this guy, Peter Singer from Australia, who had just done a book on animals called *Animal Liberation,* came down to see me in Washington and I said to him, ''I think I can help.'' It was a thought I had, which was that we should take all of these animal cases—the baby seals, the whales, the beagles having their throats cut, experimentation on primates, all of these gruesome cases—and have a commission determine whether or not they constituted inhumane treatment.

So I'm handing that statement out at the subways, and I think it's a brilliant idea. A reporter comes to see me at the subway, one of the local sheets, a young fellow, and he seems to be impressed with the idea. And then that afternoon he calls me up and says, ''Well, I've been talking to other people, and would you like to know what they say?''

I say, ''Sure.''

He says, ''Well, I have been talking to Miss Alice Herrington.'' That's a good reporter. He says, ''Let me tell you what she says.''

I say, "Sure."

He says, reading from his notes, "She says they don't need a commission. It's all cut and dried. We know the inhumane things that exist. We know what has to be outlawed. In fact, Koch is the kind of guy that if he was in Abraham Lincoln's shoes at the time of the Civil War, instead of abolishing slavery, he would have formed a commission to look into it." Which I thought was a very clever retort on her part.

So I say, "Very clever on her part. And she is Ms. Savonarola. She's got all the answers. She's a zealot. And I meet them all the time. Zealots brook no dissent. There's a role for zealots. Their role is they have to push as hard as they can and they bring other people closer to the ideal, which is somewhere less than theirs and may be more than what people want. But I have a different role. My role is that of a responsible legislator and to do what is reasonable."

12

Incumbency

INCUMBENCY is a two-edged sword. If you are seeking public office and you have no record, then people will say, "Well, what's he done?" But of course there is a benefit as well, and that is that the person with no record has no record to attack or to defend. The benefit of holding office is that the official and his record are known. Moreover, the incumbent has some authority, and that power is more easily translated into news coverage. The incumbent will generally get far more news coverage than the challenger, which should be good, but sometimes is not. Those who run are generally not wealthy, but the incumbent is more easily able to raise campaign funding. In my most recent reelection campaign, I thought we used my incumbency better than we did, say, in 1981, my first reelection campaign for mayor, or in 1982, my attempt to become governor, which failed miserably.

●　　　　●　　　　●

Before going over to the Sheraton Centre Hotel to meet Walter Mondale on the evening of the New York State 1984 presidential primary, I was watching the results on television at Gracie Mansion with Stan Brezenoff—who had succeeded Nat Leventhal as my deputy mayor for operations—and Bill Rauch, my press secretary. As the results came in it was clear that the Reverend Jesse Jackson was going to carry New York City's black vote by an overwhelming margin (ultimately he got 80 percent). The implications of that did not bode well for my reelection, since most black political leaders were opposed to me and believed the time had come for New York to join Chicago, Detroit, Washington, Atlanta and Los Angeles, and elect a black mayor. There had been a lot of discussion in the press about the huge voter-registration drive Jackson's people had mounted in the black community, and Jackson's showing in the black community in the City of New York was very impressive.

Most of Gracie Mansion was still being renovated (I was moving from the private quarters and living in the public parts of the building, one step ahead of the painters), so the three of us were sitting in the west parlor of the Susan Wagner Wing, which I used as my den. I said, ''It is very important that next year we make sure to get my vote out. We should try a huge registration campaign, and then get them to the polls."

Stan said, referring to the television screen, "These results certainly show that it can be done, that an old-fashioned street campaign can still be effective."

Bill said, "Of all the people you know in the City of New York, whom would you trust most to run such an operation?"

I said, "Jim Capalino."

Jim had been a member of my congressional staff; had been a commissioner in my first mayoral administration; was now a developer in the private sector well on his way to becoming a millionaire; had run the 1977 mayoral street campaign; and is an organizational genius, a tyrant, and brooks no screwups from those who work for him. I admire him, like him, and trust him totally.

Bill said, "Do you want me to call him or do you want to call him?"

I called Jim several days later, and over the course of the following seventeen months what Jim Capalino did was extraordinary. Early on in the planning for the 1985 reelection campaign, I decided that the campaign dollars should be split basically evenly between the television campaign and the street campaign. That was very different from what had been done in my past campaigns. There over 80 percent of the campaign funds had been spent for television commercials. However, in 1985 we knew that 99+ percent of all New Yorkers knew me and had an opinion on my mayoralty. I had no recognition problem. My problems, as we viewed them prospectively, were getting my record of achievements across on television and getting my voters to the polls.

I thought that convincing David Garth of the importance, in this instance, of the street campaign would be a difficult matter. I was wrong. David had not, so long as I had known him, run a campaign that involved large expenditures for the mail and telephones that are used for vote-pulling. He is not normally interested in street campaigns, because with almost religious fervor he believes that the thirty-second TV commercial has far greater impact than the letters and literature you receive in the mail, the volunteer calling on the telephone, the free transportation to the polls, and the volunteers in the street handing out literature or carrying campaign posters, or distributing buttons, and palm cards on election day.

I therefore took this issue up gingerly with David, but I was committed to prevailing even if he disagreed. I had a meeting with him alone, and I said, "David, I believe we should spend fifty percent of the money that we take in, whatever it is, on a street campaign and fifty percent on television." There was a long silence, about fifteen seconds, and then he said, "Okay."

I believe that that single strategy paid off more than all else combined. David used television brilliantly, and Jim Capalino used the telephones and the mails and the volunteers in the streets brilliantly.

In 1981 black New Yorkers constituted barely 17 percent of the registered Democratic electorate. In 1985 they represented nearly 30 percent. Hispanic Democrats had increased their participation nearly threefold, from 5 to 13 percent of the Democratic primary registrants. Jews, once as much as 45 percent of the Democratic voters, had declined to only about 22 percent of the vote in 1985. Similarly, the Catholic vote had declined as a percentage of the total Democratic vote in the past four years. What all that meant was that the groups that were initially, by most politicians, considered most likely to vote for me had declined substantially as a part of the total Democratic vote. The Jackson registration drive coupled with the changing demographics of the city had altered significantly the ethnic makeup of the primary voter pool.

What Capalino accomplished with his pulling effort was simple in concept yet extraordinarily difficult in execution. By the use of the direct-mail operation and the field operation, he managed, in the face of the shifting demographics, to keep the ethnic composition of the actual primary vote roughly equivalent to what it had been in 1981. The participation of pro-Koch groups rose 5 percent over 1981. Added to this was my very strong showing, 70 percent, among the Hispanic primary voters and my running nearly even with Denny Farrell among the blacks. These factors combined to give me an overwhelming vote by any standard in the primary.

On the TV time that we purchased, meanwhile, Garth showed mini-documentaries of people talking about specific neighborhood projects that had improved the lot of New Yorkers. These commercials served to get my record out. We knew that if we ran the campaign on my record my opponents would finish far behind.

When the primary was concluded I sent David the following note which truly expressed my feelings.

Dear David:

Some, entirely justifiably, call you a media wizard, others a genius in campaign strategy. I call you "friend."

When it is all said and done our relationship which really began at the end of 1976 has been and will continue to be an extraordinary one. I could not have been elected in 1977 without you, and I could not have achieved the enormous victory of 1985 without you. Your commercials have been in the past and this year in particular light-years ahead of your colleagues in the field. But beyond your extraordinary ability there are for me two things that make you special: your intellect and the intensity of your friendship when you extend it. I am lucky that you have extended it to me.

The incumbent has the benefit of choosing among first-rate political operatives who have generally been previously known and tested by him. As I said, in this case Jim Capalino had handled the street campaign for me in 1977 when I was first elected mayor, and David Garth had handled the strategy and media in all my campaigns since 1977. The challenger is generally going into new waters and is less able to rely entirely on known and tested people. That is not where the problems for the incumbent come. The problems come from the rush of events with which the officeholder must deal effectively every day. And in 1985 I had my share of "events."

•   •   •

On the twenty-fourth of December of 1984 Bernhard Goetz shot and wounded four black youths who, he has said, sought to mug him.* For some time Goetz was at large, and descriptions of what had occurred on the subway car, with which many people could identify in fact or in their dreams, and descriptions of him as tall and blond with aviator glasses were sufficient to convince some New Yorkers that the subway gunman was a vigilante, while others believed he had acted in self-defense.

On the day of the shooting, I immediately said to the press, "Vigilantism will not be tolerated in this city. We are not going to have instant justice meted out by anybody." Several days later, on December 28, when a little more was known about the alleged muggers, I said, "You have a right to protect yourself. You don't have a right to revenge. I hope he [the gunman] comes

*Of the four youths involved in the Goetz case, at this writing, three have had additional scrapes with the law. James Ramseur was found guilty in April, 1986, of raping and sodomizing a pregnant woman; Barry Allen was convicted of chain-snatching and, more recently, pleaded guilty to a new robbery charge, relating to another chain-snatching incident; and Troy Canty pleaded guilty to a robbery charge resulting from an incident that occurred prior to the Goetz shooting. The fourth, Darrell Cabey, is permanently paralyzed from the waist down and is partially brain-damaged as a result of Goetz's bullet.

in, because maybe he can establish his case." Three weeks later, after Goetz had turned himself in, I said, "We don't know if he is a victim or a villain. If the action was in self-defense, then it is not a crime. But if he went past self-defense and engaged in revenge, then it is a crime."

On January 26, following a grand jury's indictment of Goetz for illegal possession of a firearm but not for the shooting, I said, "I believe in the grand-jury system. Since they did not indict on any of the charges relating to the actual shooting, apparently they did not find that there was sufficient evidence to indict on those charges. I have no fault to find." I applauded their indicting him on the illegal possession of a gun. On February 7 I said, "My opinion is that the grand jury did the right thing, and I agree with them in the Goetz case." On March 1, I said I was going to "take a step back" from the case because Goetz had been saying some "flaky things" such as proposing that 25,000 New Yorkers be permitted to carry guns. I called that proposal "Looneyville."

I was asked a lot of questions by reporters that implied I had changed my position on Goetz. In fact there is no contradiction in these statements. The easiest thing in the world is to say, "I will have no comment on pending litigation." And sometimes that is the appropriate thing to say. But when you have a case that is on the network news every night, which the whole town is speculating about, which threatens the racial fabric of the city and in which you are in no way personally involved, I do not believe it is leadership to stand silent.

At every step of the way in the Goetz case I said what I said based on the facts as they were publicly known. What reporters have a hard time grasping is that where you have a situation that is evolving daily, the responsible public official will have a position that may change in ways that common sense dictates. It doesn't mean you are contradicting yourself. Some people would say, "Don't take a position until the matter is totally disposed of." That could take years. That's not leadership. That's writing history.

In the course of the 1985 campaign Archbishop John J. O'Connor was elevated to the cardinalate. I went to Rome for his elevation, and I enjoyed myself. I have said to people that in the last eight years I have been in more churches as mayor than I attended synagogues in the last sixty years. It's gotten so that I can tell when they've shortened the service leading to the mass. On a number of occasions a Catholic supporter will say, "When are you converting?" And I will respond, "That's a high compliment you pay me, but not in this world, maybe the next." I am a proud Jew—regrettably not sufficiently observant.

When then-Archbishop O'Connor first arrived in New York it was clear to me from that moment that we shared many aspects of personality and that we were going to hit it off. He hit it off with me when in his opening remarks during the homily at his first service at St. Patrick's he said, and the crowd loved it, "How'm I doin'?" Then, adding to it, when we stood in line in the vestibule of the cathedral after the service to shake his hand, he walked up to Governor Cuomo and said, "Mayor, I've always wanted to meet you."

And the Governor, surely pained, says, pointing to me, "He's the Mayor, I'm the Governor."

I'll never know whether the Cardinal did that purposely. I know he doesn't care for the Governor's positions on abortion—many of which, I should say, are similar to mine—but the difference is that I'm not a Catholic and therefore I don't have the obligations to the church that Catholics have. I think it's fair to say the Cardinal is unsympathetic to the Governor, and he has made that clear over the past several years. And the Governor must be in pain. He doesn't seem to know how to deal with it. And he surely worries about it vis-à-vis his expected run for President.

Now, of course, I have had my substantive differences with the Cardinal, too. We differed, for example, on my Executive Order 50. That order stipulated that private agencies that contract with the city to deliver services or sell goods must not discriminate in hiring, as the city does not discriminate vis-à-vis its own employees. That is, when the city hires it does not discriminate on the basis of race, religion, physical handicap, sex or sexual orientation. Executive Order 50 said the private contract agencies must follow the same guidelines or lose the city's funding. Well, the Archdiocese of New York, of which Cardinal O'Connor is the head, contracts with the city to deliver over $80 million annually in services including foster care, day care, Headstart, and special education—all good programs, and needed by the city.

The Cardinal decided he would take on the issue of prohibition of discrimination on the basis of sexual orientation. He decided he would initiate a lawsuit to strike down that executive order. And he ultimately won that lawsuit. The Court of Appeals, New York State's highest court, finally ruled that while my executive order might be laudable, I needed either City Council or Albany legislation to authorize me to do this. I have been trying to get such legislation for many years and so far to no avail.

Throughout the 1985 campaign there was always the question of whether my support of gay rights, my problem with the Cardinal and this lawsuit, would in some way turn off Catholic voters who were traditionally for me and upon whom we were counting to come out and vote for me. We certainly didn't want to see them turned off. I personally believe that on issues of morality if you say what you honestly believe and people believe that you are not just being political, they're not going to vote against you on that one issue even if they disagree with the position you've taken. This would be true of the death penalty, abortion, gay rights and a few other issues. I've never wavered on these, and so far as I've ever been able to tell I've never suffered as a result. Nonetheless, if you are a rational person, you worry about it.

But as Cardinal O'Connor said at his elevation in Rome, when I was in attendance at a dinner also attended by others of his friends and admirers, "Only in New York can a cardinal and a mayor sue each other and still be friends." And we have stayed friends through it all.

Toward the end of the campaign I was invited by Harriet Michel, president of the Urban League, to attend an anti-apartheid presentation in Washington. In the room in Washington with us were Mrs. Coretta Scott King, Harry Belafonte, Cleveland Robinson, Julian Bond, and Jesse Jackson. I was the only white public official there. In my comments I called for divestiture, the use of the Sullivan Principles, all the things I had been saying and doing in New York. Then, following the speeches, in the questions and answers, one of the reporters asks, "Mr. Mayor, are you upset that Israel still trades and sells arms to South Africa?"

So I say, "I am as upset with Israel's trading with South Africa as the black Americans at this table with me must be upset that there are forty-six black African states now trading with South Africa. And as Americans we must all, together, be upset that our country is trading with the South African government and with all other countries that do the same. But let me say it is unfair to single out Israel. Let's instead ask the forty-six black African states, the United States, the European countries and Israel to, together, cease their economic and diplomatic relations with South Africa."

Jesse Jackson, standing behind me, says to me as I leave the chair, "You are some piece of work. We should sit down and talk."

I said, "Absolutely, Jesse, after the election."

Okay, so now after that we take a bus ride to where the scheduled march to the State Department begins. I sit down on the bus next to former Manhattan Borough President Percy Sutton, and Jackson gets on and sits down across the aisle from me. On the bus we continued the discussion of Israel and remarks made by him and by me in the 1984 presidential primary. We talked for about three quarters of an hour, and it was very friendly. He said he thought Israel was "a light to the world," and therefore under heavy moral obligation.

I said, "Israel only wants to be treated equally. What is unfair is to ask them to go into the fire ahead of everyone else. Jews don't believe they will get to heaven before you or before anyone else. So we don't want to be treated differently. Supporters of Israel like myself are upset to have Israel constantly singled out on South Africa when there are these forty-six black states that are trading every day with South Africa and in huge amounts, and two of them have agreed to protect South Africa's borders from infiltration by rebels."

He said, "But the forty-six black African states are landlocked. They have no alternative."

I said, "Well, Israel is *diplomatically* landlocked. It also wants to protect the Jewish community in South Africa. The Vatican says it can't recognize Israel, out of fear that Christians in Arab lands will suffer. Well,

Israel similarly fears that Jews in South Africa will suffer if Israel rejects South Africa. If it's okay for the Vatican, why shouldn't it be okay for Israel?" No answer was forthcoming.

After that we got onto the subject of minister Louis Farrakhan. I said it was distressing to me that Farrakhan had been able to attract ten thousand blacks to a speech that he had recently given in Washington, and that at that speech, as it had been reported, Farrakhan had spewed his racial bigotry and anti-Semitism. I said to Jackson, "Your worst mistake was not your calling New York 'Hymietown.' It was your not rejecting the support of Farrakhan. You repudiated his statements but not his support."

He said, "I believe in redemption."

I said, "Okay, but Farrakhan never asked for forgiveness. I don't believe that because of your belief in redemption you would have accepted the support of Adolf Hitler."

He said, "I wouldn't have."

I said, "It's the same thing."

He said, "If I had repudiated Farrakhan I wouldn't have picked up three Jewish votes."

I said, "I don't know, but it would have been the right thing to do." In my head I was thinking, That's a very political assessment for a minister—to be thinking not about what's right, but rather about what helps him politically.

●   ●   ●

When I ran for reelection in 1981 my political opponents formed a loose group called the "Coalition for a
Mayoral Change." In 1985 the personalities were somewhat different but the intent was the same with two
other groups. Following the Jackson campaign and his
"Hymietown" remark a group of some one hundred
prominent New York black and Jewish leaders had had
several meetings to discuss repairing relationships. As it
happened, this "Black-Jewish Coalition" included some
of my most vocal opponents. So, and I have a flair for
descriptive language, when I was asked after one of
their meetings what I thought about their activities I
said, "There is no question that for many of them this
is a camouflage operation intended to put together a
group against me. Some are there because they want to
create better relationships, and I applaud that. And they
may very well be being used by others of this group's
membership—that is, a cabal, whose major effort is to
replace me."

Well, of course I loved it, because I was speaking the
truth and holding my opponents up to derision, but
Garth went crazy. He did not like the controversy on a
subject involving black–Jewish relations. I didn't mind
because I know that a number of these particular people
are outright phonies and simply using the issue for
political purposes and primarily to attack me, and bring
me down if they could. I will tell you I did them more
damage by jarring them with the "cabal" reference
than they did me. And I will tell you something else. In
late September of 1985, after the primary was over (and

in that primary these same individuals who were in leadership positions were against me), I was told that in October both Farrakhan and Rabbi Meir Kahane were coming to speak in the City of New York. It delighted me to be able to send to this coalition's membership a letter which asked them to do the appropriate thing vis-à-vis these two bigots. One black and one Jewish. I was told my letter caused consternation at their next meeting, and that the first forty-five minutes were spent discussing who gave me the membership mailing list. Then they discussed Jack Newfield's demand that any denunciatory letter on their part commenting on Farrakhan and Kahane should also denounce me. Hazel Dukes, president of the New York State NAACP, said, to her credit, that she would have no part of that. Their letter, which was read at the rally held outside Madison Square Garden a few days before Farrakhan's meeting there, was read by Stanley Lowell, a leader of the "cabal." It had to pain him to know that I had by my challenge to them compelled them to take a position stronger than they might otherwise have taken, because they did not like putting people on record so forcefully against Farrakhan. There were some black leaders who simply did not want to denounce Farrakhan, out of physical or political fear, or sympathy perhaps for some of his views.

Also early on in the primary campaign, another coalition, this one known as the "Coalition for a Just New York," was formed by my opponents for the expressed purpose of finding a candidate to run against me. Their meetings went on for weeks. They interviewed possible candidates. There were stories in the papers. The coalition ultimately nominated Herman (Denny) Farrell, a black assemblyman from Harlem and the Democratic County Chairman of Manhattan, to run, thus alienating Herman Badillo, a Hispanic, and the whole Hispanic wing of the coalition and some blacks who preferred Badillo. When Denny announced his candidacy on the steps of City Hall, Herman Badillo's supporters were there to heckle him and call him "traitor." I remained silent in the midst of this. What could be better than dissension among one's opponents? A revealing insight was given afterward by Jack Newfield, who was smuggled by a Hispanic security guard into the back of the meeting where the coalition, with primarily blacks present, selected Denny Farrell. Newfield told Henry Stern how shocked he was to hear the anti-Semitic and anti-Puerto Rican comments from some of those present as they decided to select Farrell in order to stop Badillo. Newfield later told Stern, "You can tell the Mayor that everything he has said about anti-Semitism among the black leaders is true."

Seeing she could not get the coalition's backing, Carol Bellamy, the President of the City Council, announced her candidacy although earlier she had said she would endorse the coalition's choice. I said when Badillo was still a candidate, "I think she's trying to cut Herman off at the knees, or at the pass. That's not nice, Carol."

Now, as I said earlier, when your opponents are

fighting amongst themselves, the best place to be, as a general rule, is above the fight. When Bellamy came into the race the first thing she tried to do was to knock Denny Farrell off the ballot. According to Carol's lawyers, Denny didn't have enough valid signatures on his nominating petitions. So she filed a challenge with the Board of Elections, and that whole process was begun. That is a process that was sure to produce acrimony between the two of them, and it did.

For my part I wanted the debates to be few and the participants many. So I said, "I hope Denny gets back on the ballot. If Carol withdraws her challenge to Denny's petitions, I'll give her another television debate."

This was a mistake. It served to divert attention from their squabbling and gave them an opportunity to attack me. Denny said he didn't want my help and called my sympathy "crocodile tears." Carol accused me of talking "out of both sides of his [my] mouth." That kind of statement served their purposes better, and when they could they escalated them. As the three-way campaign progressed they began doing what challengers will always do: they attacked my administration's record, they issued public releases, they called for more debates, all the usual techniques to get public attention. And the question for me was: How do I respond? Garth's constant admonition to me, as he put it, was "Stay cool, stay cool." I was thinking to myself, If I listened to him I'd be in the shower all day.

My problem in this area is a simple one. I am not capable of blathering pap. I'm not happy or comfortable engaging in mush statements. If I'm going to say something it's going to be substantive and at the least provocative. Hopefully it will also have some humor. That's my style, it's me. I couldn't change it now, at sixty-one years of age, if I wanted to. And I don't want to.

So as I am being attacked by Carol Bellamy and Denny Farrell and as their supporters are yammering away at me, I decided that the best way to keep Garth happy and keep my opponents out of the papers is for me to say nothing. Well, now, how does one say nothing? Easy. You declare a one-hundred-day moratorium on all political statements. Right after Carol announced, she and her staff were issuing two or three press statements a day attacking various programs and initiatives of my administration and me personally. You have to understand this was new for her, because prior to running she was relatively retiring, modest and courteous; now just the opposite. I sort of summed it up when I said of her at the debate sponsored by the New York *Post,* "I don't tell you that if you compared her with some other people that she wouldn't be better [for mayor]. But I tell you that, based on what she has done for seven and a half years, where for seven years she closed her mouth, and for six months since ambition kissed her on the lips we hear from her every day, she's not herself."

I also said, "These attacks are to be expected. They are politically motivated. I will not comment on them. I'm declaring a one-hundred-day moratorium on political statements.'' The moratorium was not a carefully planned strategy. It was not discussed in advance with Garth. It just occurred to me, so I said it. Sort of a trial balloon. And to my surprise everyone accepted it. So then when I saw over the course of the next few days that it was taking hold, and therefore I could stay with it, I sort of enhanced it by saying to the reporters in response to a question about one of Carol's statements, ''Of course you know about the hundred-day moratorium. And you should know that the hundred days start from the day of the last political question asked of me. So ask at your peril.''

Meanwhile, of course, I was having my own three or four press conferences a day announcing the various governmental programs we were implementing—housing starts, education initiatives, law enforcement, park dedications, etc.—and my comments were getting covered in long news stories, while the charges of my opponents were, minus comments from me, reduced to little metro briefs deep inside the paper.

This is the power of incumbency. Let me give you another example. As I mentioned in an earlier chapter of this book, a biography of me which was written by three City Hall reporters and which was intended to be a hatchet job was released in the middle of the primary campaign. I was lucky enough to see a copy of this book before it was leaked to the press. There was very little new news in it, and what there was—particularly relating to Ron Dellums and the episodes I related earlier—I made public with my comments in a single day, and then ignored. For this reason I believe the book got very little notice in the press and deservedly so, because it is not a good book. It did not sell well. And in the end it was probably a political plus for me, because the average person seeing the book in the bookstore probably thought, Gee, this Koch must be something to have books written about him. I think the three authors counted on my attacking their book and thereby helping its sales.

Another example of the same thing would be the cartoon that appeared in *Penthouse* magazine. It is a caricature of me drawn with the idea of making me look like a lanky King Kong perched atop the Empire State Building. Clearly it was intended to be unflattering.

Garth called and said, "Ignore it."

I said, "Better yet, I'm going to say I like it." And I did. When the reporters asked me about it I said, "I haven't looked so good since I was twenty-four. I'm going to use it as a campaign poster."

When Bob Guccione, the publisher of *Penthouse*, was interviewed on TV he was clearly angry. This was not the reaction from me he had expected, and it wasn't helping his sales.

We handled the primary debates in a similar fashion. I decided early on that I didn't want to debate only with Bellamy. She couldn't get center stage without me and I didn't wish to help put her there. We decided at first that I would appear only with Bellamy, Farrell and the so-called minor candidates: Dr. Fred Newman, Gilbert Di Lucia and Judah Rubinstein. None of them was getting much attention, none of them had any new ideas or credibility, and my second thought was, Why give any one of them a platform? I said to Garth, "I don't think I should debate at all."

He didn't think I could get away without any debates at all, but we did think we could accomplish no one-on-ones. I began by announcing I would not debate at all. "My record over the past seven years is known," I said. "I don't need debates to get it out. Who remembers anything from earlier presidential debates? 'Where's the beef?' 'There you go again'? What does it accomplish? If the best debater should be mayor, then let's go find the captain of the Harvard debating team and make him or her the mayor." Very strong, you know, to kind of stun them. I have found that is the best way to negotiate with the press. You begin with the most extreme plausible position and then allow yourself to get pulled, slowly, into a compromise.

Ultimately we had five debates, one hosted by each of the four major citywide newspapers. They were not so-called "TV debates," since TV carried only a few minutes on the six o'clock news. And one total "TV debate" hosted by the League of Women Voters and with every encouragement by us for them to use the least-watched TV channel in the city, which they did, and with all six candidates in attendance. That show had the lowest ratings of any show in that time slot (5 percent share, 3.4 rating, last on the Nielsen scoreboard) and deservedly so. The format was excruciatingly boring.

Now, what can happen if you do this? What is the downside? The downside would best be shown by describing my experience with Gabe Pressman, who is the dean of the New York local television political reporters. Gabe decided he would bait me and threaten that if I didn't come to his debate he would have it without me and that he would have an empty chair representing me. I couldn't care less, because I knew that few would be watching his show.

But every time Gabe interviewed me about anything, including when he was attacking me unfairly about my relations with the black community, he asked me again and again if I was coming to his debate, and I would say no. His staff from Channel 4 called my staff: "Is he coming?"

"No, no!" And so at the end of Gabe's evening news commentaries almost each night he says, "And we asked the Mayor if he was coming to our debate and he said, 'No.'" It became a joke.

Finally as it gets closer to primary day and Gabe is still at it seeking to badger me, I say, "Gabe, I am certainly not going to come on your show. I will not be bullied by you!" To his credit, Gabe responded, "If I'm a bully, then I have learned it at the feet of the master." He played my comments and his on his news program, and it was hilarious.

The sweetest satisfaction was, of course, the results: 64 percent of the entire primary vote, 65 percent among women; 70 percent among Hispanics; trailing Denny Farrell, the black candidate, by only two percentage points (40-38 percent) in the black community; 82 percent of the Irish vote, 78 percent of the Italian, 75 percent of the Jewish. I carried fifty-six of the sixty assembly districts. Practically a clean sweep.

I particularly enjoyed, forgive the immodesty, Gabe Pressman's editorial following the primary:

CONGRATULATIONS, MR. MAYOR, the Democratic voters have spoken giving you the mandate you wanted. By a margin of two to one they've said you've been a good mayor and they want more.

You ran an intelligent, effective campaign, winning on the strength of your own personality and your record.

More somber in victory than some expected, you were looking ahead to deal with poverty you said was a priority, economic growth, jobs, education—New York's future, you said. With one out of three children in this town living in poverty, it's a vital concern.

You are a complex man. Sometimes, I have found you ornery and abrasive, and I'm sure you return the compliment. But I've never doubted your love for the job and the city. And your spirit and administrative skills are to be admired.

Conscious now of your place in history, you probably want to be remembered as a guy who tried to improve the city, leave it better than you found it. In a real sense, the people of New York are your extended family. You have the respect of many. You've been accused of a lot of things, Mr. Mayor, but you never go stale. If you win in November, your third term can be a new beginning for you and for us.

As a result I sent him this note:

September 17, 1985

Dear Gabe:

I very much appreciated your commentary on Sunday night and I thought in the spirit of Rosh Hashanah it would be a good time for me to write and express my desire for a renewal of our formerly friendly and constructive professional relationship in the year to come.

For my part, I must admit that several issues during the primary campaign sorely tested some of my relations with the press. I was particularly incensed by attacks upon my personal honesty and upon the integrity of my administration. Particularly, I resented the charge that large political contributions paved the way for special consideration in this government. I very much respect and support the check and balance provided by the press on government. Many of the alleged "flip-flops" that Carol Bellamy charged me with were a reflection of government responding with common sense to evolving and changing situations and constructive criticism from the press. I see that as a strength and not a weakness of the government. I will always hold my ground when I believe I am right on the merits but if I am convinced otherwise, I am the first to admit that I can be wrong.

Without taking the general election for granted, I look forward to my third term with greater anticipation and enthusiasm than the two that have preceded it. I believe as a city we are poised and ready to make significant progress over the next four years in solving some of our most intractable problems. I look forward to that challenge and will seek to lead this city with the cooperation and support of all its diverse segments.

Happy New Year.

All the best.

> *Sincerely,*
> *Edward I. Koch*

•   •   •

An analysis of the primary-election results showed that there were only two groups that did not vote for me. The first was the Satmar sect, which is a Hasidic Jewish group, many of whom live in the Williamsburg section of Brooklyn. This group is against the existence of the State of Israel on the grounds that a Jewish state should exist only after the Messiah returns. In addition to that, the Satmar are death on wheels on gay-rights legislation. And, most important for them, they are opposed to the resource recovery plant, the garbage incinerator (one of eight planned for the city) which is to be located in the former Brooklyn Navy Yard in Williamsburg, and which I have led the fight for on the Board of Estimate. In the Satmar's area I got 29 percent of the vote, while Carol Bellamy got 63 percent. This is particularly significant because the last thing in the world the Satmar as a community would approve of is a woman mayor.

On Sunday, October 27, the New York City Marathon was held. The race starts in Staten Island and runs for twenty-six miles through every borough and many of the city's's ethnic neighborhoods. I started the race, as I have done for the last seven years, by firing the cannon. Then I watched as nineteen thousand runners passed before me over the Verrazano Bridge—a glorious sight. In prior years after shooting off the cannon I would go to the finish line two hours later to greet the winners. I decided that this year I should track the route of the runners ahead of them and stop at each of the watering stations set up by volunteers. There were about ten such stations set up in each of the boroughs. I loved it as I sped along ahead of the runners by car. At each station I got out of the car to drink a cup of water, to the cheers of the spectators lining the streets. I did that until I got to Satmar country in Williamsburg.

When I arrived there I told my driver that I wanted to get out of the car and walk for a few blocks. The men on the street were dressed in their black hats and coats, and the married women wore their decorous wigs. The Bible requires each married woman to wear this wig in public so as not to show her hair to any man other than her husband. There was no applause for me as I walked by. In my head I simply decided to do what I do at ball games, where they always boo politicians. I raised my arms high in the air with thumbs turned up, as though the spectators were cheering me. One Satmar man in his midthirties said to me, in his East-European–inflected English, "Mayor, we don't want the incinerator." I turned toward him and said, "I lost in this neighborhood and you're getting two." Of course it was said jocularly.

On Sunday, November 3, the weekend before the general election, the Satmar cooked up a new technique against me, or at least one that had not been used for several hundred years. I was scheduled to go to Boro Park, a lively and commercially productive section of Brooklyn that is populated in large measure by the Hasidic Jewish community. The purpose of my visit was to participate in the dedication of Bobov Promenade, a street-name change to honor the Rebbe of the Bobover community. "Rebbe" is the affectionate, respectful diminutive title given to a rabbi of great scholarship and renown. This Rebbe, Rabbi Schlomo Halberstam, has a glorious history of surviving the Holocaust and saving other Jews in Poland. He led his flock across the sea to America and they settled in Boro Park. I have met him on a number of occasions. We like each other even though we don't communicate much when we are together. His usual words are "Have a piece of cake, have a drink" (referring to wine or schnapps). And then he gives me his blessing which consists of "Everything you want you should have." At that particular moment all I wanted was to be reelected.

We had been told that one of my opponents, Rabbi

Lew Y. Levin, who is an ultra-Orthodox rabbi, would be there. He was the candidate of the Right to Life Party, and his platform consisted of denouncing me as supportive of gay-rights legislation. He said that I was bringing Sodom and Gomorrah to New York City. At the *New York Times* debate that was all he talked about. And then he engaged in insulting behavior by declining to shake hands with me. He said it was for religious reasons, the religious reason being, I later learned, that he, along with others, intended to "excommunicate" me. That was the surprise that Levin's ultra-religious group of zealots had in store for me in Boro Park: a demonstration and an excommunication ceremony.

When my car got to Boro Park, by chance we were stopped at an intersection as the demonstrators' bus approached. It happened to be where I was getting out of the car. When they saw me it was like a collective primal scream of rage from inside that school bus. I simply laughed and gave them my thumbs-up salute, which evoked more screams from them. I kept walking through the neighborhood to the site of the ceremony.

Before the ceremony I went into the Rebbe's house, and as I was walking in I noticed that among the two thousand people in the crowd, two men were engaged in a fistfight.

I said to my security guard, "Stop them. We shouldn't allow them to fight."

He said, "Mayor, keep walking."

I listened to him and kept walking into the house. I

had some cake and wine and received the Rebbe's greetings and blessings.

When I came out of the Rebbe's house my advance man, Peter Kohlman, said to me, "Mayor, it was very interesting out here. There were about four fights. The Bobov people recognized the others who were infiltrating and who would have demonstrated against you. They beat them up and then delivered the bodies, still breathing and able to walk, to the police."

Obviously if the police had seen the fights they would have intervened. But I laughed when Peter told me that, thinking, Only the Bobov would be able to tell the difference between their black hats and frock coats and those of the zealots.

The reporters were there and they asked me about the zealots. I said, "This is an exploitation of very sensitive and sophisticated religious principles for vulgar political purposes. I am a proud son of Israel and a proud Jew. And," I went on, "this is what their counterpart zealots did to Spinoza. At least I'm in good company."

When I spoke at the ceremony I referred to an incident that had occurred inside the Rebbe's house. He had pointed to someone, saying, "This is Mr. Katz. He is a real Hasid." I had said to the Rebbe, "What do you mean, a real Hasid?" He said, "If you are a real Hasid, you pick a Rebbe to follow."

So when I was out on the platform where the Bobov were cheering me, I turned to the Rebbe and said, "I asked you what it means to be a true Hasid. And you told me it is someone who picks a Rebbe to follow. I want you to know that I am a true Hasid. I am picking you to follow.''

His face lit up, and the Bobov applauded. From four blocks away I thought I could hear the gnashing of teeth of the zealots, and I loved it.

The other group that I did not win with was the most militant gay activist group on Christopher Street. There I got 40 percent of the vote to Bellamy's 54 percent. My problem there is that while I believe in gay rights, I do not believe I should impose my will by political threats on members of the City Council who for religious reasons are opposed to gay-rights legislation. So I have the Rabbi Levins on the one side saying I am turning the town into a Sodom and Gomorrah, and the militant gay activists on the other side saying I am not working hard enough for gay-rights legislation, or on AIDS, or on getting them the imprimatur on an equivalent lifestyle. What I have always said is, "If you are being attacked by the most militant activists on both sides of the issue you must be doing something right.''

The homosexual community itself is split on what the Catholic Archdiocese of New York should do with respect to providing facilities for those suffering from AIDS and what the city's role should be in the financing of those church-operated facilities. I have applauded the efforts and courage of Cardinal O'Connor in providing hospice facilities for AIDS sufferers who need interim accommodations after they leave the hospital and before they go home, and who will in all likelihood die shortly. You have to understand that these facilities are not welcomed into neighborhoods. Who but the most dedicated wants AIDS patients living next door? Nonetheless, the City of New York and the Archdiocese of New York are seeking to provide these facilities and others. The City of New York last year spent $160 million, including the state and federal share, on AIDS programs. We are doing more than any other city in America. But it is a drop in the bucket compared with the need for services for victims and money for research. We are constantly trying to find more and better ways to deal with the catastrophic effects of AIDS.

On Friday, October 25, 1985, Mother Teresa called City Hall. She said she wanted to speak to me about an AIDS shelter. I was out of the office, so Victor Botnick, my health adviser, spoke to Mother Teresa. She was at a convent in the Bronx. She told him that she had spoken with Governor Cuomo on the phone and wanted to persuade him and me of the need for a hospice for youngsters. Victor recognized that he could never persuade her over the phone of our need for an adult facility and not a children's facility, so he asked if she could come to City Hall to meet with me. She said she preferred to do it on the phone.

Victor said to her, "It isn't possible to do it all on the phone."

She said, "It is difficult for me to come down."

He said, "I will send a police car for you."

She said, "A police car?"

He said, "Yes, with lights and sirens, like with the President."

She said, "Pick me up at two-thirty."

At 2:45 P.M. she was delivered to City Hall in a police car complete with lights and sirens. I went outside and met her on the steps of City Hall. She had another sister with her. We then went into my office and chatted for about a half hour. Mother Teresa is Yugoslavian by birth and speaks English with an Anglo-Indian accent. I believe she is in her seventies. She is gnarled, bent over, exceedingly intelligent, has a wonderful smile, is tough and knows exactly what she wants to do and the power she has by virtue of her saintliness.

She told me and those assembled at the meeting that she preferred to open a shelter for children.

I said, "Mother, we don't need a shelter for children. We have plenty of people who want to take care of the *children*, but we don't have anyone to take care of the gay *men* and we need you to do that."

She said, "But if it is a children's shelter, my nuns can sleep in the rectory."

I said, "Why can't they do that if adult males are there?"

She did not answer.

I said to her, "There is less fear in the community in which this shelter will be. It is in Greenwich Village and there is a large homosexual community there. They will receive it quite well."

She ended the conversation by saying in her quaint accent, "Well, if we open the hospice I want to see every one of you [referring to Dan Wolf, Bill Rauch, Victor Botnick and me] washing and brushing the floors." And then she laughed—knowingly.

I thought to myself, Mother, they say AIDS can't be contracted by casual contact. But it will be a long time before I would be willing to brush and wash the floors. That seemed to be the opinion shared by all of us in the room. We are not saints.

After the meeting I walked her outside. She got into the police car and off she went, lights flashing, sirens screaming. The following week an announcement was forthcoming from the archdiocese that Mother Teresa and her Sisters of Charity would be opening an AIDS hospice for adult men on Christopher Street. And who's going to picket Mother Teresa?

These are examples of what incumbents can do. As I said earlier, I think we used the incumbency aspects of the campaign better in 1985 than in 1981.

•　　　　　•　　　　　•

In the 1985 general election I received 76 percent of the vote, a point higher than my 1981 margin, and the highest vote in terms of percentage in the city's modern era. There were literally thousands of good people who by volunteering in the campaign helped make that result possible, and I am grateful to them all.

In politics, as in the rest of life, winning is better than losing. And it is especially rewarding when you can be proud of how you played the game.

Index

Photo Credits

We wish to thank the following for the use of photographs from their collections. Every effort has been made to verify sources. Any errors will be corrected upon notification.

1. UPI/Bettmann
2. Carol Greitzer
3. UPI/Bettmann
4. Wide World
5. Wide World
6. H. J. Fields
7. John and Mary Condon
8. Image Bank
9. Henry J. Stern
10. Dan List
11. New York *Daily News*
12. Ronay Menschel
13. Dev O'Neil
14. Philip I. Beane
15. UPI/Bettmann
16. Ronay Menschel
17. John and Mary Condon
18. John and Mary Condon
19. John and Mary Condon
20. John and Mary Condon
21. New York City Housing Authority Photo Unit
22. Wide World
23. UPI/Bettmann
24. UPI/Bettmann
25. John and Mary Condon
26. John and Mary Condon
27. Wide World
28. Wide World
29. Ronay Menschel
30. Wide World
31. Neal Boenzi/*The New York Times*
32. New York City Metropolitan Transportation Authority
33. UPI/Bettmann
34. Wide World
35. Wide World
36. UPI/Bettmann
37. Holland Wemple
38. UPI/Bettmann
39. Wide World
40. UPI/Bettmann
41. UPI/Bettmann
42. Wide World